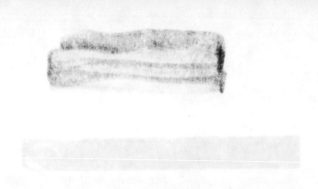

NICKELODEON THEATRES AND THEIR MUSIC

Denver's Isis Theatre, circa 1915

NICKELODEON THEATRES

AND THEIR MUSIC

by Q. David Bowers

author of
Encyclopedia of Automatic Musical Instruments,
The Moxie Encyclopedia, etc.

The Vestal Press, Ltd.
Vestal, New York 13850

Library of Congress Cataloging-in-Publication Data

Bowers, Q. David.
  Nickelodeon theatres and their music.

  Bibliography: p.
  1. Moving-picture theatres--History--Pictorial works.
2. Silent films--Musical accompaniment--History and
criticism--Pictorial works. I. Title.
PN1995.B64   1986   792'.0973   86-5594
ISBN 0-911572-49-X
ISBN 0-911572-50-3 (pbk.)

THE VESTAL PRESS, LTD.
Box 97
Vestal, NY 13850

Write for catalogue of other Vestal Press publications.

CREDITS AND ACKNOWLEDGMENTS

With fewer than ten exceptions, illustrations in the book are from the author's reference collection. The bibliography gives information sources and suggested reading topics. In particular, reading through a large file of *Moving Picture World* and *The Billboard* furnished many ideas and engendered enthusiasm. A debt is also acknowledged to the Musical Box Society International, the Automatic Musical Collectors' Association (AMICA), the American Theatre Organ Society, and the Theatre Historical Society for providing ideas and contributing to the author's interest in the subject. Several pictorial items were loaned by Tom B'hend and earlier appeared in his publication, *The Console*. David L. Junchen, the well-known theatre organ historian, contributed several illustrations and helped the author annotate the Wurlitzer theatre instrument shipping list through the year 1915. Arthur Reblitz, one of America's best known historians in the field of automatic musical instruments, provided helpful suggestions. Louis Rosa, formerly associated with the Wurlitzer Company, provided certain material. Farny Wurlitzer, now deceased, was a friend of the author and provided much information concerning Wurlitzer instruments. Leah Weisse, curator of the Regional History Center, Northern Illinois University, provided a copy of an early Wurlitzer catalogue. The Larry Edmunds Bookshop sold the author an archive of trade magazines formerly owned by the William Fox Studio Library, while Jan and Larry Malis sold him a vast file of material earlier owned by the publisher of *Photoplay*. Raymond N. Merena, the author's business associate in Bowers and Merena Galleries, Inc., encouraged the project and helped make it possible.

The author's secretary, Mary K. Valley, corresponded with many sources, compiled many of the author's research notes, and assisted in other ways. Typesetting was done by Margaret E. Graf. Proofreading and graphics work were accomplished by the author and by the Graphics Art Department of Bowers and Merena Galleries, Inc., with Jane McCabe, Linda Heilig, Sarah Whitten-French, and Jane Fernald. Triaxon, of Binghamton, New York, sized and reproduced many of the original photographs, advertisements, and other material. Staff members of The Vestal Press, including Harvey N. Roehl and Gil Williams, helped in many ways.

Author's Preface

In 1985, while contemplating an archive of 5,000 or more pictures of old theatre buildings in my reference collection, I decided it would be interesting to compile some of these into a volume tentatively titled *The Nickelodeon Theatre Scrapbook.* The term *nickelodeon* is derived from *nickel,* the price of admission, and *odeon,* the French word for theatre. In modern times, nickelodeon has also referred to coin-operated musical instruments of various sorts, but in the early part of the present century a nickelodeon was a five-cent theatre and nothing else.

At first I contemplated simply illustrating buildings in which motion pictures were shown, limiting the book to theatres built prior to 1915. Then, the more I thought about it, the more I felt that it would be appropriate to discuss the music used by these theatres—for, unquestionably, the appeal of any film was heightened by the use of musical accompaniment. The only problem was that nickelodeon theatres in themselves could have made a book of many hundreds of pages in length, while a treatise on electric pianos and orchestrions used in theatres could make another equivalent book. Still another book could be produced on the subject of theatre pipe organs!

So, I decided to cover the highlights, to touch the more important things, to illustrate not thousands of theatres or many hundreds, but, rather, to show some of the more interesting theatres of the nickelodeon style, interspersing photographs of airdomes, opera houses, and other buildings which showed motion pictures. At the same time, I desired to include illustrations of later transitional theatres, buildings from the beginning of the palatial era, such as the Isis Theatre in Denver.

Curiously, although many dozens of books have been written on the cradle days of the motion picture in America, not a single one prior to the present work has been devoted to the nickelodeon theatre. Part of this undoubtedly is due to the practice of later writers copying the information (and errors) of such early historians as Robert Grau, Epes Winthrop Sargent, and Terry Ramsaye, none of whom had much to say about the nickel theatre. Likewise curious is the nearly complete absence of use by recent historians of two turn-of-the-century publications crammed with early theatre information: *The Billboard* and *The New York Clipper.* Perhaps it is because few archives contain copies of these ephemeral magazines. On the other hand, the reader desiring to learn about David Wark Griffith, an early director, literally can accumulate a pile of books about him! Although books and articles about Griffith, Charles Chaplin, and Mary Pickford abound, where are the recent books about the early days of Carl Laemmle? And, yet, with apologies to the memory of David Wark Griffith, Laemmle was probably the most significant figure in the industry during the 1905-1915 decade. Of course, it can be argued that such a comparison should not be made, for Griffith, the director, was an artist, while Laemmle was a showman. Early motion picture history, as evidenced by books, has many gaps. Perhaps the present volume will inspire historians to rediscover the nickelodeon and give it the recognition it deserves. Likewise, in printed histories of film making and exhibition, and in the countless memoirs of old timers, scarcely a paragraph anywhere is to be found about photoplayer instruments, and there is precious little on the early days of the theatre pipe organ. What did appear in print is apt to be puzzling, indeed ludicrous, to the present-day historian. For example, *Moving Picture World* published a column on theatre music circa 1915, but it is abundantly clear that the editor had little knowledge concerning pipe organs.

This book, then, will take you on a tour of theatres, primarily of the 1905-1915 era, prefacing the trip with some historical background and concluding the journey with some information concerning orchestrions, photoplayers, and theatre pipe organs. Pictures of actors and actresses of the era are interspersed.

Nickelodeon theatres sprang up like wildfire during the period from 1905 to 1910. By the latter year there were 8,000 to 10,000 or more such establishments, according to various estimates. All that was needed to set up a nickel theatre was a vacant storefront, a projector, some kitchen chairs, a bedsheet for use as a screen stretched across the back wall, and some rented films. Out front, a sign painted on a glass window, or, more pretentiously, outlined in electric lights, helped draw the crowds in. Such names as Gem, Princess, Idle Hour, Eagle, Electric, and Bijou Dream were seen all across America. Sometimes the theatre name reflected the price charged, such as Nickel, Nickelodeon, Nickel Treat, Nickelette, or Nickeldom.

In addition to nickelodeon theatres specifically set up as such, thousands of opera houses, town halls, municipal auditoriums, summer camp buildings, church meeting rooms, and other locations were pressed into service as movie houses, with the program often interspersing film strips between vaudeville acts or stage plays.

For the price of a nickel, a wonderland of screen action awaited the nickelodeon patron. *The Great Train Robbery* thrilled millions, as did filmed visits to Niagara Falls and the White Mountains, and the spectacle of an express train rounding a curve at 60 miles an hour. Here was heaven. The troubles of the outside world, what was happening on Main Street outside of the theatre, were forgotten—and the viewer was transported to a land of vicarious thrills and delights.

After about 1910, enterprising movie theatre owners realized that films were more than a novelty. Movies were here to stay and were often more profitable than vaudeville and stage productions, the latter involving many people, elaborate facilities, stage crews, and other expenses. The age of the movie *palace* dawned. The Paris Theatre on Denver's brightly lighted Curtis Street (called the Broadway of the West) opened in 1913 and represented an investment of $250,000. Seating 2,200, the picture palace gave a ''high grade program'' for a nickel. However, the nickel was to be a short-lived admission ticket, for already many competing establishments were charging a dime, twenty cents, or even a quarter.

Not far away on Curtis Street, Samuel L. Baxter, who had come to Denver in 1906 and who had first operated a nickelodeon theatre there, complete with kitchen chairs and illumination by candles on the interior, was inspired by the success of the Paris Theatre and converted his Isis Theatre to a palace of musical splendor. Seating 2,000, the Isis featured a $50,000 Wurlitzer Hope-Jones Unit Orchestra, the largest Wurlitzer pipe organ installed in a movie house up to that date.

In the meantime, the Liberty Theatre in Seattle, fronted with a sign 40 feet high depicting the Statue of Liberty illuminated with 1,200 lights in eight different colors, continued to create a sensation. During the first few weeks after its opening, crowds extended several blocks from the ticket booth, and the police had to be called to control the mass of people. The motion picture palace concept, called by one author ''an acre of seats in a palace of splendor,'' took hold. The nickelodeon theatre faded from the scene, as did the nickel admission charge. Films became more sophisticated, stars such as Charlie Chaplin and Mary Pickford captured the hearts of millions, and a new age in motion picture exhibition was born—but that's another story.

Music is intertwined with the nickelodeon theatre and its successors. While later establishments of large size, such as the aforementioned Paris and Isis theatres in Denver, were apt to have orchestras, or pipe organs representing an entire human orchestra, earlier nickelodeons were content with a piano (often rented) played by a performer of uncertain ability. Before long, theatre owners recognized that an electric piano costing just a few cents per day for current did just as well. Such instruments were apt to be played continuously from morning until night.

By 1910, orchestrions, consisting of automatic pianos with pipes and drums added, were a common fixture in theatres. On the inside they were apt to be played non-stop, and on the outside they faced the street where they broadcast ragtime, marches, and other lively tunes to entice more people into the Silver Palace, the Crystal, or the Bijou.

In *Music Boxes, Their Lore and Lure*, published in 1957, Helen and John Hoke relate the tale of an orchestrion ''of heroic proportions—10 feet high and six feet wide,'' which was brought to the old Banner Theatre in Los Angeles, a nickelodeon, ''where it accompanied silent films in all its splendor. Inside were a piano, three sections of organ pipes, bass and snare drums, cymbal, triangle, tambourine, and a melodious 30-bar xylophone. When talking pictures came in,'' the text continued, ''the owner was faced with a giant music maker he could not use, and it was an unbelievably formidable task either to move or dismantle it. He decided to wall it in, and did so! Years went by while collectors ran down every lead for the vanished machine. In 1952, during the remodeling of the theatre, workmen were astonished to uncover the long-lost, walled-up orchestrion—and Robert Huish spent 18 months painstakingly restoring it. The day it was ready, it was christened with a bottle of champagne, and the deep, rich orchestrion again rang out *A Bicycle Built for Two*. The orchestrion's long silence was over.''

I first read those words in 1960 and was intrigued by them. Later, I learned that the orchestrion in question was a Wurlitzer Style 29-C Mandolin PianOrchestra, and that PianOrchestras were sold by the hundreds to theatres, including three of them nearly side by side on the same street in San Francisco!

Fascinated with self-playing musical instruments, I decided to acquire a representative collection. Beginning with a small Regina music box in 1960, my holdings grew to include several varieties of coin-operated pianos and orchestrions. My curiosity grew along with my acquisitions, and I eagerly sought to learn the history of these marvelous music makers. I made the acquaintance of Harvey and Marion Roehl, who were putting the finishing touches on their *Player Piano Treasury* book, published in 1961. After reading every page in the book for what must have been a dozen times, I visited the New York Public Library and other places in search of still more information. Wurlitzer instruments in particular fascinated me, and soon the seeds were sown for a book concerning them, which eventually was published in 1966 and titled *Put Another Nickel In*. Described were many varieties of PianOrchestras and other Wurlitzer instruments.

As part of my research for this and other books (including *The Encyclopedia of Automatic Musical Instruments*, published in 1972), I made a number of trips to The Wurlitzer Company in North Tonawanda, New York, where Farny Wurlitzer (born in 1883 and well past retirement age) showed up at the office every day. Farny soon became a friend and generously answered the countless questions I asked. I learned not only of Wurlitzer coin pianos and orchestrions, but also of the activities of Robert Hope-Jones and of the Wurlitzer theatre organs built using his ideas. After his death, I acquired the golden oak office desk which he had purchased in 1911 and which he used continuously throughout his career. I have often contemplated the discussions and transactions which took place over this desk during the 60 years it was in Farny's office.

In the meantime, I had gathered much information about photoplayers, or pit organs as they are sometimes called—instruments used to provide accompaniment for silent pictures. Typically, a photoplayer consisted of an automatic piano flanked by two side chests containing organ pipes, played automatically by a paper roll. A nationwide search for photoplayers ensued, aided by the mailing of postcards to several thousand theatres.

Around that time I had occasion to hear my first theatre organ, a Wurlitzer in the Tivoli Theatre, Chattanooga, Tennessee, shown to me by Bob Johnson, who demonstrated its abilities by playing ordinary 88-note player piano rolls on it. A more marvelous sound I had never heard! This began my involvement with theatre pipe organs, and before long I purchased from Bob Johnson a Wurlitzer Style 260 Special, a three-manual, 17-rank organ originally installed in the Howard Theatre in Atlanta. Later, I sold the same organ to J.B. Nethercutt, who set it up as a featured attraction in his San Sylmar museum in California. Later, a number of other theatre organs came my way, primarily while I was conducting a business, Hathaway and Bowers, Inc., with Terry Hathaway. A Wurlitzer Style 135, a two-manual, four-rank instrument with a piano console using 88-note player piano rolls, an organ removed from the White Theatre, Fresno, California, was an early purchase. Years later it was sold to a San Francisco enthusiast.

Beginning in the 1960s, Richard C. Simonton, a businessman and entrepreneur who was interested in the history of organs and who assisted with the founding of the American Theatre Organ Enthusiasts (name later changed to the American Theatre Organ Society), was a close friend for many years. Each Saturday night the Bijou Theatre, built in the lower level of Dick Simonton's North Hollywood, California home, was opened to friends and visitors. Living not far from there at the time, I went to the Bijou on countless occasions to watch classic films and to hear many recitals on his Wurlitzer organ. Gordon Kibbee was the traditional ''house organist'' and was there more than anyone else, but Gaylord Carter and others played from time to time. Often, those associated with old-time movies would be there as well, including silent film star Harold Lloyd, whose movies such as *Safety Last* and *The Freshman* are as hilarious as any I have ever seen. Interestingly, Harold Lloyd, who had achieved worldwide fame in the 1920s, was reticent in the 1970s to have his films shown to modern audiences, for he felt that they might be criticized in view of later advances in film making. However, the laughter that filled Dick Simonton's Bijou Theatre quickly dispelled any such thoughts!

On another occasion, Dick Simonton and I conferred about the Wurlitzer organ originally installed in the Paramount Theatre in New York City. The organ, a particularly large model, had been removed from the Paramount and brought to California, where it was hoped it would be installed in a Los Angeles theatre. These plans collapsed, and Dick Simonton called me to ask if I would like to acquire it. The answer was affirmative, and before long it was delivered to the Hathaway & Bowers building. No sooner had this been done, than Dick Simonton learned of a group of enthusiasts in Wichita, Kansas, who suggested setting it up in the new municipal auditorium there. Would I mind parting with it? Having no immediate plans to install it, I consented, and soon the organ was on its way to Kansas. On another occasion, a large Wurlitzer organ from the Capitol Theatre, Detroit, was purchased from David L. Junchen and subsequently sold to J.B. Nethercutt, who didn't need it for San Sylmar, for he already had the Style 260 Special, so he donated it to the Oakland Paramount Theatre, then undergoing restoration as a civic project. Over the years I acquired other theatre instruments of varying sizes and specifications, including the 1985 purchase of the beautiful Wurlitzer Style Publix No. 1, a four-manual Roman console organ originally installed in the Minnesota Theatre, Minneapolis, in 1928. In 1959 this was acquired by Reinhold Delzer, a Bismarck, North Dakota, enthusiast who rescued it from the theatre just before the building was torn down to make room for the greatest of all civic improvements—a parking lot! The 1963 convention of the American Theatre Organ Society was centered around this particular instrument and was held in Bismarck.

In 1968, *The Console,* a monthly magazine put out by Tom B'hend, announced that I was working on a history of the theatre pipe organ and would publish it within a year. With the pressures of business, writing other books, and with many other activities, I never did write the theatre pipe organ book, but I still may do this someday.

In the meantime, in conjunction with my interest in musical instruments once used in movie palaces, I formed a collection of old photographs, literature, books, and memorabilia relating to nickelodeon theatres, opera houses, and later palace-style structures. I credit Tom B'hend and *The Console* for inspiring much of my early enthusiasm for the subject. This enthusiasm was amplified by collecting and then reading early issues of important trade magazines in the field: *The Billboard, The New York Clipper, Motion Picture News, Exhibitors Herald,* and *Moving Picture World,* each of which is a treasure trove of information.

The present book primarily covers the public exhibition of motion pictures in America from the 1890s through 1915, including the nickelodeon era. After 1915, the quaint nickel theatre was forgotten, and kitchen chairs in movie houses were replaced by plush seats set in gilded frames, all made possible by increased admission prices. In 1915, $2 was the price charged to see Griffith's *The Birth of a Nation* on its first run. When *Moving Picture World* in 1916 published a feature issue on the history of film exhibition, it was careful to preface a series of articles with a statement that much of the history, especially of the decade 1895-1905, had been lost, and that even at that date there were many conflicting statements, ideas, and historical versions.

Q. David Bowers
February 28, 1986.

THE SATURDAY EVENING POST

An Illust... ...ly
Founde... A.º D... ...anklin

MAY 17, 1913   5c. THE COPY

SHOWING TO-DAY
IN
3 REELS

THE GREAT WHITE WAY

The Showdown—By Josephine Daskam Bacon

Robert Robinson, one of the most popular magazine illustrators of the early part of this century, did many covers for "The Saturday Evening Post," including the May 17, 1913 issue. A bearded old-timer is shown groping in his pocket for a nickel needed to see "The Great White Way."

Reel I
NICKELODEON THEATRES

The Early Years

The passersby scanning the posted program for the week commencing Monday, April 20, 1895 at Koster & Bial's music hall, New York City, weren't aware that they were contemplating what was to become a memorable event in history: the first showing of a motion picture to a paying audience in America. Located at Broadway and 34th Street, at the spot which later became the site of Macy's Department Store, Koster & Bial's offered that week eight entertainment items. William Olschansky was billed as "The Russian Clown," while Cora Caselli was an "Eccentric Dancer," and the Three Delevines performed their original act, "Satanic Gambols." Paulinetti & Pico, Mr. and Mrs. Decreux-Geralduc, and the Brothers Horn were also on the ticket, but what ultimately proved to be the biggest attraction was the eighth item, "Thomas A. Edison's latest marvel, The Vitascope," presenting selections such as *Sea Waves, Umbrella Dance, The Barber Shop, Burlesque Boxing, Kaiser Wilhelm Reviewing His Troops, The Barroom,* and other topics.

The first actual performance apparently took place on April 23, 1896. The next morning the *New York Times* reported that "an unusually bright light fell upon the screen, then came into view two precious blonde persons of the variety stage, in pink and blue dresses, doing the umbrella dance with commendable celerity. Their motions were all clearly defined."

The idea of pictures in motion was hardly a new concept in 1896. Beginning decades earlier, numerous parlor toys, many of them made in France, used the principle of persistence of vision to create moving images. The Thaumatrope, developed in 1825, consisted of a circular board with the image of a parrot on one side and an empty cage on the other. When spun on its axis, the bird appeared to be within the cage. Another early device, the Phenakistiscope, invented by Joseph Antoine Ferdinand Plateau, featured images painted on a flat circular board, spun in front of a mirror, and viewed through tiny slits in order to separate the images. It was Plateau who concluded that 16 images per second furnished the optimum speed for reproducing movement.

Perhaps the most popular of all was the Zoetrope, made by William George Horner in the 1830s. This device consisted of a circular drum with a series of slits along the upper outer edge. Around the inside were placed interchangeable printed strips. When viewed through the slits on the opposite side of the drum, when the device was rotating, the images appeared to move. Acrobats jumped up and down, lions bounded through hoops, and clowns did headstands. Thousands of Zoetropes were sold throughout the 19th century and were in the form of small toys, held by a handle on the bottom of the drum or mounted on a small stand. The Praxinoscope was a somewhat similar device but consisted of a removable strip placed around the inside of a rotating drum, with a series of mirror facets at the center of the drum. When rotated, the images viewed through the mirror facets appeared to move. Certain Praxinoscope devices were quite elaborate, including the coin-operated Praxinoscope-Theatre, which featured moving pictures as well as a music box and animated dolls and which was used, among other places, to entertain patrons waiting for trains in Swiss railroad stations.

In 1872, Eadweard Muybridge was commissioned by Leland Stanford, a railroad mogul who at one time served as governor of California, to help him settle a bet as to whether during a horse race all four hooves of the animal left the ground simultaneously. Muybridge rigged a series of cameras in a row, each tripped in sequence as the horse went by, creating a group of still pictures freezing the motion at various instants. The project demonstrated that all four hooves did indeed leave the ground at once. Muybridge went on to photograph many other things. Later, some 20,000 of his images were published in 11 large volumes titled *Animal Locomotion*. On May 4, 1880, Muybridge used a projector, his Zoogyroscope, to display on a screen pictures of dogs, deer, other animals, and athletes to members of the San Francisco Art Association. Around the same time, Dr. E.J. Marey, who in 1874 had devised his "photographic revolver," refined the device so that it could take 100 photographs per second. This single camera gadget (as opposed to a row of many separate cameras used by Muybridge) was an early forerunner of the motion picture camera.

In 1888, Thomas Edison enlisted the assistance of William Kennedy Laurie Dickson, a new employee, to work on a device for recording photographic images. Named the Kinetograph, the machine underwent development and refinement. By 1890, it and the Kinetoscope, a projector, were used to record and show pictures in synchronization, more or less, with an Edison cylinder phonograph.

In 1892, the Kinetoscope was made in the form of a nickel-operated peep show. It was hoped to have production models ready for the World's Columbian Exposition to be held in Chicago in 1893, but the deadline could not be met, although an early account relates that at least one machine was shown there. Meanwhile at the Exposition the Anschutz Tachyscope, a coin-operated device which featured a circular glass plate revolving within a cabinet, with pictures on the outer rim of the disc appearing in succession as a light flashed, attracted attention. By February 1894, after the fair had run its course, some 25 coin-operated Kinetoscopes were ready and were sold to Frank Gammon (who had been secretary of the Awards Committee of the Columbian Exposition) and Alfred O. Tate. The idea of an accompanying phonograph was dropped for most units sold, but a few peep shows were of the Kinetophone type and used cylinder records with music. Of the 25 units, 10 were installed in an arcade at 1155 Broadway, New York City, while five went to Atlantic City and ten to Chicago, where they were displayed in a parlor in the Ashland Block on the northwest corner of Clark and Randolph streets. The New York installation made its debut on Saturday, April 14, 1894, when a total of $120 was taken in. In the period of nearly a year from April 14, 1894 to April 1, 1895, the New York City parlor grossed $16,171.56. By November 1894, Kinetoscope parlors were operating not only in the United States, but in France, England, Denmark, and other countries. Within a year or so, over 900 peephole Kinetoscopes had been sold. Among the early film subjects were Minnie Renwood in a serpentine dance copied from Loie Fuller, the Sisters Leigh in their umbrella dance, and several boxing matches.

The development of a Kinetoscope to project images against a screen in a theatre was encountering difficulties. In 1896, Edison purchased the rights to Thomas Armat's "Vitascope" and subsequently marketed it under the Edison name. Armat, a Washington, D.C. realtor, had contrived the device after seeing an Anschutz Tachyscope at the Columbian Exposition in 1893. The Vitascope was short-lived in Edison's hands. A few months later, after having made some improvements, Edison dropped the Vitascope and marketed the Projecting Kinetoscope.

Other pioneers in the development of motion picture projection were Woodville Latham and his two sons, Virginians who devised the Panoptikon in 1895. Using a film measuring about 70mm wide, twice the width of Edison's, the Panoptikon image was sharper and clearer. Although some exhibitions were given in New York City and other locations, the venture was not a commercial success.

In France, Antoine Lumiere and Louis, his eldest son, operated a factory which employed over 300 people in the making of film. To expand their market, they sought to develop motion pictures, which they did with success. Studying Edison's devices, the Lumieres made several improvements.

On December 28, 1895, they opened a moving picture show in the Salon Indien in the basement of the Grand Cafe, Paris. Seats were priced at one franc each. In the beginning, little attention was paid to the novelty, but soon it caught on, and crowds flocked to see the pictures in motion. Typical early programs included such features as workers leaving the Lumiere factory, the sea, a gardener tending to his duties, and various city scenes. More exciting were such Lumiere subjects as a train rushing toward the audience and a hapless man caught in the intricacies of a folding bed. A novelty film showed the demolition of a wall, then the sequence was run backwards, and the wall miraculously reassembled itself.

At a time when Edison was not interested in theatre projection of his films, the Lumieres made many advances, some of which, such as 16 frames per second projection speed and 35mm film width, became standard in the industry. Other experimenters in Germany, England, and elsewhere devised further improvements and innovations. Still others were concerned with the art of motion picture photography. Georges Melies, a Frenchman, experimented with unusual sequences, and a few years later created an early science fiction feature, *A Trip to the Moon*.

Two months after the memorable Vitascope performance at Koster & Bial's, an exhibition of the Cinematographe, the projection device of the Lumiere firm, was arranged at Keith's Union Square Theatre, a leading New York City vaudeville house. Invitations to the June 29, 1896 performance were sent out to the press:

"The pleasure of your presence is requested at a private exhibition, the first in America, of the famous Lumiere Cinematographe, to be given at this theatre tomorrow, Saturday, forenoon, at 10:30."

The public, excited by earlier Vitascope exhibitions at Koster & Bial's and at theatres in B.F. Keith's circuit, responded favorably to the Cinematographe. In numerous Keith houses, the Cinematographe replaced the Vitascope system.

THE EDENGRAPH

A Motion Picture Machine--Dust-proof and Flickerless

Below a rear view of the Edengraph mechanism is shown. Note that the complete mechanism is enclosed in a practically dust-proof metal envelope.

PATENTED DEC. 1, 1903.

The above illustration shows in detail the construction of the mechanism and the simple method of threading the film.

PATENTED DEC. 1, 1903.

The many radically new features are all fully described in a handsomely illustrated catalog mailed on request.

EDENGRAPH MANUFACTURING CO.

GEORGE KLEINE, Pres.

135 West Third Street, : : : : New York

SELLING AGENTS:

Kleine Optical Company, 52 State Street, Chicago.	Clune Film Exchange, - Los Angeles, California.
C. B. Kleine, - - 19 East 21st Street, New York.	Amalgamated Film Exchange, - Portland, Oregon.
General Film Company's Offices.	Amalgamated Film Exchange, Seattle, Washington.

The Edengraph projector was named after the Eden Musee, a New York attraction.

Writing years later in 1916, E.W. Sargent told of the early showing:

"The first formal appearance of the Cinematographe was June 29 [1896], when it came well down on the regular program as befitted the headlined attraction. It was not easy to tell from its reception how it really did appeal to that first audience. Many seemed to regard it as some fake, and others, better informed, viewed with wonder but offered scant applause. The films were not particularly interesting, the best liked being the Dover Pier with a high tide breaking over the wall, and the picture of the two Lumiere children. Indeed, it was the subjects that later caused the Cinematographe to be dropped in favor of the Biograph. What was wanted then were local views, and the pictures of Dead Man's Curve, where the Broadway cable cars had to make the run from 14th to 15th Street without loosening the grip, and the 6 o'clock rush at the Brooklyn Bridge. These were received with greater favor than European landscapes, views of the Lumiere employees leaving their factory, or glimpses of the Exposition at Geneva, Switzerland.

"Close on the heels of the Cinematographe came the Eidoloscope at Koster & Bial's; an effort to trade on the name of Edison. They were then giving the evening performances in the roof garden, and this would seem to be the first open air projection of record. In the fall, Oscar Hammerstein opened his new amusement enterprise, now the New York Theatre, and its variously-named sister theatre, but then known as the Olympia, and the Lyric. Here was shown the American Biograph, and the star feature was the 50-foot length film of William McKinley, then the Republican presidential candidate, on the lawn of his home in Canton [Ohio]. This was the first use made of the motion picture as a campaign device."

The Biograph firm first began business in December 1895 as the American Mutoscope Company at 841 Broadway, New York City. In 1899 the name was changed to the American Mutoscope & Biograph Company, by which time the outfit had seven European branches as well as outlets in India and South Africa. By 1902 it was stated that the New York parent company was capitalized at $2 million. In 1909 the corporate name was changed to the Biograph Company.

On October 12, 1896, the *New York Mail & Express* carried an announcement concerning the show at Hammerstein's Olympia: "Major William McKinley will appear tonight in New York for a great throng of people, which will include members of the Republican National Committee and, in all probability, Mr. and Mrs. Garret A. Hobart. Major McKinley will not make a speech, [but] he will talk with a friend, and then retire to his dwelling, which, it may be remarked, will appear along with him.

"The new wonder of instantaneous photography and enlarged reproduction of photographic plates, called the Biograph, is the medium through which the distinguished statesman will make his appearance, apparently on the lawn of his house in Canton, full life size, and in action so perfectly natural that only the preinformed will know that they are looking upon shadow, not upon substance... All of this is to be at Hammerstein's Olympia tonight. The Biograph seems to be the limit of realism in enlarged photographic reproduction. It is constructed on a principle similar to the Vitascope, which succeeded the Eidoloscope, and is said to be as far ahead of its former invention in the perfection of its startling realistic reproductions as the Vitascope is ahead of the Kinetoscope, which was regarded as a marvel of inventive genius. Instantaneous photographs of figures in motion are first taken by an entirely new process on a great number of rapidly revolving plates. These are enlarged, and with a powerful set of lenses and in an intense steady white light the pictures are thrown on the screen with such rapidity that every motion is secure in the instantaneous photograph, even to the driving wheels of a locomotive running at 60 miles per hour..."

On the following day the same publication noted: "The scene of the McKinley and Hobart parade at Canton called forth great applause, but when a few minutes later the audience caught sight of the next president himself, 'in the flesh,' pandemonium broke loose for five minutes. Men stood up in their seats and yelled with might and main, and flags were waved by dainty hands that would fain cast a vote on November 3rd for the good cause. To satisfy the audience, the Major was brought forth again with like result. There he stood on his much betrampled lawn at Canton, talking to his son. Leisurely, he read a telegram of congratulations, and then, turning, he came toward the excited audience, until it seemed as though he were about to step down into their very midst. But, at that moment came the edge of the curtain and he vanished around the corner to address a delegation of working men."

On the same day the *New York Tribune* reviewed the performance, noting in part: "The audience went fairly frantic over pictures thrown on a screen. Several machines for the throwing of moving pictures had been shown here, but the new Biograph, for all its horrible name, is the best of all of them. The biggest part of the enthusiasm came when a view of the McKinley and Hobart parade in Canton was shown. The cheering was incessant as long as the line was passing across the screen, and it grew much greater when the title of the next picture appeared: 'Major McKinley at Home.' The Biograph showed some other interesting pictures, notably one of the Empire State Express rounding a curve, which was one of the best, if not the very best, motion pictures that has yet been exhibited here."

Concerning the train, the rival *New York Times* said: "The finest of all these pictures was one of the Empire State Express going at 60 miles speed. The train is seen coming out of a distant smoke cloud that marks the beginning of a curve. The smoke puffs grow denser on the vision, and soon coach after coach whirls to the front, and it seems as though the entire left-hand section of the house would soon be under the wheels that are racing for New York." The same account noted that other pictures in the program included *A Stable on Fire*, Joseph

4

Jefferson in the *Drinking Scene of Rip Van Winkle, Tribly and Little Bille,* and *The Washing of a Pickaninny by His Mother.*

Interest spread rapidly, and on November 3rd the Baltimore Sun informed readers that the Biograph furnished a nice intermission to minstrels at Ford's Opera House, and that among topics shown was a visit to Niagara Falls. On November 16, 1896, a reporter for the same paper, who had gone to New York City to visit Koster & Bial's, which had been exhibiting Biograph films for several weeks, wrote: "To my mind the Biograph is so far superior to the Cinematographe as the latter is to the Vitascope. I have seen all three of these inventions, the Vitascope at Bunnell's Grand Opera House and the Cinematographe at Poli's Wonderland Theatre, and can, therefore, compare their respective merits from the point of view from actual observation..."

Many press releases appeared in Chicago, St. Louis, St. Paul, Kansas City, Detroit, and other American cities.

From the commercial beginning in 1896, to shortly after the turn of the century, the motion picture was considered to be an addition to a vaudeville show or stage program and served as a filler or curiosity. Exactly when the first theatre expressly for the showing of motion pictures was set up is a matter of historical controversy. Among the claimants was William T. Rock, who later became president of the Vitagraph Company, who stated that he opened a storefront theatre in New Orleans on July 18, 1896.

In the cradle years of motion picture exhibition, films tended to represent objects in motion—such as trains, waves, amusement park rides, and the like. There were exceptions, however, with a short Edison film titled *The John Rice-May Irwin Kiss,* filmed for the Kinetoscope in 1896, causing a sharp reaction, with many do-gooders suggesting that such romantic situations be banned from public showing.

Europe was the scene of much motion picture activity. Georges Melies, whose *A Trip to the Moon* caused a sensation, produced many other widely acclaimed pictures, with many incorporating interesting novelty effects. Pathe Freres was formed by Charles Pathe and three of his brothers. Hundreds of different film subjects were produced. Business was so good that a branch was later opened in Bound Brook, New Jersey. In France, the Lumieres continued their activity, while in England such individuals as James Williamson, Cecil Hepworth, and G.A. Smith made advances in film technology, including editing and splicing together film sequences in order to make the action more continuous. At the time, most other producers simply projected all that the camera saw.

There was much pirating, and no sooner did one firm produce a subject than several others made unauthorized prints. Later, motion picture production companies incorporated their logotypes and trademarks on room and building walls and other parts of the scenery in order to curtail the copying practice, but enterprising film laboratory personnel often blanked out the trademarks on each feature, frame by frame.

In 1897, Enoch Rector produced on 1,000 feet of film the sequence of the Corbett-Fitzsimmons boxing match held at Carson City, Nevada. Audiences were thrilled, and for the next decade or more, pugilistic encounters were in great demand. In the same year, J. Stuart Blackton, who earlier was on the staff of the *New York World,* founded the Vitagraph Company, whose first feature film was *Burglar on the Roof.* Later, the Vitagraph Company was to achieve great fame and success.

In the meantime, the American Mutoscope & Biograph Company, of which William Dickson, formerly associated with Edison, was a principal, continued to loom large on the American scene. The Mutoscope, an arcade device which offered a series of printed photographs mounted on a drum and turned by a handle so that each one flicked into view in sequence, quickly became popular, and by the turn of the century thousands were in use all over the world. Like the Kinetoscope, the Mutoscope was often arrayed in long rows in parlors or galleries. Unlike the Kinetoscope and other early arcade devices which used motion picture film, the Mutoscope remained in use for many decades. In 1955, when Disneyland opened in Anaheim, California, one feature of the Penny Arcade on Main Street was a double row of coin-operated Mutoscopes, antiques rescued from an earlier era.

The much-acclaimed Biograph projecting system soon became a fixture in theatres all across America and Europe. Indeed, in England *biograph* became a generic word for the motion picture theatre. The Biograph firm was a prolific producer of film subjects. Many who were to become prominent in filmdom in later years, Mary Pickford, Mack Sennett, and David Wark Griffith among them, got their start with Biograph.

Not everyone liked motion pictures, and years later in *Moving Picture World* a critic wrote: "Motion pictures were at first a vaudeville 'headliner'—a world's wonder that drew the curious by the thousands, but they quickly degenerated into the 'chaser'—the last number on the bill, a position which none wanted, and were used to drive the people out of the house. The light was uniformly bad in those days, and the film was almost always 'rainy' and indistinct, a condition which compelled the audience to get out as a matter of self protection." However, advertisements and articles in contemporary trade publications, including *The Billboard* and *The New York Clipper,* indicate that motion pictures were alive and well and that the field was rapidly expanding during the late 1890s and early 1900s.

The idea that films were used to chase people out of the theatre, and that, as such, films were bad, has been reiterated by a number of later writers, most of whom were echoing what they had read elsewhere. One early writer, a person who was on the scene in the 1890s, presented what seems to be a more accurate view. Writing in *Moving Picture World,* May 12, 1917, James S. McQuade observed:

"[In the 1890s] travelogues, taken on the engine of a moving train, had been used as the closing number of

5

high-class vaudeville programs throughout the country, an unusual honor; for, as the writer knows by experience, the last number was always considered in those days the most attractive on the bill, so that it might hold the audience and send them away pleased and with something to talk about."

The Nickel Theatre

At the dawn of the 20th century, vaudeville was still king, but the motion picture was making a serious challenge to the throne. All across America, opera houses, town halls, and theatres were packed with audiences that came to watch and hear stage performances of *Uncle Tom's Cabin, East Lynne, Hazel Kirke,* and other dramatic productions, as well as monologuists, acrobats, singers, and musicians. The Hippodrome, Keith's, Orpheum, and other vaudeville circuits were raking in money, usually charging 10, 20, or 30 cents admission, depending upon the location of a particular seat. Involving dozens of people employed as actors, stagehands, ushers, and helpers, the operation of a vaudeville theatre was a major business enterprise.

Before long, vaudeville theatre owners, amusement park operators, and others involved in public entertainment realized that motion pictures, which involved little operating expense in their showing, could, for a nickel admission, earn more money than shows featuring live performers. The number of films shown at opera houses and vaudeville theatres increased, and instead of being one item on the program, films appeared several times during a show. It was but a short step to the showing of films exclusively, perhaps on two or three selected nights each week. In the meantime, moving pictures were drawing crowds into tent shows, called "black tops" by the trade, for the top of the canvas was dyed black to keep out the daylight. Some black-top picture shows followed fairs and carnivals, while others were set up at amusement parks, and still others traveled from town to town independently. Often a single operator would own a dozen or more traveling shows. The demand for film subjects was intense, and more production companies sprang up. An idea of the variety of films available in the early days can be gained from the November 1902 catalogue of the American Mutoscope & Biograph Company, 248 pages in length, which offered nearly 2,500 motion pictures for sale!

What some historians view as the first establishment set up specifically for the commercial showing of motion pictures in America was Thomas L. Tally's Electric Threatre, which opened in Los Angeles at 262 South Main Street in April 1902. Earlier, the same entrepreneur operated Tally's Phonograph and Vitascope Parlor, 311 South Spring Street, Los Angeles, also known as Tally's Phonograph and Kinetoscope Parlor. In 1902, he set up a projector and screen in the rear of his arcade, separating the pictures from the parlor by means of a screen with peep holes. The motion pictures proved to be more popular than the coin-operated peep shows, the division screen was removed, and soon the Electric Theatre was billed as providing "up-to-date high class motion picture entertainment especially for ladies and children."

Publicity given to Tally's Electric Theatre spurred others into action, and within a few years patrons of every small and medium-size town and city in the United States could part with a nickel and see express trains in action, ships coming into dock, athletic contests, the rides at Coney Island and other amusement parks, Yellowstone, and various other scenic attractions.

In the same year that Tally's Electric Theatre made its debut, 1902, what is believed to be the first film exchange was set up by Harry Miles at 116 Turk Street in San Francisco. The idea caught on, and soon exchanges were located in other major cities. Now, the movie theatre owner could change his program often by renting the subjects he wanted. Earlier, in 1895, a pioneer exchange of sorts was set up whereby the owners of Kinetoscope peep shows could trade in old films for new ones, but Miles' 1902 exchange is believed to have been the first for projected movies.

The Great Train Robbery, produced, photographed, and directed by Edwin S. Porter for the Edison Company in 1903, achieved wide fame. The story progressed in narrative form, changing from one location to another, telling a story and building to a climax, with irrelevant footage deleted. Later, historians were to recognize it as the most important film made up to that time. Edwin Porter was to be deified by a generation of film historians as was his contemporary, David Wark Griffith. Unlike Griffith, who boasted of his accomplishments in full-page advertisements in trade publications, Porter was a modest man.

Around the turn of the century a popular amusement park "ride" consisted of an old street car with panoramic motion pictures projected to each side. Mounted on rollers, the car seemed to be moving. Those seated could look to either side and see the landscape whizzing by. In 1904, or earlier, George C. Hale and Fred W. Gifford, of Kansas City, built a similar device, but one resembling a Pullman railroad car, open at one end, across which was stretched a curtain displaying pictures projected from the back side. The reproduction was life size and gave the illusion of a fast-moving train, as the car "in motion" progressed down the track. Mechanical devices under the unit caused it to tilt, shake, quiver, and jolt, an illusion added to by sounds of a locomotive whistle, train bell, and rushing wind. The experience was memorable to those who participated, and by word of mouth the crowds increased. An early exhibition of the device, named Hale's Tours, took place at Electric Park in Kansas City and consisted of two "Pullman cars" with an ornate facade. The cost, including the projection equipment, was $7,000. Paying an admission of 10c, about 60 passengers filled each car 20 or more times a day, more on weekends. At the St. Louis World's Fair, 1904, Hale's Tours drew record crowds. Riders could take a cog railway up Mt. Pilatus in Switzerland, or climb Mt. Lowe in Southern California, or go through the Canadian Rockies or tour New Hampshire's scenic White Mountains. "It was difficult to realize, after such a ride, that one had not actually been

New York City's Union Square early in the twentieth century. Union Square featured many sidewalk attractions, including Automatic Vaudeville, a large penny arcade lined with banks of automatic phonographs, music machines, and skill devices. An interior view of the same establishment is shown immediately below.

Hale's Tours consisted of a long gallery built in the form of a railway car, with the interior train seats facing toward a movie screen. Shown were travelogues taken from the front of a moving train, thus giving the illusion of an actual journey, an effect aided by shaking and rocking the car, clanging a bell, and simulating the sound of escaping steam and rushing wind. Hundreds of Hale's Tours installations were set up all over the world. The novelty first attracted widespread attention at the St. Louis World's Fair in 1904.

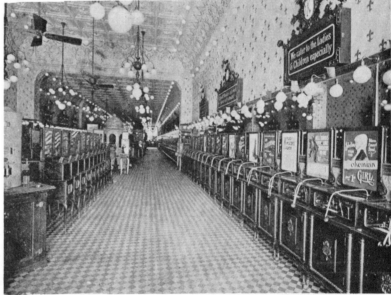

ABOVE: Interior of Automatic Vaudeville located on Union Square at 48 East 14th Street, New York City. "The greatest place of amusement on earth for one cent" the establishment advertised. Along the right wall are dozens of coin-operated phonographs, while along the left are coin-operated peep shows.

LEFT: The American Mutoscope & Biograph Company, a leading pioneer film maker, sold thousands of Mutoscope arcade machines. Shown at the left is a circa 1903 model in an ornate cast iron case with scrollwork at the bottom and an eagle motif to each side of the top. The subject "America Wins" is featured on the machine illustrated.

in Switzerland, the illusion was so perfect. It was startling to be shunted from the luxurious Pullman car out into a noisy, crowded park or street," an early report noted.

An early installation featured a sign lettered: "HALE'S TOURS AND SCENES OF THE WORLD, Trains Every Ten Minutes" and noted that the attractions included *A Trip Through Rugged Scotland* and *A Ride Through The Rocky Mountains of Western Canada*. While many films were especially made for the Hale's Tours show, more often standard film subjects would be shown to the audience, which was receptive to just about anything. Hale's Tours caught on like wildfire, and soon units could be seen in Winnipeg, Portland, Seattle, Toronto, Spokane, and other places. Improvements were made, and later cars seated 65 to 72 people each. William A. Brady in 1905 acquired the rights for 10 eastern states. The following year, Ward Gifford, representing the owners, went to Europe and Africa to set up installations. Hong Kong, on the coast of China, was another popular spot, according to early accounts. In most cases, territorial rights were sold, with Hale and Gifford sending technicians to supervise the various installations. In Chicago, Hale's Tours played on State Street, while in New York City the first was set up on the corner of 14th Street and Broadway. Eventually, more than 300 Hale's Tours cars were set up by Hale and Gifford in the United States, with 200 or more being erected by purchasers of territorial rights. It is said that the sum of $100,000 was paid for the British license alone. With so many exhibition points, the supply of film quickly became a problem. In the beginning, a film program was run for a week, then changed. Films were transferred through commercial exchanges, which passed the features from one Hale's Tours to another.

The novelty of Hale's Tours soon faded, and it was realized that a storefront-type theatre had better seating advantages, could be set up more cheaply, and required no licenses. George C. Hale went on to become the fire chief of Kansas City, later entering into the manufacture of fire-fighting apparatus. Fred W. Gifford became a leading Missouri attorney, while his son, Ward Gifford, who installed many of the Hale's Tours, became a newspaper writer.

Just as the precise time and location of the first theatre specifically set up to show moving pictures in America is a matter of controversy, so it is with the inception of the term *nickelodeon*. The most plausible account has it that on June 15, 1905, John P. Harris, earlier associated with the vaudeville theatre, and Harry Davis, his brother-in-law, opened a motion picture gallery in a store at 433-435 Smithfield Street in Pittsburgh, Pennsylvania. They decorated the front ornately, sold tickets for 5c, hired a pianist to accompany the film, and called the establishment The Nickelodeon. The first program included *The Great Train Robbery*. It was reported that the establishment took in over $1,000 per week. Harris opened other nickel theatres but eschewed the Nickelodeon name for them in favor of Bijou Dream.

John R. Freuler, who later became president of the Mutual Film Corporation, invested $450 in a storefront nickel theatre in Milwaukee in 1905. Carl Laemmle, who was to go on to great fame in the field, had a nickelodeon in Chicago about the same time, while Adolph Zukor, who later controlled the Famous Players Film Company, had one on 14th Street, near Broadway, in New York City. In the early days "Pop" Lubin, who operated a film laboratory, had a number of nickelodeons in Philadelphia.

"The moving picture business in Boston and New England had its origin in a little store on Boylston Street, close to the corner of Washington Street in what is now the main lobby of the Hotel Brewster," according to an account published in *Moving Picture World* in 1916. "Here in the winter of 1894-5 Frank J. Howard and Charles Sheafe, as partners, opened the first motion picture house in New England. The machine they had was one of the very first Edison Kinetoscopes. It was a big box-like affair, and the average reels were 42 feet.

"The first two films shown in New England were *May Irwin's Kiss* and *The Empire State Express*. The first moving picture show consisted of 82 feet of film. A little later this was extended to 600 to 700 feet per show. The price charged was 10 cents. The show house consisted of a plain store, the window light shut off by dark colored paper tacked over the glass. The screen was a plain cotton sheet, and the seats were kitchen chairs bought at a second-hand store. The operator stood on a table at the back of the hall. The show lasted about 20 minutes. The film ran out of the machine into a wastebasket. The film at that time cost 40 cents a foot. Today [in 1916] it costs about 10 cents a foot in spite of the increased cost of material and production.

"Right after the *May Irwin Kiss* and the *Empire State Express* came the Courtney-Corbett fight picture. Then in turn came the *Seminary Girls*, a 150-foot film, which, to the moving picture managers of the day, was considered the greatest film that could ever be produced. Its production marked a new era in the making of moving pictures. It pictured a dozen or more seminary girls, dressed in pajamas and nightgowns, fighting pillow battles, and for action was all to the good.

"The same winter that Howard and Sheafe were running their picture house on Boylston Street, two other stores were opened as moving picture houses, one on Tremont Street by the Read brothers, both of whom have passed on, and one on Boylston Street. The first moving picture operator in New England was Harry Rosendorf, who for years was an operator in Boston, and who had an interest in a motion picture house in New Hampshire. For the first eight months of 1896 no new moving picture subjects were received, but Howard and Sheafe continued to run their moving picture house, using the same subjects day after day, and people from all over New England came to see the wonderful moving pictures.

"Sheafe and Howard then parted company, and Mr. Sheafe retired from the business. Mr. Howard opened up the first film exchange in New England in the Jefferson Building, at 546 Washington Street. He ran the moving pictures in connection with a nickel-in-the-slot business. During his spare time he exhibited the moving pictures before clubs and societies in New England.

"The development of the business during this period showed two strange tendencies. The moving pictures were not taken up by theatrical managers, but were promoted by the nickelodeon managers. At this time—1896 to 1900—the thousands of nickel-in-the-slot machine emporiums throughout New England had seen their best days and were beginning to show decline. It was therefore to the moving pictures that these men turned. During this time the moving picture business was practically at a standstill. It had its ups and downs. This was the climactic period of the industry. Edison was practically the only producing company, and subjects were few and far between. It was at this time that foreign films began to come in at odd periods.

"The development of the industry was very slow between 1895 and 1905. During this time Mr. Howard was selling Edison machines and selling film. His customers came principally from shoe workers, grocers, textile hands, and others from the mill towns, who, hearing of the new moving pictures, came to Boston, bought an outfit with a couple of films, and started in the show business. Ninety percent of these ventures were failures, principally from the fact that the men had no knowledge of electricity, knew nothing of the moving picture machine, were in total ignorance of the show business, and, in fact, were totally unfit for promoting *any* amusement enterprise."

The same issue of *Moving Picture World* gave a history of film exhibition in Pittsburgh, apparently erroneously placing the date of Davis' early nickelodeon enterprise at 1903:

"A review of the history of the exhibiting business in Pittsburgh must logically begin with the discussion of one man, the father of the moving picture theatre, Harry Davis. The name of Harry Davis stands forth more conspicuously in this field than that of probably any other individual, not because of his extensive interest at the present time [in 1916] but because he was the first to see the limitless possibilities of the screen.

"Mr. Davis opened the first moving picture theatre in this city on Smithfield Street, two doors from Diamond Street, Pittsburgh, in the year 1903. He named the house The Nickelodeon, and thus coined a title that has clung to the picture theatres through all the steps in its development… The Nickelodeon seated 200 people and, despite the small capacity, was considered a veritable 'gold mine' from the very beginning. The house was open from 8 o'clock until midnight, and the shows lasted only 15 minutes to a half an hour, in which manner entertainment was provided to three to four thousand daily.

"One of the most notable features of The Nickelodeon was its music. Not that a symphony orchestra, or even a pipe organ, was as yet even dreamed of by Mr. Davis as a possibility for moving picture entertainment. The musical setting was supplied by a lone pianist—who was none other than the well-known composer of popular melodies of today, Harry Carroll. Mr. Carroll, who had not yet written *Within the Loop* nor his ballads such as *The

Trail of the Lonesome Pine*, received the staggering salary of $6 per week.

"Within a year after The Nickelodeon was opened, Mr. Davis had some eight or ten Nickelodeons scattered about in the different sections of the city. While The Nickelodeon was the first moving picture theatre in the world, Mr. Davis does not have the distinction of having opened the second, which was established in Warsaw, Poland. A certain Pole, whose name is not recalled here, passed through Pittsburgh shortly after the opening of The Nickelodeon and carried back with him the idea which he immediately put into effect. Another year saw the establishment of Davis' picture theatres in Philadelphia, Rochester (New York), Buffalo, and Detroit, besides a total of 17 in the Pittsburgh district alone."

In later years, several other historians credited Davis with almost single-handedly starting the motion picture business in America. In reality, the most he did was create the "nickelodeon" name.

In Atlanta, the story went something like this:

"In November 1906 Atlanta's first moving picture house was opened by S. P. Robbins on Viaduct Place and was known as the Viaduct. It gave fifteen minute shows with single reels and had a seating capacity of about 150. It was poorly ventilated, but it was a success from a financial point of view.

"In February 1907 a company composed of L.P. Daniels, S.P. Robbins, and L.H. Lansdell opened at 46 Whitehall what was known as the Twin Theatres. A broad partition divided the theatre, and a fifteen minute show was given on each side, with a five cent admission. Daniels, a successful clothing merchant, financed the theatre and for several years it was the leader. A graphophone was placed in the lobby; this was looked after by a Negro boy, who did his work so well that department stores within the block threatened all manner of injunctions. Daniels was firm in his belief that a theatre without music was a failure, and he compromised the matter by muffling the horn of the instrument with a ball of cotton and restricting the music to certain hours.

"In the fall of 1907 two theatres were equipped on the north side, both on Peachtree Street, the Pastime and the Elite. In November 1908 two prosperous furniture men saw the future in moving pictures and partitioned off a portion of their store, equipped it with the best, and started the Vaudette Theatre. From the start their theatre was a success.

"In 1908 many small theatres sprang up, but they soon went out of business. Poor equipment and inefficient operators, as well as old pictures, caused the decline in patronage. During the same year the Savoy on Peachtree Street was opened by a theatrical man named Posey. It started well but declined."

Other Early Installations

In Louisville, Kentucky, the story, as related by *Moving Picture World*, was similar:

San Francisco, Cal., Dates Back to the Year 1894

Peter Bacigalupi was First Dealer--Greatest Development Has Come Since the Earthquake and Fire of 1906

ONE of the pioneers in the moving picture business on the Pacific Coast is Peter Bacigalupi, of the firm of Peter Bacigalupi & Sons, 908 Market street, San Francisco, now handling phonographs and automatic musical instruments. Mr. Bacigalupi was interested in the moving picture industry from 1894, when the first machines were brought here, until the great fire of 1906, when he turned his attention to other lines. His memory is clear on the early days of the industry and he has some interesting relics to show of the pioneer days. Among these are business cards he had made shortly after the first films were brought to the Coast. Whenever a film became torn or badly worn it would be cut up and a section pasted over a hole cut in a business card, making a souvenir that was in much demand in those days. One of the most interesting relics in his possession, however, is a card establishing the date when moving pictures were first shown here. This reads as follows:

San Francisco, June first, 1894.
This is to certify that Captain John F. Ryan, United States Government Diver (a Christian), was the first man who paid to see the Edison Kinetoscope west of Chicago.

(Signed) HOLLAND BROS.

This was written in the back of a business card bearing the following wording:

Edison Kinetoscope,
Holland Bros.,
Ottawa, Canada.
Foreign Agents.
Represented by A. Holland.

"When Holland Bros. brought the Edison Kinetoscope to the Pacific Coast," said Mr. Bacigalupi, "I closed a deal at once for the five machines they had, paying $2,500 for them. These were set up in a store in the Chronicle Building at Market and Kearney streets and people stood in line to see the pictures, paying a fee of 10 cents. This was before a screen was used, one person monopolizing a machine during the run of the film, which was, of course, very short. Backed by himself and others E. H. Amet of Waukegan, Ill., commenced the manufacture of a machine called the Magniscope, but only a few were made.

"Walter Furst was the first man to have a five-cent show here, his house being located on Market street about where the Odeon theater now is, this being known as the Cinegraph. At first vaudeville was given upstairs and when the performance here was over the audience would go to a room below where moving pictures were shown, everyone standing to see them, there being no seats. At first ten cents was charged, but later the vaudeville was eliminated and straight pictures were shown at five cents.

"One of the first attempts to use a screen in connection with moving pictures was made by a man named Wright who came here from Portland and worked for the late Charles L. Ackerman, the attorney. He took one of the coin-in-the-slot machines, turned it on its side and with but a few changes threw a picture on a screen. He later opened a theater on Market street, near Ffith, where the Lincoln

Peter Bacigalupi, San Francisco, Cal.

Market now stands, and this house, with the one conducted by Walter Furst were among those destroyed by the fire of 1906.

About 1898 D. J. Grauman entered the field, after working for Walter Furst for a time, opening the Unique theater on market street, near Mason. He made a big success of the business and bought a large part of the films I was importing at that time. In 1900 I made a visit to Paris and bought a large quantity of Pathe, Gaumont and other foreign films and sold most of these to Mr. Grauman upon my return. Most of these films came in lengths of from fifty to one hundred and fifty feet and sold at about $25 for the shorter lengths. Some of these early subjects would be very interesting now. For instance, among the first films shown here were some featuring Ruth St. Denis, the dancer, Sandow and Anna Belle Moore.

"Among the first Biographs brought here was one showing Pope Leo XIII. I brought this to the Orpheum and at the

Unique Theater, Seattle, Wash., First Picture House of Miles Bros., Herbert Miles in Lobby.

same time brought John Brandlein, an operator, to the city, and he is still to be found here. The pictures of Pope Leo were also shown in Metropolitan Hall on Fifth street, but although they were excellent, about the best that had been shown here up to that time, the attendance was very light. Mrs. McEnerney, wife of the well known attorney, was an enthusiast over this picture, and saw it many times.

"At the time of the fire of 1906 my headquarters were at 786 Mission street, up to then, and I was doing a big business in moving pictures, Edison machines and penny arcade goods. I operated two of the latter, one being on Market street, at Stockton, and the other in the historic old Bella Union theater on Kearny street. When I lost the Edison agency it was taken over by George Breck, the supply man."

This page from "The Moving Picture World," July 15, 1916, gives a version of the early days of motion picture exhibition in San Francisco.

"Trial Marriages," a 1907 Biograph film, promised viewers many "humorous possibilities." The hero goes from one girl to another, finally deciding that bachelorhood is best.

11

ABOVE: An advertisement by the Great Northern Special Feature Film Company, New York, offers two feature subjects and invites film exchanges to contract for them on a state by state basis. Film exchanges, which flourished beginning in the 1903 to 1905 years, provided a ready way for nickelodeon theatre operators to obtain fresh material on a rental basis. Note that the advertisement states that Great Northern produced two features per month and supplied posters for its films.

LEFT: The Chicago Photo-Playwright College apparently operated from a post office box and was one of many learn-by-mail operations set up to satisfy the demand for those desiring to become part of the growing motion picture industry. This particular outfit offered a special prize and noted that: "No experience or literary ability required."

A popular young man has a problem many people wish they had. He solves it in the best way, of course!

Kate or Alice, Sue or May—
Whom shall I take to the photoplay?
They all are fair and fascinating,

And all extremely captivating.
Whom shall I take? I've got a "hunch!"
Guess I'll have to take the bunch.

"The moving picture industry took up its first home in Louisville at Fifth and Market streets, with the Dreamland Theatre opening April 6, 1904. This theatre is said to have been the second in the country with a regular moving picture front. A small storeroom was converted, the front painted white, and many incandescent lights installed. It was operated by Irvin Simons, Sam Lorch, and Alex Kraemer. It probably seated about 150 people. In 1906 the Columbia, later known as the Bijou, was opened on Fourth, near Market. This theatre seated about 250 people and had a very elaborate front and was the last word in moving picture theatre construction of the day.

"The largest photoplay house in the world in those days fell to this city when the Hopkins Theatre was opened for photoplays in 1908, after having run as a vaudeville house for years. It was operated by O.T. Crawford, of St. Louis, who was interested in some smaller theatres and the local film exchange, and J.D. Tippet. The house had a seating capacity of 2,400 on the first floor, a balcony and two galleries.

"Shortly after the Dreamland was opened, this concern leased a building on Fourth Street, near Walnut and painted up an entrance representing two passenger cars. Travel scenes were shown on the inside of the theatre, and, while of a great educational value, these did not prove profitable. A similar show was given at Fontaine Ferry Park for one season."

The same era saw activity in many other cities, including one of Ohio's leading metropolises: "The first picture theatre in Cleveland, the American, was started in November 1904 by William Bullock, brother of Sam Bullock. The American was located on Superior Avenue, near East 6th Street, the heart of the downtown section. It seated 320 persons and was regarded as a marvel of up-to-dateness, as the box office receipts showed nightly.

"Bullock, being the son of William Bullock, a veteran magic lantern and dissolving view operator widely known in England, fitted into the moving picture business as naturally as if he had been born in it. As part of his equipment in the American, Bullock brought with him a few hundred stereopticon slides to supplement the moving picture machine and the limited number of reels then obtainable.

"Within a year after Bullock opened the American, there were about a half a dozen picture theatres in Cleveland, principally what were known as 'store' shows. One of the first men to open a 'store' show was Frank M. Kenney. In 1905, Kenney opened the Clark Theatre in a store room near Clark Avenue and West 46th Street. For nearly four years Kenney operated this theatre with only 125 seats, but the place was always crowded. In 1909, Kenney built a modern 400-seat house opposite his store show."

In Maine the following is said to have occurred:

"Bangor's first moving picture theatre was The Nickel, opened in August 1906 in a modern building that had just been completed. The builder, John R. Graham, had made arrangements with the Keith interests for the opening of a moving picture house in a new block and, as a result,

the best skill of architects was brought to bear to make a theatre that would compare very favorably indeed with any then in existence for showing film productions. So, Bangor was particularly fortunate in having a splendid show house for its early motion picture plays—not the first pictures, for they had been shown in the old Opera House on Main Street as far back as 1899.

"Bangor attended The Nickel first out of curiosity and liked the pictures so much that the new house became a bonanza. The programs were short; people could come in at any hour of the afternoon and evening and see the beginning of a picture showing people chasing a miscreant colliding with a policeman. There were no dramas at first—mostly scenes of upsetting a pan of flour, etc., also views of scenery taken from the front or rear end of a train. But these captivated theatregoers, and so rapidly did the pictures improve that the people kept on coming.

"The novelty and all the other factors mentioned combined to keep The Nickel and the other theatres that started up shortly after crowded all the time. A Mr. Howe was the first manager of The Nickel, and he was succeeded by several managers in rapid succession. Early in 1907, James P. Forrest, a Bangor theatrical manager of considerable experience, became manager, and held that position for two years, with credit to himself. In May 1909, Stephen Bogrett, a manager of experience, came to Bangor to succeed Mr. Forrest as manager of The Nickel. Mr. Forrest took over the management of the Gaiety Theatre, which was established by the Keith interests in Norumbega Hall.

"Both The Nickel and the Gaiety, the latter devoted to vaudeville with moving pictures, prospered greatly until the day that will always be remembered in Bangor's history, April 30, 1911. On this day a $3,000,000 conflagration struck Bangor, and it wiped out The Nickel and the Gaiety so utterly that nothing but the office safes remained to show that there had been a theatre there. This concludes the history of the first Bangor motion picture house.

"Inspired by the success of The Nickel, three other houses opened in 1908 and 1909, the Graphic, the Gem, and the Union."

In the same recollections-packed issue of *Moving Picture World*, the claims of Philadelphia were advanced:

"There is no American-born citizen, and comparatively few of foreign birth, in the United States today who does not know in more or less detail the prominent place the city of Philadelphia occupies in the history of this country. Like unto its inseparable connection with history of the United States is Philadelphia's relation to the moving picture industry in America.

"Besides being among the first centers to exhibit the moving picture, it was in Philadelphia that Dr. Coleman Sellers, a Philadelphian, conceived the ideas for and built the first moving picture machine in 1858, which device, though crude, formed the nucleus around which the moving picture industry of today has been developed. [Sellers took a series of still pictures of his children, posing his children slightly differently in each advancing sequence.

The San Francisco fire and earthquake, April 18, 1906, made headlines around the world. Film makers rushed into production with graphic depictions of the disaster. The Biograph film advertised here was made by using "a model city, constructed in our studio from photographs," augmented by footage from the actual event.

Florence Lawrence starred in many Biograph pictures and became known as The Biograph Girl, although, in keeping with Biograph policy, her name appeared nowhere in the credits.

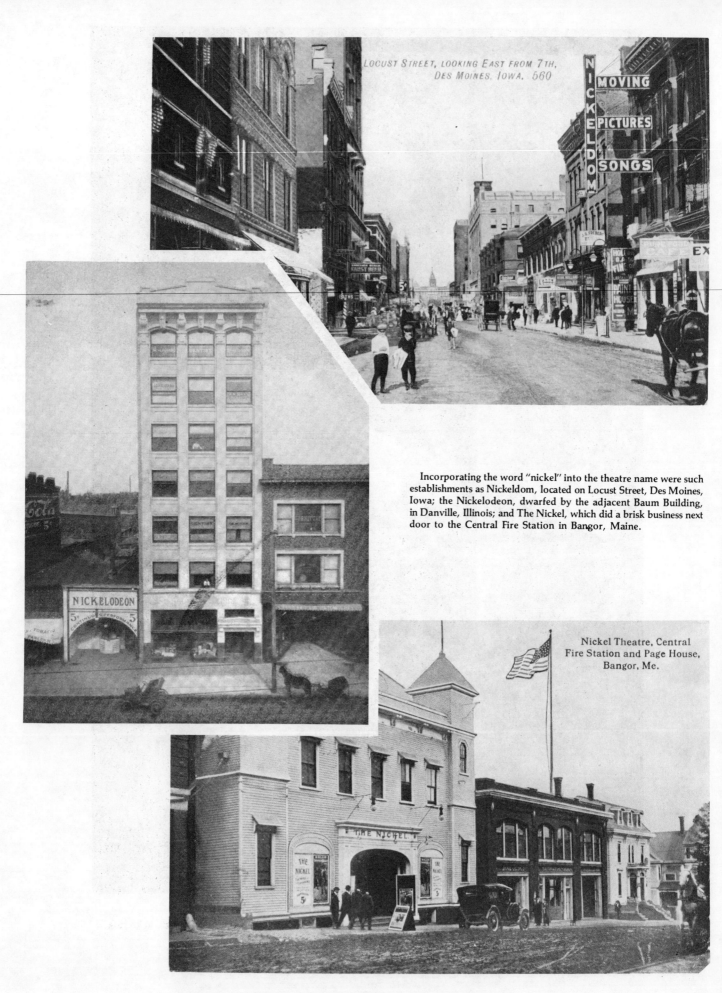

LOCUST STREET, LOOKING EAST FROM 7TH, DES MOINES, IOWA. 560

Incorporating the word "nickel" into the theatre name were such establishments as Nickeldom, located on Locust Street, Des Moines, Iowa; the Nickelodeon, dwarfed by the adjacent Baum Building, in Danville, Illinois; and The Nickel, which did a brisk business next door to the Central Fire Station in Bangor, Maine.

Nickel Theatre, Central Fire Station and Page House, Bangor, Me.

MOVING PICTURES

WE FURNISH COMPLETE OUTFITS

FOR

- 5-CENT THEATERS
- TRAVELING EXHIBITORS
- STREET ADVERTISING
- LODGE WORK
- CHURCH ENTERTAIN-MENTS
- PUBLIC SCHOOLS

AT THE VERY LOWEST PRICES

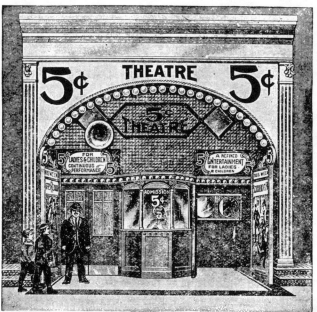

SEND FOR OUR 160-PAGE SPECIAL CATALOGUE

OF

- MOVING PICTURE MACHINES
- STEREOPTICONS
- GAS MAKING OUTFITS
- ILLUSTRATED SONG SLIDES
- LECTURE SETS OF VIEWS
- MOTION PICTURE FILM

AND FULL LINE OF SUPPLIES

THE NEW 1908 MODEL MOTIOGRAPH

THE NEW "MOTIOGRAPH" MOTION PICTURE MACHINE is the greatest machine ever made for 5-cent theater work. The "Motiograph" is the most powerful, the most strongly and substantially constructed motion picture machine on the market. It is a machine that will stand the hard wear and tear of continuous service that is demanded in 5-cent theater work. In the sharpness and clearness of the pictures, freedom from flicker, ease and convenience of operation, strength and durability, it surpasses any machine yet constructed. It is made with fireproof magazines, and automatic safety fire shutter. It complies with all fire ordinances and all rules of the board of underwriters. It is the latest, most practical, and the best motion picture machine made, not only for 5-cent theatre work, which is the hardest test to which a motion picture machine can be put, but for any class of moving picture work. For complete description, full specifications, and prices, send for our big special catalogue of stereopticons and motion picture apparatus which will be mailed to you free of charge.

THE MOVING PICTURE BUSINESS has grown to immense proportions, developing into a world wide enterprise, involving an invested capital of millions of dollars. Like the advent of the telephone or the graphophone, the moving picture machine was at first regarded as more or less of a curiosity, but when the possibilities of this new field became better known it grew more and more into favor with the public and recently has sprung into such popular favor that there is scarcely a city of any size in this country which does not contain a moving picture theater with an ever increasing number of regular patrons.

TRAVELING EXHIBITION WORK is today more popular than ever. An excellent plan is to map out a route which will take about a half year to cover, arranging your bookings several weeks or months in advance. Your advertising matter is sent on in advance so that when you reach each city you have only to give your exhibition, collect the receipts for the evening, and then pass to the next city. When you have finished your route it will then be time to start and go over the same ground again with a new lecture and, if your previous exhibition has been one to deserve appreciation, you will rapidly develop a steady patronage which will be worth many dollars to you in future years.

STREET ADVERTISING is a comparatively new but extremely interesting branch of exhibition work. For this business it is only necessary to have a good stereopticon outfit, such as those described in our special catalogue of these goods. You will also require a number of stereopticon views and a considerable quantity of attractive advertising slides. You then arrange with the merchants of your city to show their advertisements for a certain amount each night, and by stretching a screen upon the side of a building and placing your machine across the street, you can project your views and slides upon the screen. The novelty of this exhibition will attract many people, and you will be surprised to find how many will stop and remain for hours to watch these pictures. The merchants also feel the effects in increased business. This work can be done in your own city during the evening, as it does not in any way require all of your time.

CHURCHES, LODGES, AND SCHOOLS. Many of the largest churches are now using the stereopticon and find that it not only increases their attendance but creates a real interest in the subject of the day. Various organizations of the church will find the stereopticon a most profitable matter for their consideration. Lodge work is made far more interesting by the use of the stereopticon, and we furnish any secret society slides needed, a list of which is given in our special stereopticon catalogue. Schools and colleges are installing the stereopticon in many of their lecture rooms with most excellent results. These features and many other valuable and important facts regarding the stereopticon and moving picture business are fully described in our big 160-page Special Catalogue, which will be sent free, to any address, upon request.

THE 5-CENT THEATER IS HERE TO STAY. It fills a want that has existed in every community for a moderate priced form of clean, up to date amusement. This business offers attractive inducements to anyone with small capital who wishes to establish himself in a profitable and permanent business of his own. Almost any vacant store room can be made into a five-cent theater by removing the glass front and replacing it with a regular theater front similar to the illustration shown on this page. A show of about twenty minutes is given, and the low price of admission is an inducement which many people cannot resist.

SEND FOR OUR BIG 160-PAGE FREE CATALOGUE OF MOVING PICTURE MACHINES.

THIS IS THE LARGEST CATALOGUE of moving picture machines, stereopticons and exhibition supplies that has ever been published. This big catalogue fully illustrates and describes all of the apparatus used in public exhibition work, such as moving picture machines, stereopticons, gas making outfits, illustrated songs, moving picture film, etc. It shows exactly what is needed for a complete outfit, tells how to select the best machine, gives valuable hints and suggestions for the beginner, and will prove an invaluable guide to anyone who is interested in exhibition work of any kind.

EVERY MACHINE FULLY GUARANTEED. Every moving picture machine, stereopticon, gas making outfit, or apparatus of any kind that is described in our special moving picture catalogue, is sold under the terms of our binding guarantee to be entirely satisfactory to the purchaser, or it may be returned to us at once, and the entire amount of money will be promptly refunded, including also the transportation charges on the shipment. No other machine on the market is sold under such a broad and liberal guarantee, a fact which is worthy of your careful consideration and which speaks volumes for the quality of our merchandise.

Don't fail to send for this BIG SPECIAL CATALOGUE. It will be mailed to you **ABSOLUTELY FREE.**

Even Sears & Roebuck got into the nickelodeon act. Above is a page from a 1908 catalogue.

No. 15. Apollo Theatre.   CHILLICOTHE, Ohio.

ARTKRAFT Theatre Fronts
Do the Trick

The outward appearance of Places of Amusement have much to do with the Patronage.

Fronts and Interiors that are artistic, clean and inviting (not necessarily expensive) attract the continual entertainment seeker.

Let us tell you all about Artkraft Fronts, Ceilings, Sidewalls and Stage Fronts. Catalogs and Designs Free.

THE CANTON METAL CEILING COMPANY

1953 Harrison Avenue.
CANTON, O.

ABOVE: A baby elephant cavorts in the entry to the Apollo Theatre, Chillicothe, Ohio, in this 1910 postcard scene. The facade appears to have been ordered from the Canton Metal Ceiling Company (see advertisement to the left). Also shown in the above view is the Dreamland Theatre, to the right, with what seems to be a draped piano in front of the right-side doors.

LEFT: Circa 1910 advertisement for Artkraft Fronts. "Fronts and interiors that are artistic, clean and inviting (not necessarily expensive) attract the continual entertainment seeker," the copy notes.

BELOW: The Kanneberg Roofing and Ceiling Company, also located in Canton, offered "new designs every day." Made of pressed metal, plaster, or composition, ornate fronts by various companies were sold by the thousands.

LOBBY AND STAGE FRONTS

Let us hear from you right away if you are about to build or remodel. New designs every day. Special drawings made free. Built to any dimension.

DESIGN BOOK FREE

Send pencil sketch with full measurements or a blue print if you have one. Our suggestions will please you. Ask for design book.

THE KANNEBERG ROOFING AND CEILING COMPANY
Manufacturers "Electric Eclipse" Signs   Canton, Ohio

18

Hello Rena come to see me, I booked [illegible] your [illegible]

Out in the woods in Catawissa, Pennsylvania, the Dreamland offered "Life Motion Moving Pictures" and "Illustrated Songs" for an admission charge of a nickel. Featured on the day this photograph was snapped, in August 1908, was a film about New York City. The day's illustrated song was "Down in the Vale of Shenandoah."

The Peerless 5-Cent Theatre, Owosso, Michigan, in August 1908.

When the pictures were viewed in rapid succession, the children seemed to be in motion.]

"The first public showing of a moving picture on the screen in Philadelphia was made in the old Bijou Theatre, on Eighth Street, below Vine [in 1901]. This demonstration was made as a side attraction at the Bijou Theatre, then conducted by the B.F. Keith Company as a vaudeville house."

It was recalled that Siegmund Lubin set up Philadelphia's first large moving picture theatre, which was located in the heart of the city's business district.

The first theatre in Baltimore was said to have been set up by a Mr. Brown, who fitted up half of a penny arcade with a motion picture parlor comprising 35 seats, which had been bought from the YMCA. "On the opening day, before any of the show had begun, a fire broke out in the operating room and the place was closed." The second theatre to be built in Baltimore was erected by J. Howard Bennett in 1907 and was called the Little Pickwick. The show consisted of one reel a day from the Chicago Film Exchange rented at a cost of $4 per day. He ran the reel off in 20 minutes on days except Saturday, and on this day he allowed 12 minutes to the reel. On Saturdays he would exhibit to 6,000 or 7,000 people. He had no music and employed one doorman, one cashier, one operator (not licensed), and used a phonograph. The seating capacity was 112, and the weekly expense was less than $100.

The first moving picture theatre in Kansas City, Missouri, also involved a penny arcade:

"In 1898, Carl Mincing brought an old Edison moving picture to Kansas City and, on the second floor over a penny arcade he owned, established the Arcade Theatre, at 720 Main Street. The equipment was not extensive, consisting of a machine, a very poor screen, a platform for the machine, 200 ordinary folding chairs, and an orchestra organ, the first of its kind in this section.

"One reel per show was the extent of each performance, the length varying from 50 to 300 feet. Generally the shows lasted 15 minutes, with a similar intermission so as to allow the operator time to rewind the film. About 15 shows per day were given, which were attended to by the same force of helpers. In the beginning each picture was shown until the film wore out, but as the industry became more active changes came more often, and for some time one week was the limit for a single picture.

"The admission charge was five cents, and each performance found the house packed. The theatre was a moneymaker from the first day."

In New Orleans, "the Electric Theatre was a success. So many nickels and dimes poured into the coffers that the owners built a second house, the Dreamland Theatre, on St. Charles Street, in 1906. These were rather small affairs, just to feel out whether the vogue of moving pictures would last, and so was their third theatre, The Grand, 1033 Canal Street, which was built during the following year. With the success of their three small houses, the owners were determined to build bigger and better.

After three years of prosperity the Bijou Dream was constructed on St. Charles Street at a cost that most everybody figured would prohibit profits from the venture. The sum of $25,000 was a mighty big wad to throw away, people thought."

In Portland, Oregon, the first moving pictures were said to have been exhibited in 1897 at Cordray's Theatre. The first theatre set up especially for films was The Nickelodeon, built at Sixth and Alder streets in 1908. "The show was opened by a man whose name has been forgotten, but who sold out soon after opening to A.B.L. Gellerman, who conducted it successfully for a long time. One reel constituted a show, and five cents was the price of admission. Then S. Morton Cohen entered the Portland field with the Imperial Amusement Company and operated the Hippodrome, Orpheum, and Casino."

Arthur Hotaling, a pioneer, gave his recollections in 1916 of the earlier "good old days" in the business:

"It was in the very late spring of 1896 that I went down to Atlantic City to see what might be doing. I was not so old that it bothered me any, but the year before I had seen a living picture show on the boardwalk. It was there I met motion pictures for the first time. I paid my ten cents like the rest to look them over, but the front of the house interested me more than what I saw inside. There was just one strip across the front that called attention to 'Edison's Latest Invention, the Vitascope,' and the box office man sat huddled in his little pen indifferent to everything but the occasional demand for a ticket. I spent the rest of the evening in front of the place, lamenting the lack of showmanship, and the next morning I hunted up the owners, two brothers named Kiefaber. I told them what poor showmen they were, with all the confidence of my youth, and they agreed with me. It was easy to come to terms, and I went to work for them.

"As a showman, one of my best assets was an ability to handle a brush, and the first thing I did was to plaster the front with banners. The two star films were Cissy Fitzgerald in her dance and the *John C. Rice-May Irwin Kiss*, and I decorated the front with these in vivid color. Then I fixed the entrance so that the curtain could be drawn back to display the screen. If we saw anyone in the crowd getting interested, we would drop the curtain, and he would have to pay his dime to see the rest. Generally, though, we would show part of the Fitzgerald picture and I would make a 'spiel' about the kiss picture. Business picked up...

"September came and with it the end of the season at the shore. The Kiefabers prepared to put the machine in storage for the winter, but I persuaded them to tour the state, and opened in Newark. It was pretty hard sledding, the public did not know what pictures were and apparently did not care ten cents' worth...

"[Next year] the summer of 1897 was just getting under way, and Fred Chaplin had a Kinetoscope in a store. This was the second of the exhibition Kinetoscopes, the first being practically the same as the Vitascope, except for the name. This was a smaller model, a very light

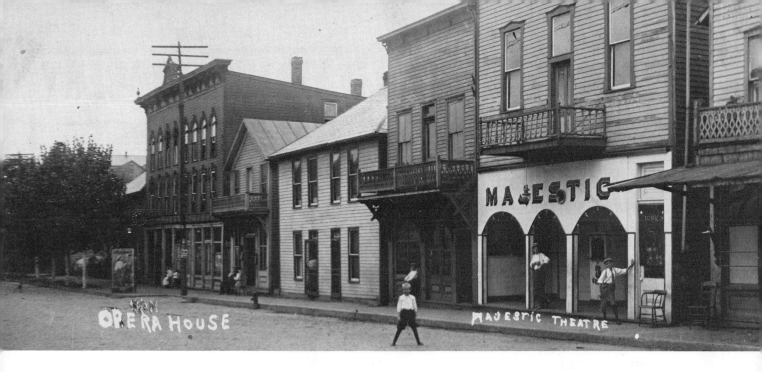

A view of Valley Street, Corning, Ohio, in October 1908 shows two places of entertainment. Down the street is the Opera House, while to the right is the Majestic Theatre, a nickelodeon. The facade style of arches lined with electric lightbulbs was a popular one, and many nickelodeons used this format. A chalkboard at the right side of the theatre proclaims the evening's attractions.

The Peerless Theatre, a typical nickelodeon of the 1908-1910 era, sported a latticework facade. A sign notes that the programs were changed each Monday and Thursday and that the current song was "Good Night Beloved, Good Night," by Miss Edith Devins of Bradford, Pennsylvania.

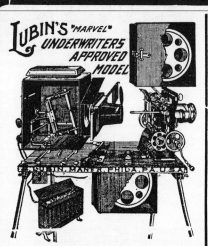
Siegmund Lubin, a Philadelphia optician, entered the motion picture business in the 1890s. Before long, he owned one of the largest film laboratories as well as a string of nickelodeon theatres.

Lubin unabashedly copied the films of others, hiring technicians to erase or blot out the trademarks of the films' original makers. In other instances, he pirated successful pictures by filming his own versions, sometimes with the same title, as with the "Great Train Robbery" mentioned above in a 1905 advertisement. The name was the same as the Porter classic. Brazenly, Lubin proclaimed his version to be the "Most Popular Picture Ever Shown."

Below is shown the Lubin studio, with its glass roof which permitted indoor filming.

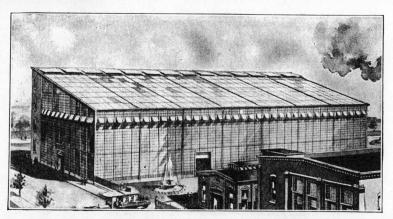

Lubin Factory, Showing the Glass-Roof Studio

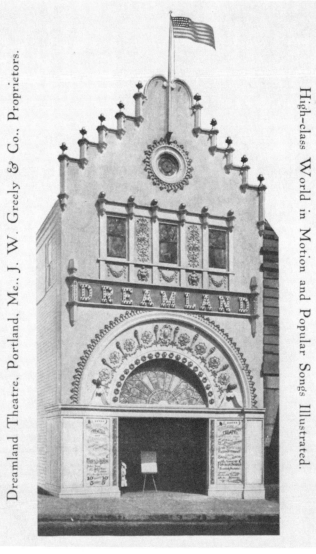

Dreamland Theatre, Portland, Me., J. W. Greely & Co., Proprietors.

High-class World in Motion and Popular Songs Illustrated.

ABOVE: In Portland, Maine, a town boasting numerous nickelodeon theatres, the Dreamland posted an admission charge of 5c for children and 10c for adults. Just inside the front door was a penny arcade.

RIGHT: The Big Nickel, also in Portland, had a similar admission structure, as this notice indicates.

BELOW: Announcement slides were a feature of most theatres and were projected while films were being changed or rewound. Topics included advertisements, advice, and song lyrics.

America's Biggest and Best Picture Shows

Continuous Performance Daily From 10.30 A. M. to 10.30 P. M.

Big Nickel

ADMISSION 10c
CHILDREN 5c

Monday, Tuesday and Wednesday
OCTOBER 5th, 6th and 7th
PARAMOUNT PICTURES Presents
The World's Foremost Photoplay Actress
MARY PICKFORD
In The Celebrated Romantic Comedy

SUCH A LITTLE QUEEN

By Channing Pollock
Produced By The FAMOUS PLAYERS FILM COMPANY
In Five Reels Of Motion Pictures

Thursday, Friday and Saturday
OCTOBER 8th, 9th and 10th
PARAMOUNT PICTURES Present

WILLIAM TELL

The Most Enthralling Of All Romances
AN ALL-STAR CAST
In Five Reels Of Motion Pictures

Every Friday & Saturday — "The Mutual Girl"

Big Nickel

The Princess Theatre, South Framingham, Mass.

Princess was a popular nickelodeon name, and here is shown a trio of Princesses. At the above left is a Columbus, Ohio theatre, while directly above is one in South Framingham, Massachusetts. To the left is the Princess Theatre located at 98 Woodward Avenue, Detroit, home of "Popular 5c Shows," which had the motto "Nothing Nicer Anywhere." Other theatre names also reflected royalty, such as the Queen, Nickel King, Royal, Prince, Court, Palace, and Majestic.

Of the dozens of nickelodeons using the Bijou Dream name across America, the one shown above, location unknown, was certainly one of the least pretentious. A notice painted on the door advised patrons that the theatre was open on Saturdays from 3 to 5 in the afternoon and from 7 to 10 in the evening.

In Bangor, Maine, the Morey Furniture Company diversified and opened the Gaiety Theatre in the center front of its building. This photograph, taken in 1910, advised patrons that the movie house was closed for the season and would re-open early in May.

Colonial Theatre, Wichita, Kansas.
The Most Beautiful Theatre in the Southwest.

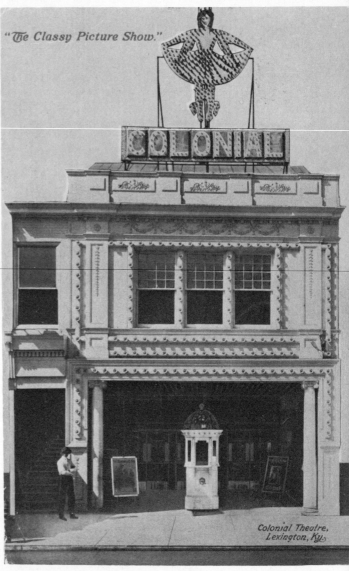

"The Classy Picture Show."

Colonial Theatre.
Lexington, Ky.

CONTINUOUS PERFORMANCE AFTERNOON AND EVENING

Colonial

SELECT VAUDEVILLE MOTION PICTURES

Colonial Theatre. Wilkinsburg, Pa.

Colonial was a popular theatre name, and dozens of such establishments were scattered across America. Shown here are theatres in Wichita, Kansas (above left, view circa 1912); Lexington, Kentucky (above, circa 1912 - at which time "A Trip to The Garden of Allah" was scheduled to appear on October 12 and 13); and Wilkinsburg, Pennsylvania (left).

ABOVE: The Boody Theatre, location unknown, packed its patrons in like the proverbial sardines. Cooling was provided by wall-mounted electric fans, a common practice at the time. Strung around the theatre walls were tuned electric bells with resonators, played from a piano keyboard down front. With musical notes coming from all directions, the effect must have been quite disconcerting.

BELOW: The Revelry Theatre, located at 47th Street and Calumet Avenue, Chicago, offered film subjects for a nickel, interspersed with illustrated songs. Ruby Harrison, "Chicago's Sweet Singer," was featured when this photograph was on the bill in 1909.

machine. It was called an Edison machine, and it might be added that the Eidoloscope was not an Edison machine. This latter used a different film and was the only machine I recalled that ran the film up instead of down through the head. The Kinetoscope was handled about as the Vitascope had been, and I quickly hooked up with Chaplin and made the place over into the semblance of a show shop. One afternoon, Chaplin told that there was a man with some films he wanted to sell, and I went over and had a look at them. At first glance I saw they were copies and said so. The salesman shrugged his shoulders and said they were all doing it. I told them that the originals were poor enough to run through the machine, let alone dupes, and that there was nothing doing.

"He did not argue, but as he turned away he slipped something into my hand with a request that I buy a drink when I was not so busy. I looked at a $5 bill and called after him to come around the next morning when I could look at them more carefully. He came around promptly in the morning, and as we needed a change of program we bought some of the best. When the deal was concluded he gave me his card with the remark that he made films and might be able to use me when I should be through at the store. The card read 'S. Lubin.' It was my first meeting with a man for whom I worked nearly 18 years."

Arthur D. Hotaling recalled that the first picture show set up in New York City might have been the showing of a prize fight picture at 204 Broadway. "New York did not take kindly to the store show, and little was done in this direction. It was not until 1905 that the store exhibition came back to New York."

The advent of the nickelodeon theatre did not spell the demise of the vaudeville houses, at least not in the beginning, for in larger cities vaudeville remained alive and well. Indeed, until the late 1920s, when talking films became popular, vaudeville acts were an important part of many theatre routines. As nickelodeons were opened all across America, vaudeville theatres continued to feature films on their bills. Some vaudeville houses joined what they couldn't fight, and converted to the showing of films exclusively. In small towns in particular, opera houses, town halls, and other pre-existing places of public entertainment were fitted with projection booths and screens and became the local cinema.

By the time that nickelodeon theatres became popular, many films had been standardized to a length of about 1,000 feet and contained rudimentary plots. Sometimes two or three subjects would be joined together in order to achieve the required 1,000 feet, which was equal to a reel of film. Often these were turned out by film companies which produced one or two subjects a week, usually without a script, working impromptu from sketchy notes. Actors and actresses were not featured prominently. It was not until after 1910 that the so-called star system became popular. Early posters were apt to mention just the title of the film and the production company, with no mention of individual performers.

Since the novelty of a given film was short-lived, it was not unusual for a theatre to show several different films every day. This was no problem, as the rapidly expanding industry turned out dozens of different titles each month. Soon, the 1,000-foot or "one-reel subjects" were supplanted by two-and three-reelers, with intermissions between each reel, unless the theatre was fortunate enough to have two projectors. Films were acquired in one of two ways: purchase or rental. They could be bought outright for so much per foot, 10 and 12c being common prices. Thus, most trade advertisements for feature subjects stated their length in feet. Dozens of film exchanges sprang up, and rental became more popular, thus providing for frequent changes of subject matter.

The Success of William Fox

Upton Sinclair, one of America's best-known writers during the early part of the present century, told of his own experience with early moving pictures at the Eden Musee and how William Fox, the subject of a biography written by Sinclair, had his initiation into the field:

"I well remember seeing the first pictures in a place called the Eden Musee on 23rd Street in New York City," Sinclair wrote. "There were wax works and all sorts of horrors—President Garfield being shot, and the Chicago anarchists making bombs, and a policeman who looked so lifelike that you went up and asked him the way to the labyrinth of mirrors or whatever delightful thrill you were seeking. Then you went into a little court with palm and rubber trees, and sat in rows of chairs, and there was the image of the 20th Century Limited train. It trembled and jumped so that you almost put your eyes out, but nevertheless it was so real that you could hardly keep from ducking out of the way as it bore down upon you. A tremendous adventure!

"It happened that on 14th Street there was a place called the Automat with phonographs, punching bags, weighing machines, chewing-gum machines, and, of course, Kinetoscopes. The Automat was one of the sights of the town, because no employees were needed, only a watchman. You dropped your nickels in a machine, and down in the basement there was a track running under the machines and a little car running on the track, and as it passed, the machines spilled their nickels into it, and then the car ran around to the other side of the room and dumped the nickels into a funnel, from the other end of which they emerged, all counted and wrapped and ready for deposit in the bank. It was almost as marvelous as the Chicago Stock Yards, where a hog was dropped into the machine at one end, and sausages and buttons and haircombs came out the other end."

Upton Sinclair went on to tell how William Fox, who in the 1920s built a chain of palace-style theatres and who became one of the best-known figures in the motion picture industry, knew of the Automat in the early days and was impressed by it:

"The Automat pleased William Fox, and he made it known that he was in the market to buy an establishment of that sort. Soon there came an agent suggesting that there was one at 700 Broadway, Brooklyn, owned by a

ABOVE: The Arcade Theatre, Los Angeles, offered any seat for a nickel and invited patrons to "Come In and Laugh." The three-reel program lasted an hour. Note the large eagle above the ticket booth, the caryatid figures along the wall, and the other ornate decorations.

BELOW: In Cleveland in 1911 this nickelodeon offered "Real 'First Run' Pictures—Changed Daily—The Day the Makers Release Them." Currently showing was "The Outlaw and the Female Detective."

In the nickelodeon era, facades ranged from the exceedingly ornate to the plain. At the upper left is the Butterfly Theatre, Milwaukee, which billed itself as the "Most Luxurious, Exclusive, Refined Photo-Play House in America." At the time the above picture was taken, "The Early Life of David Copperfield" was among the features. Note the large electric butterfly sign, with a goddess at the center, at the top of the facade. At the upper right is shown the Liberty Theatre, Third and Main streets, Los Angeles. A dime admission was charged. Below is shown the Dreamland, a counterpoint to ornateness, a theatre located in Livermore Falls, Maine, circa 1911.

Dreamland Theatre, Livermore Falls, Me.

While the patriotic parade of little folks, most of whom were carrying flags, catches the eye at first, in the background two nickel theatres, side by side in the same building, offer film subjects, including "Roosevelt Hunting Big Game in Africa." The right-side theatre boasts a brass phonograph horn emerging from a porthole above the lobby sign.

In East St. Louis, Illinois, the Electric Theatre offered the latest films in 1910. Local citizens, probably including those pictured here, called the place The Nickelodeon.

man named J. Stuart Blackton, then president of the Vitagraph Company of America and destined to become one of the big moving picture millionaires."

Fox visited 700 Broadway by appointment. It was all he could do to fight his way through the large crowd in attendance. Later in the same week, also by appointment, he visited for the second time and was met with an even larger crowd. Enthusiastic, he bought the establishment. In Fox's words:

"I took charge of it on the following Monday, and only about two persons dropped in all day! I realized that someone had supplied the crowd on the two former occasions when I had gone to see the place. This was sometime in May, and I was told that business was always bad in the summer."

The year was 1903, and Fox ruefully contemplated what to do with his unfortunate investment. The story, written by Upton Sinclair, continues:

"How was the crowd to be induced to enter the Fox Automat? Quite recently he had been to a showing of the new 'moving pictures.' He had seen a picture of a tree, and the leaves of the tree had moved, and the man behind him had said that it was a trick, someone was shaking the curtain, but William Fox, with his inquiring mind, had talked to the operator after the performance was over and asked to have the trick explained. No, the screen had not been shaken; the pictures actually did move of themselves. The operator showed the film, which was nearly twice as wide as it is now, and did not run on sprockets, but merely through a groove. The length of the film was then 100 feet.

"Fox investigated further. He saw the pictures of the 20th Century Limited, and a still more marvelous production, a little story told in front of the camera, called *The Life of an American Fireman*, then another one, still more thrilling, *The Great Train Robbery*. He saw the public pouring in to witness these spectacles, and he examined the premises rented and noted that there were some rooms upstairs used as a dwelling. It occurred to him that he might rent these premises also, and put out the tenants and turn it into a showroom for the new picture stories. If he took the people up by the front stairway, and after the show sent them down by the rear stairway, they would enter the nickelodeon at the rear and have to walk past all of the machines, and very probably they would drop some nickels on the way.

"[He set up] a showroom with a screen, and 146 chairs, and some display posters outside informing the public that moving pictures were to be seen. But, alas, the Brooklyn public didn't know what moving pictures were, and nobody went upstairs. Fox stood outside for a whole day, gazing anxiously at the public, regretting that he had no personal charms to lure them into the establishment."

The next day a magician was set up in front. Tricks were performed, a crowd gathered, then the magician closed his act, stating that the performance would be continued upstairs and, for the moment, the admission was free. Going into the building, the public learned about moving

pictures, enjoyed them, told their friends, and within a week "there was such a crowd that the police had to be called in to control them. At last Fox had found a real gold mine! Here was the way to a fortune plain before him, and his one task was to get there before the others. He got two friends to join him, and began renting stores on the crowded avenues of Brooklyn, and in each one they set up a screen and a projection machine and rows of chairs—of which the total must not exceed 299. Up to that limit you could have a 'common show' license; but if you had 300 chairs or more, you were a theatre, and the fire laws took strict charge of you. So, presently, here was William Fox with 15 show places in Brooklyn and New York… Not since the days of the 49ers had there been such a way for the little fella to get rich as in this new business. Everything depended upon a location where the crowds were passing. Fox found that in order to get the right location, it would often pay him to lease the whole building—even though the fire laws required that the upstairs tenant be turned out before moving pictures were shown in the building. He conceded the idea of combining motion pictures and vaudeville, with the admission price of 10c for any seat in the house."

Fox went on to greater things. Soon he learned of a burlesque theatre located at 194 Grand Street, Brooklyn. In dilapidated condition, the theatre had not been occupied for two years. After paying $20,000 for the land and building, he changed the name to the Comedy, circularized 10,000 neighborhood residents to entice them to visit, and soon was reaping thousands of dollars in profit. Then came the purchase of the Folly, a 2,000-seat theatre which was set up to give five shows a day, two hours each. From then onward it was a steady climb to fame and fortune. Later, he became one of several motion picture princes to commission an adulatory biography.

One of the first moving picture houses in Chicago was the Electric Theatre, located near the northwest corner of State and Harrison streets, opened early in 1906 by Gustav Holenberg. Business was so excellent that in a few weeks another place, the Chicago Theatre, was opened nearby. Aaron J. Jones claimed to be the very first motion picture theatre operator in Chicago, opening a movie show on South State Street on Christmas day, 1905, after having been inspired by seeing the nickelodeon theatre run by Harry Davis on Smithfield Street, Pittsburgh, Pennsylvania, a month earlier.

In addition to the Electric Theatre near the corner of State and Harrison streets, another Electric Theatre, this one owned by Ike Van Ronkel, was opened at Quincy and Halsted streets on a date stated to be February 1, 1906, although, as is the case with so many events in moving picture history, the time is a matter of dispute among historians. Still another theatre was the Nickelodeon on Halsted Street, 50 feet north of Van Buren, said to have been opened on January 1, 1906, by three partners, M.A. Choynski, Harry Cohen, and D.L. Noon.

An article in *Moving Picture World*, printed in 1916, described early films shown in Chicago:

The Washington Theatre, a nickelodeon located on Elm Street, Dallas, boasted a particularly ornate front. On the back of the picture reproduced above, signed "Billy," was a message to his family: "The big panel under the arch and all the figure work was made by me. The photo cuts off the figures at the top of the building. They are over 10 feet high. The center panel is the largest panel in the entire Southwest, and the group at the top is the only group of figures in the state of Texas. This photo is small and does not really give the big impression that the show does. It is finished in bronze, solid from the top of the marble. The head in the circle is the 'Father of the Country.' The other theatre that I am doing is in the same block to the left of this one. Some show, believe me."

A peaceful scene at the Gem Theatre, Dry Run, Pennsylvania, April 1912. "The Tenderfoot Messenger" was playing.

View of the Colonial Theatre, 426 North Main Street, Bloomington, Illinois, probably circa 1908. The titles of the film features were not stated. Given were the names of the companies producing them: "Latest Biograph Subjects" and "Selig Pictures."

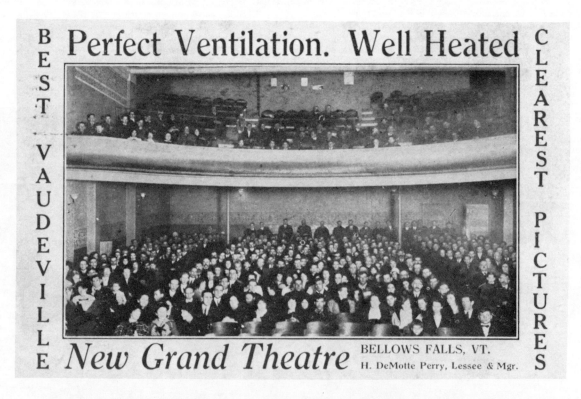

The interior of the New Grand Theatre, Bellows Falls, Vermont, 1913. The crowd shown was gathered to watch the stage production of "Arrival of Father" with James M. Wesley and Janet White, "Sam Barber & The Gold Dust Twins," and a film, "Oh You Flirt!"

A simple storefront nickelodeon was The Unique Theatorium, which advertised "New Pictures Every Day" and "Continuous Performance 2 to 5, 7 to 10."

ABOVE: The Bijou Theatre, Wallingford, Connecticut, April 1913. A group of school children gathers in front. Feature shows of the time included "The Price He Paid" and "From the Valley of Shadows."

LEFT: The Wonderland Theatre, owned and managed by F. Fowler, Troy, New York, attracts an audience seated in kitchen chairs, as shown in this 1908 snapshot.

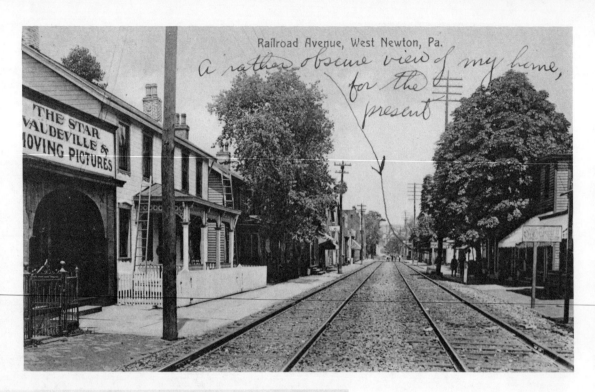

Railroad Avenue, West Newton, Pa.

A rather obscure view of my home, for the present

MAJESTIC MOVING PICTURE THEATER, CATASAUQUA, PA.

Moving picture theatres were often located away from busy commercial districts, as these three pictures illustrate. Above is shown The Star, offering vaudeville and moving pictures on Railroad Avenue, West Newton, Pennsylvania, 1910. To the left is the Majestic, Catasauqua, Pennsylvania, 1910, which offered such attractions as "A Queen of Burlesque," "Blacksmiths' Ball," and "The Postal Clerk." Below is the Indian Neck Theatre located on the outskirts of Branford, Connecticut, circa 1915.

Attracting summer visitors to a park was this small nickelodeon which offered illustrated songs and moving pictures, probably circa 1910. To the left is shown an unloading platform for an amusement park ride.

The Island Ledge Casino at Wells Beach, Maine, offered moving pictures (for a dime admission), dancing, bowling, and picnic facilities. The crowd shown here was attending an outing sponsored by a textile mill.

Park Theatre & St George Hotel, Avon, N.Y.

This trio of nickelodeon theatres includes the Park Theatre next to the St. George Hotel, Avon, New York; the Novelty Theatre, Auburn, New York, which prominently announced its 5c admission price; and the Clement located on Broadway, Dover, New Hampshire. For adults the Clement charged a dime admission, "including seat," according to the sign at the entrance.

NOVELTY 5¢ ADMISSION

COMPLIMENTS: NOVELTY AMUSEMENT COMPANY

AUBURN, N. Y.

CLEMENT

KING ART

Moving Picture Theatre, Broadway, Dover, N. H.

ABOVE: This ornate theatre, name not stated, charged a nickel to children and a dime to adults to see "His Wife" (a Lubin film) and "Sophie's Birthday Party" (an Essanay western feature).

BELOW: The Gloucester Theatre, a Massachusetts nickelodeon, was closed and had an iron gate across the entrance when this photograph was snapped.

Lots of things were going on at the Bijou Theatre, a nickelodeon located in Attica, New York, circa 1910. Features included "All is Not Gold," or, as stated on another poster, "Gold Is Not All," plus "In the Frozen North, by Selig stock players, plus the illustrated song "Call Me Up Some Rainy Afternoon." Above the entry a brass phonograph horn projected music into the street. "Here is a view of Attica's best-paying business—crowded full every night—everybody goes," noted the caption on the back side of the above picture.

B. H. STEPHENS, ARCHITECT.

In Wilmington, North Carolina, another Bijou, also a nickelodeon, was designed in the form of a Greek temple by architect B. H. Stephens. At the time the above picture was taken, the ticket office was closed, and a penny scale was placed in front of the ticket window (just above the letter J in BIJOU above).

Another view of the Bijou Theatre (also shown at the top of this page) in Attica, New York, this illustration being a bit more formal. Feature films at the time included "His Date With Gwendoline" and "The Last Performance," both Pathe pictures.

Mary Fuller, who began her film career with Vitagraph in 1907 and who later went to Edison, starred in 1912 in a movie series, "What Happened to Mary?" A clever promotion, the "What Happened to Mary?" sequences were approximately coordinated with a related series of articles in "The Ladies World," a popular magazine. The first episode, titled "The Escape from Bondage," was released July 26, 1912, followed by "Alone in New York" the following month. Each story and motion picture segment, although related, stood on its own and was a complete feature in itself. The idea was a great success, and soon "The Perils of Pauline" and other serials appeared.

The New Empress Theatre in Missoula, Montana charged patrons a dime in May 1913 to see "Cupid Throws a Brick." Other billboards showed portraits of leading actors and actresses with the Reliance Company and the American Flying "A" Company, two of the film makers of the era.

This anonymous storefront theatre boasted neither a name nor lobby signs or posters when this snapshot was taken, probably circa 1908-1910. It was still in the process of being set up, as attested by two electrical wires dangling down the front.

"In all these early theatres sensational pictures were the most popular. Mr. Van Ronkel is certain that he used film 400 feet and more in length of this type in his theatre. The most popular at the time were *Escaped from Sing Sing* (Vitagraph), *The Great Train Robbery* (Edison), slapstick comedies of a primitive kind and trick films, including *A Trip to the Moon* (Melies).

"Aaron J. Jones is certain he used pictures 1,000 feet in length in his first house, including *The Great Train Robbery*, slapstick comedies, and street-chasing scenes, such as Pathe's comedy showing the baker boy with a tray of pastry on his head being knocked down as he hurriedly goes out of the store, and the following mix-ups.

"Folding camp chairs, as a rule, formed the seats in these early primitive 'store' picture theatres. In some cases many of the people had to stand. Five cents admission was charged for one reel to a show, and as a usual thing, a phonograph was placed in the lobby to attract the attention of passers-by... Muslin screens, either plain or sized, or white walls were used, as a rule, in all of these early theatres. The financial Panic in 1907 gave a tremendous impetus to the moving picture theatre generally. During that year, 5-cent theatres grew and multiplied throughout the country. The scarcity of currency turned the amusement-loving public to the low-price picture theatres, and the oftener they went the more convinced they became that the new entertainment was not only novel, but exceedingly enjoyable and attractive.

"The Hale's Tours cars came in vogue in Chicago in the spring of 1906. Aaron J. Jones put up the first in a store alongside Schaefer's Penny Arcade at 306 South State Street (the old number), the Arcade being 308. Jones simply took out the store front and ran the Hale's car in, admitting people to the front of his store and giving them exit through the Arcade adjoining. The second Hale's Tours show was opened by Mr. Jones later in the same year, next door north of the present Orpheum Theatre.

"From the earliest days of the 'store' shows, music of some kind was used with pictures. At first the phonograph was favored because of its cheapness. Illustrated songs had been used in entertainment as early as 1904, but they were used first in cheap vaudeville houses. In the fall of 1906 they were first used in picture theatres and became quite a fixture until 1911, when they began to lose their hold on the better class of houses. They gradually dwindled until 1914, when only a few could be found in any Chicago theatres. Several small theatres and small country towns still use them [in 1916], but their day is over.

"As early as 1909, an attempt was made to play suitable selections on the piano, with drum accompaniment, for the pictures. None of these pianists at the time could improvise so much as to catch the scene of the picture accompanied, with the result that patrons with musical ears soon tired of such music and preferred the pictures alone."

The year 1906 was one of tremendous growth for the nickelodeon industry. Motion pictures were still a novelty, and the public flocked in record numbers to nickel theatres as they opened. In the entertainment trade, emphasis primarily remained on vaudeville, however, with films in use as fillers. *The Billboard*, trade journal of the field, was filled with news of performing troupes, actors, and actresses. However, each year moving pictures occupied an increasing proportion of editorial and advertising space in that publication. In 1906, slides and illustrated songs were increasing in popularity. Typically, a set of 20 slides sold for $5 or so. Projected in theatres between live acts or in moving picture houses between films, slides, accompanied by piano music, allowed the audience to get into the act—by singing *In the Good Old Summertime, A Bicycle Built for Two*, and other favorites. Many competing types of motion picture projecting devices were advertised, including the Edison Kinetoscope, with stereopticon attachment, for $75 or more, available with "an endless variety of films—50 feet or more—12c and 15c per foot," and several models of the Cameragraph, made in New York City by Nicholas Power. The Edengraph, the Motiograph and other devices each captured a slice of the market pie in the early years. Later, the Cameragraph became the dominant make.

By 1907 there were more than 3,000 nickelodeons in America, according to one report, with over 100 in Pittsburgh and over 300 in Chicago. In many localities nickelodeons had 199 or fewer seats, for those seating 200 or more had to have a theatre license. Other towns placed the license requirement at 300 or more seats. The Philadelphia, a nickelodeon theatre built in 1907, had 1,000 seats and, despite license fees and an annual rental of $35,000, garnered great profits.

In November 1907, *The Saturday Evening Post* published an article which stated that over two million people attended nickelodeon theatres each day of the year, a third of these being children. "The nickelodeon is usually a tiny theatre, containing 199 seats, giving 12 to 18 performances a day, seven days a week. Its walls are painted red. The seats are ordinary kitchen chairs, not fastened. The only break in the red color scheme is made by a half dozen signs in black and white, 'No Smoking,' 'Hats Off,' and sometimes, but not always, 'Stay as Long as You Like.' Last year or the year before it was probably a second-hand clothier's, a pawn shop, or a cigar store. Now the counter has been ripped out, there is a ticket seller's booth where the show window was, an automatic musical barker somewhere up in the air thunders its noise down on the passers-by, and the little store has been converted into a theatrelet. Not a theatre, mind you, for theatres must take out theatrical licenses at $500 per year. Theatres seat 200 or more people. Nickelodeons seat 199 and take out amusement licenses.

"For some reason, young women from 16 to 30 years old are rarely in evidence, but many middle-aged and older women are steady patrons, who never, when a new film is to be shown, miss the opening."

A month later, in December 1907, Kalem, a leading film production company, advertised *Ben Hur*, a movie based on Gen. Lew Wallace's famous novel first published in 1880. As Kalem did not seek permission to use the story, a lawsuit was brought by the author's estate, publishers,

The Royal Theatre, St. Joseph, Mo. Finest picture House in the southwest. Capacity 800.

Charging 10 cents admission were these theatres: The Colonial, Onset, Massachusetts, 1909; the Royal Theatre, St. Joseph, Missouri; and the Lyceum Theatre, Hot Springs, Arkansas. Often a show would charge a dime for adults and a nickel for children, or would charge a nickel to all patrons for matinee performances.

and earlier producers, resulting in a settlement in their favor of $25,000, thus establishing a precedent for the value of movie rights.

Operating A Nickelodeon

As the nickelodeon concept caught on, many people got into the act. Magazines and bulletins on the subject flourished, new moving picture production companies started up, hundreds of people aspired to be actors or actresses, countless different gadgets were offered for sale to the theatre owner, and all the other trappings of widespread commercial activity came into being. Many guides were available to help the aspiring motion picture theatre projectionist or theatre owner. The *Cyclopedia of Motion Picture Work,* published in two volumes in 1911, was one of the best and gave detailed instructions for the handling and operation of just about every conceivable piece of theatre equipment. One could learn how to mount a glass slide, to unpack an Edison Kinetoscope from its shipping crate, or to synchronize a phonograph record with action on the screen. For the aspiring nickelodeon owner, hints were given for starting a store-front theatre building:

"A vacant business house having been selected both for its location and for size, the process of converting it into a motion picture theatre is to remove the glass front and framing for the door and window, to replace it with a closed front a few feet back from the sidewalk line and into which are built the ticket seller's booth and the entrance and exit doors and on the inside of which is built a projection operator's booth. At the far end of the room a muslin screen about three by four yards is stretched. The room is filled with rows of chairs, either kitchen chairs or opera chairs, as the expense justified by the location will permit, and a piano is placed near the picture screen...

"The front partition of a typical theatre is placed six feet back from the sidewalk. The ticket booth extends forward from this partition. A still deeper front is desirable if the floor space can be spared; it gives advertising space, it gives the opportunity for decorative efforts without the expense of decorating the entire front of the business house; it suggests retirement in the theatre, and when the prospective patron steps off the sidewalk he feels he is already within the theatre, even before he has purchased his admission ticket."

Readers were told of a study involving three theatres in the same city block, with no other theatres within several blocks in either direction. The least successful theatre was the oldest, without an attractive front.

In another instance, a theatre had a front done in mission style, finished in a dark stain similar to that used on mission furniture. It was not successful, and the theatre changed hands. The new manager painted the front pure white and put up miniature electric lights and interesting signs. The theatre, named the Happy Hour, succeeded from that point forward.

In a further instance, a theatre was located on a side street with few shoppers passing its door. The theatre changed hands, and the new manager put in a sloping floor to make the films easier to watch, reduced the size of the picture screen in order to give a brighter picture and to reduce the jiggling of the image, eliminated a vaudeville act and substituted in its place a really good singer, and changed the program daily rather than twice a week. In addition, a new illustrated song was shown each day. The pictures and song comprised a program of 40 to 45 minutes, for which 5c was charged.

"Any town of 1,000 people will support a motion picture theatre if it is run by the right man and in the right way," the *Cyclopedia of Motion Picture Work* went on to relate. "It is found that a 'one theatre' town will pay weekly at the ticket window from 2½ to 5c per capita on its census population. A town of 1,000 people will yield from $25 to $50 per week on a show running six nights per week and on Saturday afternoon or whatever day of the week the country people use for market day, usually Saturday, but not always."

The gross revenue expected in a small town can be determined by multiplying the population by a figure of 3½ or 4c per week, the text noted. With this total in mind, "it remains for the prospective theatre manager and owner to decide whether he can bring his expense sheet sufficiently below the gross receipts to give an acceptable profit for his time and whether with such an expense sheet he can give an acceptable show that will continue to bring in money after the first few weeks, when the novelty of the theatre has worn away." It was further suggested that the manager must make himself familiar with city ordinances regulating the operation of motion picture theatres, for even small towns were apt to have such laws.

A small theatre could be set up for a modest cost. The same account noted that $150 would provide for renovating the store front and interior, 200 kitchen chairs could be had for 50c each, electric lamps and wiring cost $100, a projecting machine cost $175, and, to save expense, a piano could be rented. The total expense, including some advertising, would amount to no more than $600 by opening day. A piano was not necessary, but such an instrument was recommended, either automatic or hand-played, to accompany the films.

A very elaborate theatre front was apt to cost $500 to $2,000. For those with a more ample budget, a theatre could be provided with a sloping floor. Instead of kitchen chairs, up to 200 opera chairs could be installed at $1.20 to $1.60 each. An additional $200 to $300 could be profitably spent for inside decorations and a modern picture screen. Such a fancy nickelodeon theatre might cost as much as $6,000 when completed and would be designated primarily for a larger city.

It was noted that a "high class" nickelodeon theatre might have the following weekly expenses: rent of theatre $40; rent of film for three reels, daily change $50; carbons for carbon-arc projector $1; pianist $15; violinist $10; drummer $12; usher $2.50; electricity $18; song slides $2; cashier $5; singer $18; license $4; projector operator $18; porter $4; ticket taker $5; general expense $10—for a total week-

Those passing the Orpheum Theatre, city unknown, were bound to be attracted by the uniformed soldier or the cannon out front, to say nothing of the spelling error on the canvas stretched across the portal. Realistic props exhibited in front of the theatre were a surefire way to increase patronage, and trade journals recommended that theatre owners use their imaginations in this regard.

"The Blue and the Gray," subtitled "The Days of '61," was showing at the Bijou Dream for those caring to part with the required nickel. Helping to lure patrons through the door were a cannon, three stacked rifles, and several flags. A small sign on the front promises "All the Latest Subjects in Moving Pictures and Illustrated Songs."

MYRTLE GONZALEZ

Myrtle Gonzalez, a Vitagraph actress.

Charleroi, Pennsylvania, a town of about 12,000 people located approximately 40 miles from Pittsburgh, was home to the Palace Theatre, shown above, circa 1912. Offered was "Refined Vaudeville." At the time, vaudeville shows and motion pictures were often described as "refined" or "high class," leading the present author to contemplate whether any pictures of "unrefined" or "low class" theatres still survive! Posters noted that the Colonial Minstrels were scheduled to appear at the Palace on November 25th. Adjacent was the Electric Theatre, owned by the Palace management, which featured films. To the left is the "new" Palace, circa 1913, which shows its conversion from vaudeville to photoplays.

In Berwick, Pennsylvania, The Lyric, a storefront theatre, attracted patrons by phonograph music.

48

ABOVE: The Gem Theatre located on Lake Avenue, Hill City, Minnesota.

RIGHT: In Crookston, Minnesota, February 27, 1914, "The Truth About White Slavery," a film accompanied by a lecture, was featured. "Know the Truth and Help in the Fight Today," prospective patrons were advised. Also on the bill was "Her Father's Daughter," a Reliance film.

BELOW: The Gem Theatre was an attraction in Creston, Iowa.

This traveling show, set up in Wisconsin, featured "Best Vaudeville and Moving Pictures," a "Great Wild West Show," and "Wild West Photo Plays." Included on the program were such attractions as "Great Storm at Sea," "Jones Brothers Wild West," and "Real Wild West." Note the portable ticket booth set up out front. The entertainment was a mixture of films and stage shows, the latter featuring cowboys and Indians.

This travelling show enticed townspeople with several tattered banners arranged so as to permit an entrance and exit. Features included "Spanish Mexican Bull Fight for World's Championship" ("10 Bulls Killed," "Horses Gored to Death"), a Kay Bee film, "From Out the Dregs" ("in 2 parts") and "Harry K. Thaw's Fight for Freedom in Canada" ("These are the only motion pictures authorized by Mr. Thaw himself as taken in his cell at Sherbrooke, Canada by the well-known playwright, Hal Reid"). Thaw, a Pittsburgh millionaire, murdered architect Stanford White in a dispute over White's former lover, Evelyn Nesbit.

ly expense, not including the manager, of $214.50. This would represent an expense against receipts averaging $240 for six nights and an additional $100 for Sunday, or $340 total each week. By contrast, a small town theatre operated only during evenings was estimated to have a weekly expense, including $5 for a pianist, of $83, to yield prospective ticket sales of $110 to $150 per week.

On a bigger scale, it was suggested that a theatre building with a 50-foot front and seating 500 or more people could be built, not including the real estate cost, for $10,000 to $20,000. Such an establishment would incorporate vaudeville shows in addition to motion pictures. A structure of this type was estimated to have a weekly expense, including $91 for an orchestra of four pieces, of $860, with average receipts for weekdays and Sundays totaling $1,215.

Statistics for a large theatre located in the busiest retail district of one of the largest cities of the United States were also provided. The theatre was open 14 hours per day, seven days each week, from nine in the morning until 11 in the evening, showing three reels of film and two illustrated songs, changing the three reels three times a week and changing the songs weekly. Two singers were employed for the two songs of each program, one male voice and one female voice. Three projector operators were utilized simultaneously, two of them working motion picture projecting machines while the third projected stereopticon slides featuring announcements and songs, the same person also attending to the lights in the theatre during intermission.

A typical program was started with several announcement slides, followed by the first feature film. At the end of the first film, stereopticon song slides were shown, with the audience singing. At the close of the song, the second feature film was projected, then followed by another song, then the third film. The lights were then turned on, and the crowd was allowed several minutes to pass in and out, while a concessionnaire passed up and down the aisle selling candy. The program typically occupied about 50 minutes, while the change of audiences took five minutes. On an ordinary day, 15 performances were given in 14 hours. On Saturday, the busiest day of all, an extra performance was also given, making 16 in all.

This particular theatre represented a capital of $160,000 to remodel an existing building, rented from a landlord, for which an additional rental of $48,000 per year was paid, including heating. This theatre seated 700 people and charged 10c admission, giving full house receipts of $70. The survey showed that on the average the house was about six-tenths filled during six days of the week, with slightly higher attendance on Saturday. About 44,500 tickets per week were sold, grossing $4,450 at the ticket window. On many Saturdays the ticket sales reached nearly 10,000, yielding $1,000. Thirty-five employees, not including the manager and clerical help, were on the theatre payroll, with the day force working from 9 a.m. until 4 p.m. and the night force from 4 p.m. until 9 p.m.

It was advised that the best way to advertise films was to feature the name of the maker rather than the title of the film, for the film titles were apt to be unfamiliar. Another suggestion was to give the character of the film, such as "beautiful colored picture tonight" or "a roaring farce tonight."

Film exchanges provided posters giving specific information, such posters usually costing 5c each in the one-sheet size. Often, poster services would provide a supply of one-sheet displays for $5 to $10 per month. The theatre owner would then use those posters fitting films shown that month and discard the others. Sometimes film distributors would supply posters free. The best posters were considered to be those showing scenes from the film, rather than simply "title posters" giving the film name within a stock border.

"An electric sign, with words and letters formed by electric lamps, such as 'theatre,' 'five-cent theatre,' 'motion,' or 'pictures,' or even 'five-cents,' can be seen a long way up and down the streets," the 1911 account continued. It was suggested that lamps of about 12 watts each were ideal. A typical small sign was apt to cost about $50 and, illuminated four hours in an evening, with electricity at 10c per kilowatt, to cost 50c per day to operate.

A cousin to the store front nickelodeon was the open air theatre or "airdome," occasionally called an "airdrome" (although the latter term is better known as a name for airports). Airdomes offered the advantage of low construction cost, fresh air, and a minimum of accessories needed. During the summer, when theatres were hot inside and were not comfortable for the audience, the airdome provided a feasible alternative.

The Motion Picture Handbook, an early guide to the subject, noted: "In many of the small towns the airdome has consisted merely of an open lot with a high fence around it, seats set directly on the ground, little sawed-off 'coops' containing one projector, and a cheap as possible screen. A dirt floor is by no means satisfactory, particularly to women wearing white skirts and good clothing." At the time, in New York City the law required that airdomes must be floored, either with wood or cement, and that chairs had to be fastened down to the floor.

The same text suggested that an economy could be effected if the site selected for an airdome was already surrounded by billboards or walls of another character. However, the property had to be free from the glare of nearby lights and the distraction of nearby sound or music. And, not every property owner or apartment tenant wanted an outdoor theatre next door. There was also another problem: "Does the site adjoin a large tenement house or other buildings from which a good view of the show may be obtained without the formality of paid admission?"

In practice, relatively few airdomes were set up. Most motion picture theatres of the nickelodeon era were of the indoor type.

Big Business

The year 1908 saw the beginning of David W. Griffith as a director at Biograph. He popularized such techniques as the flashback, fade, close-up, and other novelties, later

The airdome, an open-air theatre, was popular during the days of the nickelodeon. Many were simply set up in vacant lots surrounded by fences, the Orpheum Theater & Air Dome Company enterprise shown above being an example.

The Air Dome, a Wilkinsburg, Pennsylvania open-air movie theatre, charged a dime to see "Four Big Acts" and moving pictures.

Florence LaBadie, an attractive Thanhouser actress.

View of Grand Avenue looking north, Kansas City, Missouri, June 1910. Visible to the left of the center is the Cameraphone Theatre, one of a chain of theatres of the same name. Admission charge was a nickel for the balcony and a dime for the orchestra level.

The Star Theatre on 8th Street, city unknown, offered "Good Vaudeville, Motion Pictures, and Illustrated Songs" for 15 cents general admission or 25 cents for a reserved seat. The sign leaning against the board to the left is supported by a stick. As it mentioned the theatre's street location, it probably was paraded up and down the sidewalk earlier in the day.

STATE RIGHTS FOR
SAPHO

SELLING RAPIDLY

ATTRACTIVE PRINTING

PICTURE INCOMPARABLE

HANDSOMELY COSTUMED

ORDER IT NOW!

3 REELS   2,800 FEET

WE HAVE A FEW MORE STATES OPEN FOR
DEADWOOD DICK
THE HERO OF THE BLACK HILLS
A THRILLING WESTERN PICTURE

ALSO A FEW GOOD ONES LEFT FOR THE
LAST STAND OF THE
DALTON BOYS
AT COFFEYVILLE, KANS.
WRITE, WIRE OR PHONE FOR THESE AT ONCE

OUR NEXT ══ "QUO VADIS" ══ COMING SOON

ATLAS MANUFACTURING CO., 412 CENTURY BUILDING, **ST. LOUIS, MO.**
BELL PHONE, OLIVE 2131.

In 1910 the film "Sapho" was extensively advertised and was billed as the greatest film ever made. This advertisement, placed by the Atlas Manufacturing Company, a St. Louis and New York film maker, notes that distributors could secure rights for the film on a state by state basis.

By 1910 just about every amusement park in America had a moving picture theatre. At Savin Rock, Connecticut, Mitchell's Theatre offered moving pictures ("Changed Daily"), illustrated songs, and vaudeville acts, for admission charges of a nickel and a dime.

At Sacandaga Park, located in upstate New York, the Electric Theatre offered "Latest Illustrated Songs - Moving Pictures," with the picture of the day being "The Chauffeur."

The Scenic Theatre offered shows for a nickel and a dime in Storm Lake, Iowa. In October 1909, when this picture was taken, features included "Crazed by Jealousy," "Culture of Rice," and "Fattie's Follies." Note the phonograph horn above the exit door, which blared music into the street.

In the summer of 1910 two tired bill posters stretched out on the sidewalk below their handiwork, as three onlookers faced the camera. A nickel admission was charged by the Opera House, which offered illustrated songs, moving pictures, dancers, and a magic show.

ABOVE: The Princess Theatre, owned by James Halper of Roswell, New Mexico, charged 10c and 15c admission. Then showing was "The Runaway," a Thanhouser film, while "The Madcap of the Hills," a Reliance film, was scheduled to appear the following Tuesday. Additional entertainment was provided by Carl W. Molter, tenor, who offered "new songs every other day."

LEFT: The Princess Theatre, St. Cloud, Minnesota, as shown in a 1911 photograph. Attractions included "The Fall of Troy," an Itala film distributed by the New York Motion Picture Company, and "Grenadier Roland," an Ambrosio film.

BELOW: The Bijou Dream, located at the corner of Broadway and Division Street, Camden, New Jersey, offered moving pictures and illustrated songs.

The Hyde Park Theatre, located in Hyde Park, Massachusetts displayed a lobby sign which suggested that patrons start a collection of autographed movie star photographs for 25c each.

The Elvira Theatre, located in a building named the Elvera Palace (with slightly different spelling) attracted patrons on a busy street upon which also fronted many other business enterprises. Showing at the Elvira (or was it the Elvera?) were several films, including "The Woman In Chains."

In Newport, New Hampshire, The Empire, a tiny nickelodeon theatre in a building of its own, was showing "The Spell" on the day this photograph was taken. Unlike some of its contemporaries, The Empire stayed in business for many years. Undoubtedly, the photographer was concentrating on the Citizen's Bank Building, with a sporty flivver parked out front, and The Empire appeared as an incidental subject.

The Nickeldeon offered a variation, intentional or otherwise, on the spelling of "nickelodeon." It took in a steady stream of nickels in Paris, Illinois, right next to the Paris Hotel.

claiming to have invented certain of these procedures. He requested permission to make multi-reel dramatic pictures, but Biograph was more interested in one-reel topics, the film format which had been the mainstay of their business for many years. Several years later, in 1913, he went to work for the Mutual Film Corporation. In 1915 he produced *The Birth of a Nation,* a picture depicting the Civil War and the Reconstruction era. Glorifying the Ku Klux Klan and presenting a biased view of conditions in the South, the film engendered many protests. In its initial run in larger cities, $2 was the price of a ticket to see the feature. Years later, historians were to view Griffith as one of the great figures in the early motion picture industry.

In December 1908 it was announced that all important patents bearing on the manufacture of motion pictures and projecting machines had been acquired by a new concern incorporated as the Motion Picture Patents Company, later simply known as the "Patents Company" in articles and trade literature. Licenses were then granted to the Edison Manufacturing Company, American Mutoscope & Biograph Company, Pathe Freres, Georges Melies Company, Vitagraph Company of America, Kalem Company, Essanay Company, Selig Polyscope Company, George Kleine, and the Lubin Manufacturing Company. It was stated that licensed motion pictures would be leased only for use on projecting machines made by member firms. The agreement was to take effect on January 1, 1909. By pooling their patent interests, the group sought to reenforce each other's businesses and to keep others from succeeding in the rapidly expanding moving picture industry. Rental exchanges wanting to handle Motion Picture Patents Company films had to agree not to handle the products of any other makers, a step designed to prevent new companies from gaining a foothold in the market. A cozy arrangement was set up whereby film from George Eastman's Kodak factory in Rochester, New York, would be supplied only to Motion Picture Patents Company firms.

The General Film Company, a distributing organization, was soon set up to acquire film exchanges and to fix prices. Associated with the Motion Picture Patents Company, the General Film Company had no problem persuading 57 leading distribution firms to sell out for about $2,500,000 cash and $794,000 worth of preferred stock. This was accomplished from April 1910 to January 1912.

What was envisioned as a stranglehold in the film industry was soon broken when Carl Laemmle (a New York distributor) and William Swanson (who distributed films from Chicago) broke away and encouraged other distributors to do the same. In order to provide films to show, for none could be obtained from the Motion Picture Patents Company, Laemmle set up his own Independent Motion Picture Company, nicknamed IMP, which soon grew to become a prominent force and which later developed into Universal Pictures. William Fox, the early nickelodeon theatre owner and distributor, soon was in the film making business as well, as were several others. Soon, competition was once again alive. The independent firms went on to prosper and, decades later, some of them

outlived the last of the Motion Picture Patents Company principals, the Vitagraph Company, which expired in 1925. Laemmle was the most colorful figure in the motion picture industry during the 1905-1915 decade. His flair for showmanship was in the style of P. T. Barnum.

To battle the Patents Company, the independents in 1910 set up their own outfit, the Motion Picture Distributing & Sales Company, popularly known as the Sales Company. Such firms as Eclair, Imp, Yankee, Bison, Kinograph, Lux, Powers, Thanhouser, Ambrosio, Atlas, Champion, Electragraff, Nestor, Cines, Film d'Art, Defender, Capitol, Carson, Columbia, Great Northern, and Itala joined. The Sales Company was disbanded in 1912, by which time the Patents Company was no longer a factor.

Detectives and thugs hired by the Patents Company continually harrassed the independents, who at that time were primarily centered in the New York City area. Partly to escape this continuing annoyance, the independent firms started moving to the West Coast, thus initiating a shift which would transform the center of the motion picture business to Hollywood within five years or so.

Virtually every town and city in the United States was abuzz with theatre activity. From 1908 through 1912, thousands of new establishments opened their doors. Often the same house would change hands and be given different names over a period of time. Thus, in Spokane, Washington, the Empire Theatre opened on August 22, 1908, and took in $178.70 at 10c a ticket for the first night. The Empire was run until 1912, when it was redecorated and opened as the Rex Theatre, charging a nickel admission, except for 10c for special features and occasions. On opening night in May 1912, the Rex took in $95, and on the next day the receipts were $154.20. Other Spokane theatres of the era included the Clemmer, Liberty, Casino, Class A, Lyric, Majestic, Best Show (earlier named the Dreamland), Empress, Unique, and Gem. Giving competition was the Strand Theatre, which had stage performances in addition to films, and two vaudeville theatres, the Hippodrome and Pantages, which primarily featured live acts interspersed with film features.

In San Francisco, the rebuilding of the city after the April 18, 1906 earthquake and fire brought with it the opening of many nickelodeons. Among the entrepreneurs involved were Sam Davis and his brother Mo, partners in the Davis Amusement Company, whose Davis Theatre enjoyed considerable success until a play was staged which caricatured the Irish. "Citizens of Irish blood took the matter up and pronounced the playhouse taboo," noted an account in *The Billboard.* "Following this, the Board of Public Works condemned the place as having been built contrary to the fire ordinances." Undaunted, the Davis brothers set up a new nickelodeon theatre in the Mission District. At the same time, it was noted that business in San Francisco was so good that H.G. Miller, manager of the Pacific Film Exchange, had to move to new and more spacious quarters. To supply the ever-increasing demand all across America, the Edison Manufacturing Company announced in September 1908 that it was producing two

September 3, 1909 advertisement by the Motion Picture Patents Company, the "Trust."

MOVING THE "JUNKMAN" ALONG

Carl Laemmle published many cartoons mocking the Motion Picture Patents Company, more familiarly known as the Film Trust. Above left is shown a fat Trust official raking in $2 each week from nickelodeon owners across America, an effort which yielded over $1 million per year. In retaliation, the Trust made fun of the independents, depicting their picture subjects as worn out and broken down and their features as junk. The Trust was short lived. The independents, lead by Laemmle, pirated many actors and actresses and soon were achieving greater success than the old-guard firms which made up the Patents Company.

A picture said to be of one of Thomas L. Tally's peep show parlors in Los Angeles. In the back is a wall with holes through which motion pictures projected on a screen could be viewed. Soon, Tally found that the screen pictures outdrew the peep show machines, and the Electric Theatre, set up expressly for the showing of films, became one of the first such theatres in America, with some historians crediting it as the very first.

David Wark Griffith, the pre-eminent motion picture director of the 1910-1920 decade.

THE INAUGURATION OF LAEMMLE

Films and Laemmle Service in any
5-cent Theatre or Vaudeville House

MEANS PROSPERITY FOR YOU!!

I HAVE taken "sick nickelodeons" and made them well with a liberal dose of <u>quality</u>. I have taken houses that were losing money and have turned them into big profit-makers—not with any special pet treatment, but with the same, identical class of film service that I am ready to hand out to <u>you</u>! If you want to get results, GET IN <u>RIGHT</u> WITH <u>BIG</u> PEOPLE!

EXTRA The marvelous SYNCHROSCOPE, formerly $550, is now <u>$395</u>. The maker-and-inventor has cut the heart of his price to me, and I pass the good thing along to you. But don't delay!

———— CARL LAEMMLE, President ————

THE LAEMMLE FILM SERVICE

HEADQUARTERS, 196-198 Lake Street, CHICAGO, ILL.

———— AND EIGHT MORE OFFICES AS FOLLOWS ————

PORTLAND, OREGON.	EVANSVILLE, INDIANA.	MEMPHIS, TENNESSEE.	OMAHA, NEBRASKA.
MINNEAPOLIS, MINN.	SALT LAKE CITY, UTAH.	MONTREAL, QUEBEC.	WINNIPEG, MAN.

This Laemmle advertisement appeared at the time of the 1909 Taft inauguration. Theodore Roosevelt hands Taft his "Big Stick."

March 1906 advertisement for one of several varieties of Pathe Cinematograph projectors. Also offered is a new Pathe film, "I've Lost My Eye Glasses," a comedy.

Pathe Freres (Pathe Brothers), a French firm, set up its American production facilities in Bound Brook, New Jersey. The Pathe manufacturing plant is shown here, circa 1911. Pathe was also one of the world's leading makers of phonographs and phonograph records. At the height of its business, more than 6,000 people were employed in America and Europe.

VITAGRAPH

Florence Turner

Florence Turner, one of many Vitagraph actresses.

This sign-bedecked theatre promised the viewers many things, including subjects from the Longhorn Feature Company, whose appeal was undoubtedly enhanced by the buckaroo leaning against the canopy column to the left. Other attractions included "The Convict's Story" (a Kalem film), "Buffalo Jones Lassoing Wild Animals in Africa," "At Cross Purposes" (a Selig film), and other films by Essanay, Lubin, and Vitagraph.

In Osawatomie, Kansas, the Majestic Theatre offered "Special Vaudeville Tonight" as well as "High Class Motion Pictures" for admission charges of five cents and ten cents. (August 1912)

reels of film each week and shipping the reels on Tuesdays and Fridays.

In December 1908 it was announced that an organ had been installed as an added feature of the Alcazar Theatre in Chicago. The purpose was specifically to accompany moving pictures. "Mr. Seaver, the managing owner, is the first in the field with this innovation in picture show business and, judging from the results, is but the pioneer of a large and general movement in this line," noted *The Billboard*. "Those who have enjoyed the organs now in operation in the McVickers and Auditorium theatres can really appreciate the opportunity of hearing music of that nature at the nominal cost entailed by a visit to the Alcazar." Earlier, in Los Angeles in 1905, Thomas L. Tally had installed an organ in a moving picture theatre, and still earlier, in 1898, it was said that an "orchestra organ" was set up in Kansas City, but it may have been that the Alcazar instrument was the first large organ in Chicago put in specifically for film audiences.

An interesting experience in pictures and theatres is provided by an account of the life of Martin Johnson, a young Independence, Kansas, photographer who in 1907 and 1908 sailed to the South Seas islands with novelist Jack London, London's wife Charmian, and a small crew in a 44-foot yacht named the *Snark*. Hundreds of still pictures and countless feet of moving picture film were taken of natives, exotic animals, and other scenes in this remote territory.

Returning to Independence, Martin had a discussion with Charley Kerr, a local druggist, who encouraged him to go into the theatre business. The event is related in *I Married Adventure*, a book written years later by Martin's wife Osa. Charley Kerr queries Martin:

" 'One of the boys was saying that you've got some moving pictures you took. That's right?'

"Martin nodded and told about [how he had substituted for some camera men sent to the South Pacific by Pathe Freres, but who had become ill] and how he had stopped in Paris on the way home and had bought prints of several reels from the Pathe Freres Company.

"Charley Kerr's eyes widened and he snapped his fingers as an idea hit him. 'Why don't you make a show out of it? You know—run the moving pictures, have some lantern slides made from those other pictures you took, and give lectures. I'll bet people would come from all over the county.'

" 'I've thought of that,' said Martin, 'but it would take a lot of money. You'd have to fix up a theatre, buy a projection machine, get the slides made...' "

Charley Kerr sold his drugstore to finance the project and used the money to rent a store front several blocks away. The facade was rebuilt to represent the bow of the yacht *Snark* and, inside the structure, the deck plan of the yacht was outlined in lights on the ceiling.

"Martin selected a large number of his best pictures and took them to Kansas City, where he had vividly colored slides made of them. He spent hours of agony writing and rewriting his lecture to accompany these and committing it to memory. Seats installed, the big screen hung, the projection machine set up with Dick Hamilton as operator, and the Snark Theatre was ready for the opening. Had the opening been held years later the probabilities are that great searchlights would have swept the sky attracting attention from miles around, and a radio station would have carried a description of the event into every home. All the ballyhoo available then was a phonograph set up in the lobby grinding out Hawaiian melodies—audible for not more than a block—but it was sufficient to fill the little theatre to capacity...

"The little enterprise prospered, and in a few months Charley and Martin had equipped another store as a motion picture theatre and called it Snark No. 2. There they ran current films, offered popular illustrated ballads, and found themselves launched in the amusement business."

Early in 1909 a report noted that there were 8,000 nickelodeon theatres in operation in the United States, with countless thousands in other countries; overseas counterparts taking in a stream of pennies, centimes, pfennigs, and other coins. In the meantime, in America the nickel reigned supreme. In Portland, the Big Nickel Theatre drew crowds, while Nickeldom in Des Moines, Iowa, did a booming business. Other theatres named The Nickel, Nickel Treat, Nickelette, or simply Nickelodeon paid tribute to this omnipresent coin.

The Billboard kept theatre operators posted on current events, goings-on, and other activities. The April 3, 1909 issue is typical. It was reported that the Jewel, an Omaha moving picture theatre, after being renovated and redecorated, was again open and doing a larger business than ever. "The new front is very attractive and greatly adds to the appearance of the place," an account related. In Pittsburgh it was reported that "the vaudeville houses, which are classed here now as five and 10-cent houses, are all doing nicely. This is also true of the moving picture houses. The outlook indicates that the spring season will compare favorably with that of a couple years ago."

In San Francisco it was reported that the Orpheum Theatre was doing a great business with various stage acts, but that a motion picture showing the inauguration of President Taft was also on the program of this well-known vaudeville palace. At the National Theatre, also in San Francisco, patrons were treated to a stunt billed as the Human Bridge, as well as to Coin's Trained Dogs with their "It Happened in Dogville" pantomime, a violin soloist, a comedy titled *Two Men and a Bottle,* and other features, including two reels of moving pictures. Similarly, Pantages' Empire Theatre in San Francisco, another vaudeville house, had a variety of live acts spiced with two motion picture features. Elsewhere in San Francisco, "the Victory Theatre opened this week as a five and ten-cent moving picture theatre with three vaudeville turns and an orchestra of three people," while "the Grand Central, People's and Silver Palace continued to play three vaudeville acts with their moving pictures, and all seem prosperous. The Silver Palace Theatre, Market Street, is doing a phenomenal business with moving pictures and a few

ABOVE: In Independence, Kansas, Martin Johnson, shown standing in front of the ticket booth, opened two theatres, Snark No. 1 and Snark No. 2, both named after novelist Jack London's yacht, on which Johnson had sailed to the South Sea islands. The story of Martin Johnson's adventures in film making and exhibition are told in a book, "I Married Adventure," by his wife Osa.

BELOW: Charging a nickel, the Casino Theatre attracted patrons to 214 Main Street, Oneonta, New York. Above the ticket window was a brightly painted morning glory phonograph horn.

THE CASINO
THEATRE

L. H. SHEPPARD, PROP.

214 MAIN STREET
ONEONTA, N. Y.

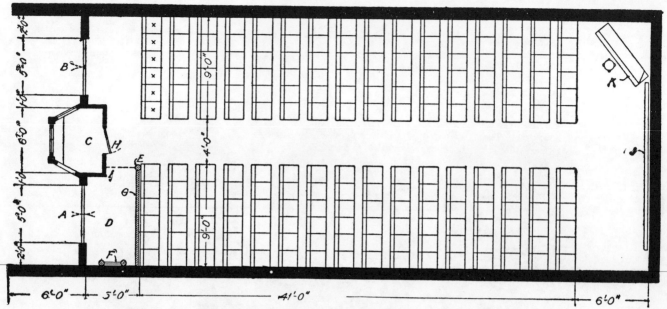

Fig. 1. Floor Plan for a Small Store-Front Theater

Floor plan for a small storefront theatre as printed in the "Cyclopedia of Motion Picture Work," 1911. The book was one of several guides to the moving picture industry and told how to set up and operate a nickelodeon, how to produce movies, and otherwise how to become involved in the field.

THOUSANDS OF EXHIBITORS
REALIZE THAT THESE TRADE MARKS SIGNIFY
Highest Standard of Film Production
AND ARE USING THE FOLLOWING PROGRAM:

Mon.—American, Champion, Imp, Nestor.
Tues.—Eclair, Majestic, Powers, Republic, Thanhouser.
Wed.—Ambrosio, Champion, Nestor, Reliance, Solax.
Thurs.—American, Eclair, Imp, Rex.
Fri.—Bison (2 Reel Subjects), Lux, Solax, Thanhouser.
Sat.—Gt. Northern, Imp, Nestor, Powers, Reliance, Republic.
Sun.—Majestic, Rex, Eclair.

AMERICAN FILM MANUFACTURING CO., Ashland Block, Chicago, Ill.
CARLTON MOTION PICTURE LABORATORIES, 540 W. 21st St., N. Y. C.
CHAMPION FILM COMPANY, 145 West 45th St., N. Y. C.
COMET FILM COMPANY, 344 E. 32nd St., N. Y. C.
ECLAIR FILM COMPANY, Fort Lee, New Jersey.
IMP FILMS CO., 102 W. 101st St., N.Y.C.
LUX FILM CO., 10 E. 15th St., N. Y. C.
MAJESTIC MOTION PICTURE COMPANY, 145 W. 45th St., N. Y. C.

NESTOR FILM COMPANY, 688 Avenue E, Bayonne, New Jersey.
NEW YORK MOTION PICTURE CO., 251 W. 19th St., N. Y. C.
GREAT NORTHERN FILM COMPANY, 7 East 14th St., N. Y. C.
POWERS MOTION PICTURE CO., 511 West 42nd St., N. Y. C.
REPUBLIC FILM COMPANY, 145 West 45th St., N. Y. C.
REX MOTION PICTURE COMPANY, 573 Eleventh Ave., N. Y. C.
SOLAX COMPANY, Congress Ave., Flushing, Long Island.
THANHOUSER CO., New Rochelle, N.Y.

The Motion Picture Distributing and Sales Company, better known simply as the "Sales Company," was set up to combat the Patents Company trust and distributed the films of several leading firms, setting specific day release dates for new titles. The opposing firm, the Motion Picture Patents Company, usually referred to as the "Patents Company," controlled the output of several film makers, and made an unsuccessful attempt to monopolize the field and to squeeze out the independent producers, who later formed the Sales Company.

THE EDISON KINETOSCOPE

New Model Underwriters' Type "B"

The Machine That Spells Certainty of Success in the Motion Picture Business

There is no other business that brings such great returns on such small investment. But the one big thing is to make a hit from the minute you open your doors, and keep the nickels and dimes coming in a steady stream.

The Edison Kinetoscope projects the flickerless, clear-cut pictures that bring the crowd back for more, night after night. You can't afford to start wrong. Send today for full particulars regarding the Edison Kinetoscope and a copy of the Edison Kinetogram.

Special New Features

Adjustable Outside Revolving Shutter, chain drive take-up, extra large lamp house with double doors and square condenser holder, set of extra heavy adjustable extension legs.

A machine able to stand up to the steady grind, which means a minimum cost for repairs.

Unequaled from every point of view.

Price, with Rheostat, 110 volt, 25-40 amperes, $225.00.

Price, with 110 volt, 60 cycle Transformer, $245.00.

Thomas A. Edison
INCORPORATED

269 Lakeside Ave, - Orange, N. J.

COMING EDISON FILMS
Tell Your Exchange You Want Them

March 5—Lost, Three Hours. 1,000 feet. Comedy.
March 6—The Yarn of the "Nancy Bell," 970 feet. Comedy.
March 8—The Heir Apparent. 1,050 feet. Dramatic.
March 9—New York Poultry, Pigeon and Pet Stock Association (Madison Square Garden, N. Y.) 540 feet. Educational.
The Patent Housekeeper, 460 feet. Comedy.
March 12—The Baby. 1,000 feet. Comedy.
March 13—Her Polished Family. 1,000 feet. Comedy.
March 15—For the Commonwealth (Produced in co-operation with the National Committee on Prison Labor). 1,000 feet. Dramatic.

March 16—Personally Conducted (A Trip to Bermuda). 1,000 feet. Descriptive.
March 19—Her Face. 1,000 feet. Comedy Drama.
March 20—Dress Suits in Pawn. 1,000 feet. Comedy.
March 22—The House with the Tall Porch. 1,000 feet. Dramatic.
March 23—Incidents of the Durbar at Delhi. December, 1911. 600 feet. Scenic.
Tommy's Geography Lesson. 400 feet. Comedy.
March 26—The Lighthouse Keeper's Daughter. 1,000 feet. Drama.
March 27—Percival Chubbs and the Widow. 1,000 feet. Comedy.
March 29—How Washington Crossed the Delaware. 1,000 feet. Historical.
March 30—A Funeral That Flashed in the Pan. 1,000 feet. Comedy.

The Edison Kinetoscope, shown here in a March 1912 advertisement, was one of the most popular theatre projection systems. Edison, who held several important patents in the projection field, licensed them to the Motion Picture Patents Company, whose investigators and operatives took legal action against anyone attempting to infringe on the patents or to show other than "approved" films on such equipment. This advertisement also tells of the release in March 1912 of numerous film features, at the rate of nearly one per day.

MURIEL OSTRICHE
(Eclair)

Muriel Ostriche, born in New York in 1897, began her film career at age 15. From 1912 until the early 1920s she starred in many films, often taking the part of a heroine engaged in daredevil stunts and other antics. She was with several film companies over the years, including Eclair, Thanhouser, Vitagraph, and World. In 1913, a poll taken to determine the most popular moving picture stars placed her as second among all women players. From about 1915 to 1919, she was also known as "The Moxie Girl" and appeared in many advertisements and promotions of that well-known eastern soft drink firm. She married an architect, Frank A. Brady, and settled in Great Neck, Long Island, where by 1925 she had two children, Gloria and Margot.

THANHOUSER FILM

SPECIAL NOTICE

Release Day Changed from TUESDAY to :: **FRIDAY**

At the request of a majority of the Exchanges affiliated with the National Independent Moving Picture Alliance, we have changed our Release Day from TUESDAY to FRIDAY. The first Friday release is

"A 29c ROBBERY"

Released Friday, April 15th.

Length, 750 Feet.   Code Word, Twenty.

The Greatest "Kid" Drama ever, and on the same Reel, THE OLD SHOE CAME BACK, 250 Feet of Corking Comedy.

THANHOUSER COMPANY
New Rochelle, N. Y.

Thanhouser was one of the most active of the early film production companies.

73

ABOVE: The Lincoln Theatre, located on Main Street, Orion, Michigan, as shown in the summer of 1916. Vaudeville acts were presented as well as a film starring King Baggot, a popular actor.

LEFT: The Star Theatre, Broken Bow, Nebraska, as it appeared on October 25, 1910. Four films were being shown that day, headed on the bill by "The Maelstrom." Note the brass phonograph horn above the ticket booth. Typically, the record player was operated by the projectionist, who often sold tickets as well.

BELOW: In Grass Valley, California, the Auditorium offered motion pictures and illustrated songs for a dime. A small sign above the ticket booth advised parents that "All Children Occupying Seats Must Pay."

ABOVE: The Royal Theatre, Litchfield, Illinois, on November 4, 1911 offered a variety of shows, including "The Lineman" (an Imp film), "He Was a Millionaire," and "The Claim Jumpers."

BELOW: The York Theatre offered a continuous program of illustrated songs and pictures, features changed every day. "The Lure of the Picture" (an Imp film) and a Sales Co. "Animated Weekly" were on the bill.

The Jewel, a Hamilton, Ohio nickelodeon, was inundated up to its ticket booth when this photograph was taken. The poster advertises "Red and White Roses," a Vitagraph feature, billed as: "Foreign conspiracy and scandal. A man of prominence is made a victim of political ambition and intrigue. Full of vital throbs."

A disaster of a different sort befell the Unique Theatre, San Jose, California, here shown after the earthquake of April 18, 1906.

vaudeville acts at 10c admission." Perhaps the large Wurlitzer PianOrchestra, an immense orchestrion installed at the front of the Silver Palace so that it could be heard up and down the street, helped draw crowds.

All around the country it was reported that vaudeville theatres found that supplementary films increased attendance.

Churches, civic groups, and others complained about the morality of certain pictures, with the result that in April 1909 the Motion Picture Patents Company inaugurated a plan to eliminate objectionable pictures by screening them before its Board of Censors. Representatives of the Motion Picture Patents Company stated: "Agitators who are now seeking legislation against the picture show will find their efforts will no longer be required. All we ask is a fair test of the reforms that this company has instituted which, of course, cannot be carried to completion in a day. No industry so vast as this one can be reconstructed in one fell swoop; but investigations are now under way in every section, and results that will surely gratify the most exacting critics will rapidly and positively be shown."

The same issue of *The Billboard* noted that the Board of Censors, composed of educational and church authorities as well as film executives, had its first meeting on 85th Avenue, New York City. Eighteen reels of film were examined and criticized. Of the 18,000 feet projected on the screen, 400 feet were found objectionable and discarded, while one reel was pronounced inartistic but passed inspection from a moral and educational viewpoint.

Another reform movement recommended that motion picture theatres be made thoroughly fireproof, not only to comply with minimum laws but to truly protect the public, and also to be well-lighted, ventilated, and clean.

In April 1909, among the Biograph films released that month was *The Drunkard's Reformation*, described as follows:

"John Wharton, the husband of a true and trusting wife and father of an eight-year-old girl, through the association of rakish companions becomes addicted to the drink habit, and while the demon rum has not fastened its tentacles firmly, yet there is no question that given free rein the inevitable would culminate in time. Arriving home one afternoon in a wine besotted condition, he is indeed a terrifying spectacle to his little family. Later, after he has slept off the effects to some extent, while at supper, the little girl shows him two tickets for the theatre, begging him to take her. After some persuasion, he consents to go. The play is a dramatization of Emil Zola's [A Gin Shop], which shows how short a journey it is from peace and happiness to woe and despair by the road of rum. Here the picture shows both the action and the psychological influence it has on the audience, Wharton especially. Here is shown a most clever piece of motion picture producing, portraying the downward path of the young man, who is induced to take his first drink; how it finally became an inconquerable habit, causing poverty and suffering for his young wife and child and death for himself,

while at the same time presenting a sermon to Wharton in front, sinking deeper and deeper into his heart, until at the final curtain fall he is changed, going downward with a firm determination that he will drink no more, which he promises his wife upon his return. Two years later we find the little family seated, happy and peaceful, at their fireside, and we know that the promise has been kept. The photography of the picture is perfect."

Gaumont, another film maker, issued *The Policeman*, billed as follows:

"This series illustrates the perpetration of a practical joke of a young lady upon her lover. She visits the offices of the superintendent of the police and while there dons the uniform of an officer. Thus attired, she passes through the office where her lover, also a friend of the superintendent, is relating his troubles. Out on the street she is called upon to perform the duties of an officer, and this gives rise to several very amusing incidents. Arriving at her home after a number of trying experiences she is glad of the opportunity to change her attire and return her troublesome uniform. At the superintendent's office she again meets her lover and both leave, happy again in each other's company."

The Chicago Film Exchange at the same time released *The Burden of Debt*, described in *The Billboard* as:

"The only child of a poor tailor lies ill in bed. They have no money to buy medicine for him, and he rapidly gets worse. One day, a rich banker comes into the store to have a suit of clothes made. The tailor borrows some money from him, giving him a promissory note. Sometime afterwards, when the note becomes due, the banker demands payment. The tailor is unable to comply with his request, whereupon the banker makes love to the wife of the tailor. The enraged tailor forcibly ejects the banker from the store. The poor man is deprived of his shop, and gets a job as a laborer. He has the misfortune to overturn a wheelbarrow load of bricks upon the foot of a visitor and is discharged. He tells his wife about his ill luck and she resolves, unknown to him, to get the money from the sale of their former possessions from the banker. He, in the meantime, has been stricken with remorse, and readily grants her request. She hastens home just in time to save her husband from committing suicide, and all ends well."

The Chicago Film Exchange, a prolific outfit, also offered such titles as *Prascovia, A Salon in 1820, The Alcoholic Doctor, For the Motherland, Father and Son, Medieval Episode, He Is the Cousin Who Eats the Truffles, Love Letters, Drama in the Forest, A Convict's Return, The New Servant, The Artist's Model's Jealousy, The Magic Games, Toward the North Pole, The Train Robbers, Fishing by Dynamite, The Beggar's Daughter, Drama in the Village, Tubbie's Terrible Troubles, Husband's Vengeance, I Want a Mustache,* and *The Blind Child's Dog.*

Oh! Rats!, a slapstick comedy released by Edison in April 1909, was reviewed as follows:

"Bridget rules the household. The agitation of this 'ser-

How I Became A Photoplayer

JUST chance! As you know, Dame Opportunity often takes a delight in ignoring those people who spend all their time on her trail, while suddenly appearing before others who are not even expecting her.

I was one of the latter. It happened when I was fifteen years old. Kalem Company had just built their Cliffside (N. J.) studio. The place

was within a few minutes' walk of my home, and I frequently had occasion to pass it.

Now, there was never a thought in my mind that I would some day appear in Motion Pictures. I was visiting some friends in New York City one afternoon when my mother phoned me, advising me to return home as soon as I could. She gave no

reason, and, considerably frightened, I hastened home.

The moment I entered the house I saw that my fears were groundless. Mother was chatting with a man whom I could recall having frequently seen in and about the Kalem studio. He proved to be Mr. Buel, the producing director. Mr. Buel had noticed me passing the studio, and it seems that I was just the type he wanted at that time.

Now, up to that time, I had posed for Harrison Fisher, and other artists, and I was the original of many of the illustrations on the magazine covers of that period. I had never had any stage experience and told Mr. Buel so frankly. He reassured me by declaring that in this event I would not have any of the mannerisms peculiar to the stage and that his work in directing me would therefore be considerably lightened.

All this occurred just two years ago. Thanks to the kindness of the directors under whom I have worked, I have obtained experience which many years on the stage might not have given me. There's "Bob" Vignola, for instance. He produced Kalem's three-act masterpiece feature, "The Barefoot Boy," in which I played the title rôle. He gave me the benefit of his great experience and helped me to do what I consider my very best work.

Would I give up Motion Pictures for the legitimate stage? I would not! Such an opportunity presented itself very recently, but I just adore my work and turned the offer down. Besides, Kalem tells me that in the future I am to portray nothing but leading rôles, playing under the direction of and opposite Tom Moore.

MARGUERITE COURTOT.

"Motion Picture Story Magazine" printed many interviews with actors and actresses, including the story of Marguerite Courtot, a Kalem Company player. In 1915, Miss Courtot related that she was a model for Harrison Fisher (who was America's best-known and most highly paid illustrator of the era) and that she was "the original of many of the illustrations on the magazine covers of that period."

VITAGRAPH

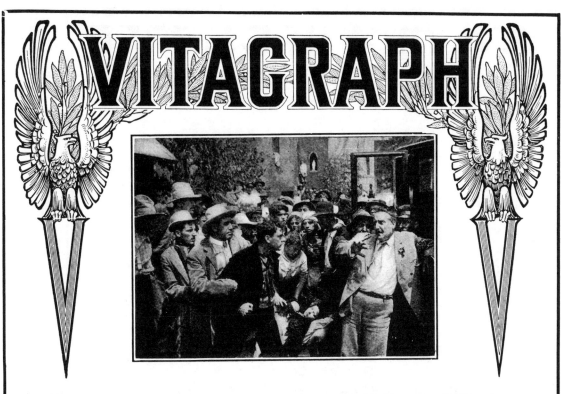

"THE MILLS OF THE GODS"

IN THREE ACTS

From George P. Dillenback's novel of same name.   Published by The Broadway Publishing Co., New York City

A Modern Drama that palpitates with fire and power.   The most vigorous acting by the greatest artists who have ever infused a reproduction of life on the stage or on the screen.

DRAMA

THE MODEL OF ST. JOHN.   The boy and the man.

ROMANCE OF A RICKSHAW.   In India.

THE ANARCHIST'S WIFE.   A deep-laid plot.

THE WOOD VIOLET.   Idyllic.

THE SCOOP.   A newspaper woman's experience.

MRS. LIRRIPER'S LODGERS.   From Charles Dickens.

SIX O'CLOCK.   Momentous.

COMEDY

THE UNEXPECTED HONEYMOON.   Up in a balloon.

THE EAVESDROPPER. } Two refined
THREE GIRLS AND A MAN. } comedies.

COMEDIES

SUSIE TO SUSANNE.   What's in a name?

ABSENT-MINDED VALET.   Fat and forgetful.

THE REINCARNATION OF BILLIKEN.   Among the cannibals.

TOO MANY CASEYS.   Real Irish comedy.

IN THE FLAT ABOVE.   A neighborly jar.

IRISH DRAMA

WILD PAT.   An Irish hero.

O'HARA, SQUATTER AND PHILOSOPHER.   A peacemaker.

WESTERN

OMENS OF THE MESA.   Drama that grips.

UNA OF THE SIERRAS.   Bright and natural.

VITAGRAPH COMPANY OF AMERICA

This 1912 Vitagraph advertisement features over a dozen different titles. Note that no names of actors or actresses are given. It was not until toward the end of the 1910-1915 era that players were regularly mentioned in movie advertisements.

ABOVE: "The Motion Picture Story Magazine," published in Brooklyn, offered pictures of popular movie stars free with a subscription order.

RIGHT: The Vitagraph Company of America invited readers of this February 1913 advertisement to order postcards featuring Vitagraph players as well as one featuring Jean, the Vitagraph dog.

BELOW: Associated Motion Picture Schools, a Chicago firm, solicited plots for motion picture plays. "We teach beginners in ten easy lessons." Apparently the firm achieved some success, as the listing of films indicates.

The Wigwam, a New England theatre, offered "High Class Vaudeville & Pictures," the latter including "The New Congressman" and "The Life of The Czar." The program for the night included stage appearances of The Komedie Trio and Paul Hollander ("Boston's Boy Tenor").

RIGHT: Conn's Theatre, Concord, New Hampshire, emphasized its fireproof construction in an era in which the memory of the 1903 conflagration at Chicago's Iroquois Theatre, which claimed the lives of hundreds of vaudeville patrons, was still vivid in the minds of many.

BELOW: Movies shown at the Arlington Theatre, Nephi, Utah, in May 1915 included "The Million Dollar Mystery," subtitled "The Borrowed Hydroplane." Stage performers Amena Ryan & Berry stopped there on May 7 and 8, 1915, and sent this picture home, noting that the town had a population of 4,000, and the theatre, which seated 800, "had a fine crowd - Saturday show full house, about 40 standing. Fine manager and stage hands."

View of Sweden Street, Caribou, Maine, showing the Powers Theatre. Showing at the time was "Bubbles," a Pioneer Film Corporation production starring Mary Anderson.

A firm believer in advertising, the manager of the Alamo Theatre, Bucksport, Maine, displayed posters showing coming attractions for each day of the week.

Three EDISON BEAUTIES

GERTRUDE McCOY

ELSIE MAC LEOD

BLISS MILFORD

Gertrude McCoy, Elsie MacLeod, and Bliss Milford were "Three Edison Beauties" of the 1914 era. These pictures are from "The Motion Picture Story Magazine," which often conducted interviews with stars and told their life stories.

Popular Actors and Actresses of the Year 1913

The *Motion Picture Story Magazine* (name later changed to *Motion Picture Magazine*) conducted a contest, which closed on January 23, 1913, inviting readers to name their favorite players.

The most popular male actor was Romaine Fielding, who was a Lubin Player. He garnered 1,311,018 votes. Coming in second was Earle Williams (Vitagraph) with 739,985 votes. The most popular woman actress was Alice Joyce (Kalem) with 462,380 votes, followed by Muriel Ostriche (Thanhouser) with 212,276 votes.

A complete listing follows:

Romaine Fielding (Lubin) 1,311,018
Earle Williams (Vitagraph) 739,985
Warren Kerrigan (American) 531,966
Alice Joyce (Kalem) 462,380
Carlyle Blackwell (Kalem) 296,684
Francis X. Bushman (Essanay) 252,750
G.M. Anderson (Essanay) 217,069
Muriel Ostriche (Thanhouser) 212,276
Arthur Johnson (Lubin) 209,800
Mary Fuller (Edison) 191,759
Edith Storey (Vitagraph) 188,161
Crane Wilbur (Pathe Freres) 186,854
Maurice Costello (Vitagraph) 183,422
Ormi Hawley (Lubin) 152,327
Mary Pickford (Famous Players) 130,592
Florence LaBadie (Thanhouser) 108,641
Clara Kimball Young (Vitagraph) 108,615
Marguerite Snow (Thanhouser) 106,518
Dolores Cassinelli (Essanay) 87,782
Lillian Walker (Vitagraph) 87,397
Blanche Sweet (Biograph) 86,791
E. K. Lincoln (Vitagraph) 86,001
Florence Turner (F. T. Co.) 84,184
Pearl White (Crystal) 82,209
Edwin August (Powers) 81,471
Guy Coombs (Kalem) 70,032
Betty Gray (Pathe Freres) 68,489
Jack Hopkins (Rayo) 67,345
Whitney Raymond (Reliance) 67,258
Florence Lawrence (Victor) 64,316
Ruth Roland (Kalem) 61,780
James Cruze (Thanhouser) 51,598
Edna Payne (Lubin) 51,243
Leah Baird (Imp) .49,739
A. E. Garcia (Selig) 49,120
Harry Myers (Lubin) 46,731
Adele DeGarde (Vitagraph) 46,567
Gene Gauntier (G. P. Co.) 43,118
Wallace Reid (Rex) 43,117
Pauline Bush (Rex) 41,153
Anna Nilsson (Kalem) 34,519
Helen Costello (Vitagraph) 30,930
Norma Talmadge (Viagraph) 30,381
Leo Delaney (Vitagraph) 29,874
Thomas Moore (Kalem) 29,784
Gwendoline Pates (Pathe Freres) 29,574
Gertrude Robinson (Biograph) 28,687
James Morrison 27,004
Paul Panzer (Pathe Freres) 26,588
King Baggot (Imp) 25,888
Mabel Normand (Keystone) 25,527
Lottie Briscoe (Lubin) 24,989
Frederick Church (Essanay) 24,808
Marc MacDermott (Edison) 23,646
George Gebhardt (Pathe Freres) 20,581
Julia Swayne Gordon (Vitagraph) 19,802
Robert Gaillord (Vitagraph) 19,560
Eleanor Blanchard 16,291
Marie Eline (Thanhouser) 16,174
John Bunny (Vitagraph) 15,596

Courtenay Foote (Vitagraph) 15,483
Thomas Santschi (Selig) 14,763
Harold Lockwood (Universal) 14,673
Augustus Phillips (Edison) 13,101
Francis Ford (Universal) 12,973
J.J. Clark (G.G.P. Co.) 12,516
Ray Myers (Broncho) 12,283
Kathlyn Williams (Selig) 12,156
Jane Wolfe (Kalem) 12,045
Tom Powers 10,937
Earle Metcalf (Lubin) 10,597
J.B. Budworth (Majestic) 10,592
William Mason (Essanay) 10,580
Howard Mitchel (Lubin) 10,259
Beverly Bayne (Essanay) 10,124
Jack Richardson (Universal) 9,055
Benjamin Wilson (Edison) 8,924
Robert Vignola (Kalem) 8,669
Marion Leonard (Monopol) 8,520
Harry Beaumont (Edison) 8,262
Mary Charleson (Vitagraph) 8,262
George Melford (Kalem) 7,891
Kenneth Casey (Vitagraph) 7,273
Helen Gardner (H.G. Co.) 7,090
Mabel Trunnelle (Edison) 6,812
Jessalyn Van Trump (Rex) 6,689
Robert Burns (Vitagraph) 6,675
Miriam Nesbitt (Edison) 6,671
Janet Salisbury (Gem) 6,614
Bessie Learn (Edison) 6,556
William Russell (Thanhouser) 6,438
Vivian Prescott (Reliance) 6,426
Dorothy Kelly (Vitagraph) 6,268
Charles Arthur (Edison) 6,214
Ethel Clayton (Lubin) 6,189
Irving Cummings (Reliance) 5,660
Mignon Anderson (Thanhouser) 5,335
Owen Moore (Famous Players) 5,260
Hazel Buckham (Broncho) 5,125
True Boardman (Essanay) 4,982

The ten highest vote getters received a library on the subject of moving pictures, including a complete bound file of *The Motion Picture Story Magazine* from its inception to date, volumes of photographs containing all of the players, Hulfish's *Cyclopedia of Motion Picture Work*, Talbot's *Moving Pictures*, and "such other books as the editor may select." In addition, each received a suitably engraved certificate. "The contest did not call for the *best* player nor the *handsomist*, nor the *best known*, but for the *most popular* one. This narrowed it down to a limited few who, after years of experience and publicity, had won the hearts of the public," the contest sponsors noted. "Many players were at a disadvantage in this contest. Some were almost unknown to the public, due perhaps to the policy of the company with whom they had been playing, or a short career in photoplay, while others have had the benefit of extensive advertising by their companies. Again, some have been unfortunate in being cast for thankless parts, while others have been assigned to play the heroic lover, or brave soldier, or gallant prince. Villains and comedians usually have small chance to be prominent in contests like this, as also have those who play inferior roles. Perhaps a fairer contest would have been one in which our readers were asked to vote for the cleverist player and the handsomist and the most versatile, and so on; or, the best villain, the best comedian, the best old man, young man, juvenile, child, etc. Perhaps, next year, something of this kind will be attempted."

At CRIPPLE CREEK

RELIANCE

by EPES WINTHROP SARGENT

EVEN at its best, Martin Mason's dance hall at Cripple Creek was a den of discontent; the home of the homeless and the outcast. It was very seldom that Mason's was at its best; at its worst, it shamed even the rough mining country.

Martin Mason, himself, square-jawed, belligerent, yet at heart a cowardly bully, believed in "keeping things lively," and in this endeavor he was ably assisted by "Dynamite" Ann, who could outswear, and outfight, if need be, any man in camp. Few remembered the coming of Ann to the Creek. She was one of the first victims of Mason's lying, luring advertisement in the Chicago papers, calling for a governess for the children of the Rev. Josiah Strong. She had come, a slim slip of a girl, eager for the country life that had so appealed to her in the crowded city, confident in the integrity of the mythical Reverend Strong, but once past her initiation into vice, she had become notorious far beyond the limits of the camp. Even Mason feared his "star" at times.

Yet there was good in the woman, the good that lies in every woman's heart, dormant at times, perhaps, but ever ready to respond to the proper appeal. She had stood, a belligerent, mighty shield, between Mason and his two motherless little daughters, Mag-gie, who was sixteen now, and Tatto, a child but half that age. It was at little Tatto's appeal that she had given up the vile synthetic whiskey that Ben, the barkeeper, dispensed over the rude plank that served as a counter.

Dynamite Ann, as a teetotaler, might have been a nine days' wonder in the camp, but close upon the heels of the first surprise had come absolute revolution. Belle Gordon, an orphan, had come to Mason's, in answer to his hackneyed advertisement, only to find that she had been duped. Ann had seen scores of girls enter the same trap. She had found a negative sort of enjoyment in watching them brought down to her own level, but there was something so childish, so appealing, in the newcomer, that she had stepped between Mason and his prey.

Even with the assistance of Reginald Duncan, a young mining engineer, fresh from college, who had arrived in the same stage with Belle, it looked dark for Ann and Belle, tho at the first set-to Reginald had floored Mason with a cleanly delivered blow. Manuel Alvarez, Mason's half-breed partner, had come to his assistance, and only the opportune arrival of Joe Mayfield, the United States Deputy Marshal, had prevented bloodshed, and perhaps murder.

Mason had good reason to fear the

The story line of "At Cripple Creek," a Reliance film, written by Epes Winthrop Sargent, was presented in August 1912 to readers of "Motion Picture Story Magazine." The story, reprinted on this and the next several pages, was much more elaborate than the simple title panels used on the film itself. It is doubtful that the film had as many embellishments and nuances as the story.

Cripple Creek, located high in the Rocky Mountains to the west of Colorado Springs, was at one time called "the greatest gold camp on earth." Cripple Creek provided fodder for news articles, dramas, and motion pictures. Certain aspects of Cripple Creek life probably weren't much different from that outlined in the left paragraph of the above text.

young deputy, especially when he was backed up by Wahkeeta, an Indian, more generally known by his translated name, "The Eagle." When the deputy left the place, he took with him not only Belle and Ann, but Mason's little girls, for Ann knew what their fate would be did she leave them behind.

With Ann to play chaperone, and keep house, Joe had established them in his own comfortable cottage. Mason had made a tentative effort to recover his children, but the threat of an appeal to the courts, backed by Ann's testimony, had discouraged him, and he found himself rather well pleased, after all, that they had gone. They had been in the way about the dance hall, and it was Tatto's plea that had caused the backsliding of Dynamite Ann, in his eyes. The incident had dwindled to bets as to how long Ann would stick, and interest in the betting on a "sure thing," with no takers, had soon lost its charm.

Ann was proud of the trust Joe placed in her, and she guarded a more precious interest still, for she loved the handsome, fearless young deputy with all the force of a love-hungry heart; a love that grew stronger because she knew it to be so hopeless, not alone because of her own evil life, but because it was plain that Joe fairly worshiped Belle, and some day, Ann felt, he would find the words to tell his love, tho now he was terror-stricken, and smitten with dumbness, when left alone with the girl.

Love seemed to be in the very air,

"AND GOD BLESS BELLE"

for Reginald, too, hung about the cottage, seeking a word with Maggie; and even little Tatto, saying her "Now I lay me" at Joe's knee, would add: "And God bless Ann, and God bless Belle, 'cause Uncle Joe loves her."

Belle could not understand why Joe always maneuvered to hear Tatto say her prayers when she was not present, until one day, under the open sky, came the child's plea. She blushed rosy red as she listened to the lisped petition, and Tatto wondered sleepily at the warmth of Belle's good-night hug.

It was at the close of one long June day. Tatto been put to bed, and Joe sat in front of the cabin, waiting for Ann and Belle to finish the supper things, that he might walk thru the twilight by the side of the lonely girl. The Eagle slipped toward him, with a word of warning, and a moment later Mason and Alvarez came around the corner. Joe made sure that his revolver was loose in its holster, and looked inquiringly at the two men. It was Mason who broke the conversational ice, after an appealing glance at his partner for assistance.

"Doin' much work on yore 'Last Dollar' claim?" he asked, with an effort to appear natural that but emphasized his eagerness.

"More than th' law calls for," answered Joe.

"Gittin' much out of it?"

"Enough to pay for picks an' powder."

"Jest about that," assented Mason, pleasantly. "Look here, Joe, I've been doin' some smart thinkin'. You've taken those kids off my hands, and I ought to do somethin' to balance th' scales. I've been talkin' it over with Manuel here, and he's willin' to let me pay four hundred dollars for that claim. It aint worth that," he added, quickly, "but we figured you wouldn't want charity, and th' transfer of th' claim would make it seem like straight business—of course every one knows what a joke th' Last Dollar is."

"Maybe I like jokes," suggested Joe. "That tunnel ought to cut the Quintock lode pretty soon, and that's th' highest-grade ore in these parts. I'll stick, Mason."

"Better sell," urged Mason. "Four hundred's four hundred, you know. Me and Manuel will put a lot of men in, on a gamble, and either make or break in a month. It will take you years."

"I'm young yet." Mayfield's voice was level, but his anger was rising behind it.

"You'll be sorry if you dont sell," warned Mason, with thinly veiled threat.

"I'll prob'ly be sorry if I do," retorted Joe. "Seein' that our business chat is over, I'll say good-night."

Muttering threats, the two companions in evil took their departure, and half an hour later Joe had forgotten all about the offer as he walked with Ann and Belle. A cry from Ann roused him from pleasant thought, and he groaned as he followed the direction of her pointing finger.

Little Tatto was a somnambulist, and it was evident that she had been walking in her sleep, for high on the cliff above stood Alvarez, holding the child, while Mason stood beside them. Joe whipped the revolver from his holster, but Alvarez forestalled him, holding the child so that her frail body served him as a shield, and Mason dropped behind the rocks.

The half-breed tauntingly held his burden over the cliff's sheer edge. The two women turned from the terrible sight, their shoulders shaken by

MASON AND MANUEL SIGHT THE SLEEP-WALKER

their sobs; but Mayfield never took his eyes from Alvarez, hoping for a chance shot before the child should be tossed to death on the cruel rocks below. In the quiet air Alvarez' voice rang out:

"You have refused to sell us th' Last Dollar claim. It costs this child her life!"

"I'll sell—I'll give you the mine!" shouted Joe, but it was too late. Already the tiny nightgown fluttered in the air as Tatto fell, and her shriek mingled with Manuel's cry of triumph. Joe muttered a curse that was a prayer, but the two women roused at the half-breed's exultant shout. Unnoticed by either party, The Eagle had come upon a lower ledge of rock, and now, steadying himself with the wild grape-vines that grew in ladder-like profusion, he caught the child in his great arms.

THEY SEE THE EAGLE RESCUE TATTO

score they held against him. If they could not get it, at least he should not profit; and so the quick mind of Alvarez formulated a plan, which should include the services of "Shifty" Ben, the barkeeper. Cripple Creek ran close to the mine. A single "shot," well placed, would rend the rock and fill the mine with water. Joe was frequently called away by his official duties. They had but to watch their chance, slip in, and place the shot that would destroy his mine.

What they did not know was that The Eagle followed as they descended into the mine, and they were too engrossed with their work to notice his wary descent after them. There was much to be done, and no time to be spared. Not until they heard the bucket descend, with Joe and Belle, did they cease their work, and hide behind the piles of quartz at the foot of the shaft.

Joe uttered an exclamation of surprise as he saw The Eagle standing there, and this was followed by an exultant shout as The Eagle presented him with a bit of ore Mason had chipped off—ore so rich that the vir-

For a moment he swayed dangerously, as it seemed as tho the vines must be torn away. The little group in the valley shuddered as it seemed each moment that the Indian must share the fate intended for the child, but at last he swung himself to safety, and made his quick, sure way down the cliff. Once Joe had saved The Eagle's life, winning his undying gratitude; now, The Eagle had brought a life in return. But in the excitement of the rescue, Mason and Alvarez had made their escape.

Nor were they content with a single effort at revenge. They knew, what Joe did not, that he had passed the Quintock lode, the richest in Cripple Creek, and that millions in high-grade ore lay behind instead of before his pick. By mischance he had tunneled thru a seam of barren rock, passing wealth on either hand. They dared not seize the mine, and Joe would not sell, thereby adding to the already long

TATTO IS STOLEN

gin gold could be picked from the seams with a claspknife.

So engrossed were they in the find, that The Eagle, for the moment, forgot the intruders. Before he thought again of them, or had time to warn his benefactor, they had rushed in upon them. Mason disarmed Joe before he could draw his gun, and Alvarez plucked the knife from The Eagle's belt in grappling with him. Belle they tied to one of the timbers that supported the roof, but the men they bound hand and foot, and left on the rocky floor. Ben, the barkeeper, brought the keg of giant powder from the end of the tunnel, and Alvarez inserted a fuse, giving plenty of length, that they might be well away from the mine before the explosion came. Then they shook the bucket rope, and were drawn up by unseen arms.

The three captives watched, with fascinated glance, the tiny spark that crept so slowly toward their destruction. Joe sought to cheer Belle, and gave no thought to The Eagle for the moment. He could hear him writhing on the floor, but in this dreadful last moment his thoughts were all for the woman he loved.

Slowly the spark crawled along the flooring, like some worm of destruction. A foot was gone—eighteen inches; the spark seemed to rise in the air. It had burned along the flooring, and now it crept up the side of the barrel. In another moment it would gain the top, and then—— Joe called a last good-by, and, with closed eyes, waited for the end; but at that moment a shadow crossed before the spark of flame. There was an instant of suspense, then a grunt of satisfaction, and The Eagle, with flesh torn and bruised by the rough rock, fell backward, with the last few inches of fuse in his teeth. He had wormed his way over to the powder, and had withdrawn the fuse but an instant before its contact with the explosive.

"No harm," he panted. "Got knife—come to you."

In a few vigorous moments he had made his way to Joe, carrying in his teeth the knife he had found on the floor of the tunnel. On his crawling up, like a faithful dog, Joe hacked at The Eagle's bonds.

Ten minutes later they were at the surface. For a second time The Eagle had defeated the schemers.

But danger shared and gone brought no courage, in one respect, to Joe. His face crimsoned as he thought of that good-by, so that when he came face to face with Belle he seemed tongue-tied and foolish; and it was Maggie, the seeing one, who took the matter into her own hands. She played her part with all the indifference of the outsider, and in five minutes she had accomplished what Joe had not been able to perform in as many months. She was still enjoying her triumph, that of the natural born match-maker, when Reginald came into the room, and Maggie, in turn, met her own Waterloo, in the war of his warm words of appeal.

Ann was the first to congratulate the happy pairs, but her heart was as heavy as her manner was gay. She knew that she could not hope to win Joe's love, and she wanted to see Belle happy; but while she went about the preparations for the double wedding with a bright, smiling face, she came to dread the long, sleepless nights that were the Gethsemane of her hopeless love. It was not until the eve of the wedding that peace was hers, and she came to Mayfield on Joe's and Reginald's wedding morning, with a face shining with renunciation and resolve.

"Joe," she said, radiantly, "I've got a wedding present that I reckon you'll like. God came to me in the middle of the night, and—I'm square with Him at last."

Joe grasped her hand in fellowship. Better than the others, he knew of Ann's struggle; of how earnestly she had sought to "square it" with her Creator for the misspent years of her life. They had talked it over many times, and she spoke truly when she said she knew it would be his most welcome wedding present.

She was the life of the wedding party, and when the minister had spoken the last words of the simple ceremony that made four hearts happy, she threw open the door to the dining-room, with a flourish.

"This way to the banquet!" she called. "All the stuff's guaranteed under the pure food act, because I made it myself. This way; dont crowd—there's plenty of room and plenty of grub for all."

Laughing, the guests trooped into

The guests came rushing into the room at the sound of the report, the men hurrying thru the outer door to give chase to the murderer. Joe gently laid Ann upon the floor. It would be useless to move her, and, as she gasped for breath, he knelt beside her.

"Good-by, Joe," she panted, thru spasms of pain. "It's all right—it's better so. Put on the stone just 'Dynamite Ann—she—lived—right.'"

THE CHILDREN ARE RESCUED

the next room, carrying Maggie and Reginald with them; but Joe lingered to claim a kiss from his pretty bride. Ann watched them smilingly. It did not hurt now: she was at peace.

She started as at the window appeared the sinister face of Manuel Alvarez. The face quickly disappeared, but along the sill lay the blued steel of a revolver barrel. There was no time to call—to warn the man she worshiped. Time only to step between him and the window, and make the last sacrifice of expiation.

The last word was barely audibly spoken, but Joe heard, and understood. Reverently he laid the toil-gnarled hands across the faithful breast, and in the fingers, of whose slim whiteness Ann once had been so proud, he placed Belle's bridal wreath of virginal white.

"She did die 'right,'" he whispered. "For no man hath greater love than this, that he gives up his life for his friend. She gave both love and life to those she served, and she died—'right.'"

vant problem' in the family of Mr. and Mrs. Green is at an acute stage.

"To leave Bridget, the domestic tyrant, in absolute possession of the house seems to be the only solution. Bobby, the son, by chance discovers Bridget's insane fear of rats. Bobby tells his father, who uses the knowledge so advantageously that peace reigns once more in the household.

"Mama enters the kitchen to see a peddler thrown through the doorway. Her protest against such conduct is immediately overruled by the servant, who forces her from the room. Poppa, arriving home, volunteers to correct matters and starts for the scene of strife. Entering the kitchen he finds the grocer in the hands of the tyrant Bridget. Interfering, he becomes the center of attack. Deluged with flour, he escapes.

"At the family 'council of war' Bridget's discharge is decided. The discharge, passed to her through a doorway on a broom, is torn to bits, and poppa, bombarded with crockery, beats a hasty retreat.

"Bobby, entering with a pet rat, shows it to Bridget—she screams and mounts a chair. Bobby's peals of laughter bring his parents, who are surprised to see Bridget madly leap through the doorway.

"In consultation, poppa decides to use rats as a means of the servant's discharge. Bringing home a cage of big ones, he places two on a dish on the kitchen table—covers them, and hides to await developments. Things happen quickly. Bridget enters and removes the cover. The rats jump out. Screaming, she mounts the chair. It is now poppa's chance. He shows her the cage of big rats, threatening to let them out—she begs for mercy. Mama and Bobby, who have prepared in advance, enter with the servant's luggage. Threatened with rats, she accepts her discharge and leaves, to the relief of all."

Of a documentary nature was *Whale Fishing*, released in early 1909 by Pathe Freres:

"This interesting picture was taken on a whaler and gives us a vivid idea of the perilous enterprise which, when viewed from a sporting standpoint, seems to be all that one with sporting proclivities could desire. The first picture shows them sighting a big fellow rolling around in the water, and the whaler starts in pursuit, getting the harpoon ready. When they get within reach they fire and hit the monster, and he dashes off—dragging the vessel behind, but it is only a short time before his strength gives out. He is then captured and dragged to shore. It is a great sight, one which is well worth witnessing, to see him being dragged upon the land where he is dismembered. This monster measured 68 feet and weighed 172,840 pounds. The amount of fat obtained from it weighed 74,073 pounds and the oil 59,524 pounds."

Other recent Pathe Freres films included *His Last Illusion Gone, The Limit for Delivery, Old Aunt Hanna's Cat, Beware of Evil Companions, Every Lass a Queen*, and *The Martins Leave Home for a Week*.

The Gaumont Company, with offices at 124 East 25th Street, New York City, suggested that nickelodeon owners install the Chronophone, "the only machine which gives perfect synchronism between the voice and the lips which any operator can work. Without perfect synchronism you simply have a moving picture machine and a phonograph, and this you can buy anywhere, and waste your money. What you want is a system and a perfect system and that is what we supply. You buy a Chronophone complete (not an attachment), including Chrono Moving Picture machine, lamp house, rheostat, synchronizing apparatus, talking machine, and connecting cable for $600."

The Chronophone was one of many experiments intended to produce sound synchronized with motion pictures. Others included the Cameraphone, Cinephone, Viviphone, Actophone, Unaphone, and Photophone, to mention just a few. In the early years none met with true commercial success. Most featured an accompanying phonograph kept synchronized by increasing or decreasing the film speed or doing the same with the phonograph record. This was fine for background music, crowd scenes, and distant portrayals, but it was a failure in close-up views of speaking actors. Another problem related to the time limit of the phonograph recording. Twelve-inch discs, the largest American standard, ran for just 5 minutes, while the standard 10-inch disc ran three to four minutes. Two-minute and four-minute cylinder records lasted as long as their name indicated. Also, the sound volume of a typical phonograph was apt to be inadequate in all but the smallest theatres.

To overcome the synchronization problem, a number of clever proposals were advanced. One suggested that the phonograph, located behind the screen so as to project the voices from the scene of the action, be directly connected and geared to the film projector by means of a long driveshaft extending under the floor. A clutch provided the possibility of adjusting one device or the other in order to bring them into synchronization. More feasible, and along the same lines, was the idea providing synchronized electric motors to both the phonograph and the projector, each running from the same electric current source and each operating at the same speed using alternating current.

Perhaps the cleverest type of "talking picture" was that performed simply by having a group of people standing in the wings to the side of the screen, or behind the screen, out of view of the audience, reciting the lines aloud as the action was projected!

From the earliest times of motion picture exhibition, films were colored, by hand in the earlier years, but later a stenciling machine was developed. This device was synchronized, with stencils being lined up with the sprocket holes in the film. Each of several stencils contained holes for a given color. A separate stencil was required for each color, and the film to be colored was run through as many coloring machines, each with a different stencil and a different color of ink.

Thus, in the 1909 era it was possible to see "sound movies in color," but the "sound" was apt to be unsynchronized, and the color was anything but a subtle blend of tonal shadings.

JANE RETURNS TO THE CITY AFTER A WEEK'S VACATION
Scene from Photoplay, "The Snare of the City"
Courtesy of *Essanay Film Mfg. Co., Chicago*

ABOVE: A scene from an Essanay film, "The Snare of the City," released in April 1911.

BELOW: This Winner, South Dakota theatre was built in 1916, at the end of the nickelodeon era. The sign notes: "The Cosmo - Opera - Photo Plays." Showing at the time was "The House of Fear," a Pathe film.

92

PETTENGILL'S OPERA HOUSE, ISLAND FALLS, ME, 20 K.

ABOVE: In the 1920s, after the nickelodeon era had ended in most places, Pettengill's Opera House, Island Falls, Maine, showed moving pictures for 5c to children and 10c to adults, with the house being scaled at 10c, 20c, and 30c for operatic and vaudeville stage productions.

BELOW: View of the main street of Cornell, Wisconsin, on April 19, 1913. The rather rustic Lyric Theatre was probably the town's main entertainment attraction.

Film Manufacturers of the 1911-1915 Era

Listed here are some of the film companies of the 1911-1915 period. A complete listing of film manufacturers and importers of the 1911-1915 era would comprise many hundreds of names. In one month during the period several *dozen* companies were formed in New York State alone! At the time, the East Coast, primarily New York City, northern New Jersey, and surrounding areas, was the capital of the film industry. By the end of the nickelodeon era, migration west had occurred, and Hollywood had displaced New York.

The listing given here is primarily taken from the *Cyclopedia of Motion Picture Work*, 1911, with supplementary additions and comments.

Adolpho Croce. Milan, Italy film maker whose features were imported into the United States. In the era of silent films many European reels were imported, with the only adaptation needed being the addition of English language title frames.

Ajax Film Company. 12 East 15th Street, New York, New York. A. J. Clapham, managing director.

"Ambrosio." Societa Anonima Ambrosio, Torino, Italy. Films imported into the United States by the New York Motion Picture Company, One Union Square, New York City, and sold through the Motion Picture Distributing & Sales Company (hereafter referred to simply as "Sales Company").

Ambrosio Film Manufacturing Company. Located at 16 Rue St. Marc, Paris, France. Films imported by the New York Motion Picture Company as preceding.

American Cinephone Company. Located at 124 East 25th Street, New York City. Controlled patents in the United States for the Cinephone, one of numerous early talking picture devices. The Cinephone was marketed through the American Kinograph Company. The Cinephone was an attachment for a popular make of phonograph equipped with an unusually heavy spring permitting it to obtain full speed and volume of sound almost instantly upon release of the brake.

American Film Manufacturing Company. Offices on the bank floor, Ashland Block, Chicago, Illinois. Made picture film under the sign of the "Flying 'A'."

American Flying "A" Studios, affiliated with the preceding. Production facilities in Santa Barbara, California.

American Kinograph Company. Located at 124 East 25th Street, New York City. J. A. Toupin, manager. Operated under the Cinephone patents. Supplied Cinephone sound records and picture film for Cinephone Talking Pictures.

American Motor Racing Picture Company. 330 East 35th Street, Chicago. Special film features were released on an irregular basis.

American Mutoscope & Biograph Company, regularly referred to simply as Biograph. Offices in New York City. Trademark, an "AB" monogram in a circle. Studio also in Southern California. Licensed by the Motion Picture Patents Company of America (henceforth referred to as "Patents Company"). Biograph, one of the pioneers in the field, produced two features each week during its height. From 1908 to 1913, David Wark Griffith produced 400 subjects for Biograph. Mary Pickford joined in 1909 and produced her first film, *The Violin Maker of Cremona*, released June 7th that year. Her next film, *The Lonely Villa*, was written by Mack Sennett. "The Biograph Girl," Florence Lawrence, starred in many films before 1910, but her identity was not advertised or made known to film viewers. In 1910 she defected to Imp, was nationally publicized, and the so-called "star system" was born.

Animated Motion Picture Patents Company. A patent-holding company controlling a patent issued to Meredith Jones for a camera making a motion picture without stopping the film behind the lens.

Animatophone Syndicate, Ltd. 11 Denman Street, Piccadilly Circus, London, England. Produced talking and singing pictures.

Aquila Film Manufacturing Company. Torino, Italy.

Atlas Film Company. Facilities at 10 East 15th Street, New York City. Manufacturing facilities in St. Louis. Manufactured films under the trademark of Atlas supporting the earth, with a picture film encircling both Atlas and the globe. A 1910 film, *Sapho*, was widely advertised as the greatest film ever made, but historians subsequently took little notice of it.

Barker Motion Photography, Ltd. Topical House, 1 Soho Square, London, England. Produced films under the "bulldog" trademark.

Bat Films. 8 Rue du President Carnot, Lyons, France.

Bavaria Film Manufacturing Company. Strassbourg.

Biograph. Name by which the films of the American Mutoscope & Biograph Company were known.

"Bison" trademark was used by the New York Motion Picture Manufacturing Company.

W. Butcher & Sons, Ltd. Camera House, Farringdon Avenue, London, England. Made films under the "Empire" trademark.

Capitol Film Company. Washington, D. C. Sigmund G. Bernstein, General Manager. Made features under the name of "Capitol Films," with a trademark of the Capitol dome within the letter C.

Carlton Motion Picture Laboratories. One Union Square, New York City. Made films under the "Reliance" trademark. Films sold through the Sales Company.

Champion Film Company. 12 East 15th Street, New York City. Mark A. Dintenfass, manager. Made film under the "Champ" trademark and the sign of a victorious gladiator. Products distributed through the Sales Company.

E. G. Clement. 8 Rue du Petites-Ecuries, Paris, France.

Columbia Film Company, 301 West 27th Street, New York City. Distribution through the Sales Company.

Continental Film Manufacturing Company. Copenhagen, Denmark.

Cosmopolitan Film Company, Ltd. London, England.

Cricks & Martin. London, England. Made film under the "Lion's Head" trademark.

Defender Film. 111 East 14th Street, New York. William H. Swanson, General Manager. Distribution through the Sales Company. At one time Swanson was also affiliated with the Rex Film Company.

Ste. Drankoff. 12 Nicolaeiwich, St. Petersburg, Russia.

Eclair Films. 8 Rue St. Augustin, Paris, France. Eclair opened an American facility and became an active force in the industry in the 'teens. One of their stars was Muriel Ostriche, "The Moxie Girl," who also starred for Thanhouser and others over a period of years.

Edison Manufacturing Company. 65 Sidewinder Road, Orange, New Jersey. Made films with the trademark of the "Circle E." Licensed through the Patents Company. Edison produced hundreds of subjects, including the famous 1903 film, *The Great Train Robbery*, directed by Edwin S. Porter, generally considered to be the first narrative film made in the United States.

Essanay Film Manufacturing Company. 435 North Clark Street, Chicago. Studios in Chicago and Colorado in 1911. Licensed by the Patents Company. Used an Indian head trademark. The firm's name was derived from the initials S and A, from founders George K. Spoor and G. M. ("Broncho Billy") Anderson. Through its California branch opened in 1908, "Broncho Billy" films were turned out at the rate of about one a week for seven years.

Famous Players Film Company. Formed in 1912 by Adolph Zukor, David Frohman, and principals of Loew Enterprises.

Film d'Art Manufacturing Company. Paris, France.

Gaumont Company, The. 57 Rue St. Roch, Paris, France, with a factory and theatre at 12 Rue de Alouettes, Paris. An American office was maintained at 125 East 23rd Street, New York City. Films were imported into the United States by George Kleine, who maintained an active distributorship in Chicago and who was a leading figure in the business at the time.

Gnome Motion Picture Company. Offices and studios at the southwest corner of Park and Tremont avenues, Bronx, New York. Licensed by the Animated Picture Patents Company.

Great Northern Film Company. The home office was the Nordisk Film Company, Copenhagen, Denmark, with an American branch maintained at 7 East 14th Street, New York City. Trademark of a "Polar Bear on the Globe of the Earth."

Hepworth Manufacturing Company, London, England. Made films under the trademarks of "Hepworth" and "Hepwix."

Hispano Films. Barcelona, Spain.

David Horsley. German Savings Bank Building, 4th Avenue and 14th Street, New York City. Made films under the "Nestor" trademark. Distribution through the Sales Company.

"IMP" trademark of the Independent Motion Picture Company.

Independent Motion Picture Company of America. 102 West 101st Street, New York City. Carl Laemmle, president. Made films under the trade name "IMP" and the trademark of an imp associated with a shield design bearing the letters IMP. Distribution through the Sales Company in 1911. The first Imp production was *Hiawatha*, released on October 25, 1909. In 1910, King Baggot joined Imp and soon became a popular star, later a film director. Laemmle fought the "trust" and later founded Universal. He was a prominent advertiser in trade journals of the era.

Itala Film Manufacturing Company. Torino, Italy. Films imported by the New York Motion Picture Company, One Union Square, New York City.

Kalem Film Manufacturing Company, New York City. Made films under the name "Kalem" and the sign of the blazing sun with the word "Kalem". Licensed by the Patents Company. Started in 1907 with $400 capital by George Kleine, Samuel Long, and Frank Marion, whose surname initials, K, L, and M, inspired the firm name.

Kinemacolor Company of America. Allentown, Pennsylvania. Made the Kinemacolor picture films and Kinemacolor projecting machine. "Kinemacolor is a process of motion pictures in natural colors by color photography direct from nature," according to an early account.

Kineto, Ltd. 48 Rupert Street, Shaftsbury Avenue, London, England. Made "Kineto" films.

George Kleine. 52 State Street, Chicago. Imported Gaumont and Urban-Eclipse films into America under a license from the Patents Company. Kleine had his fingers in many pies and over a period of time was involved in numerous projects.

"Latium" Film. Made by Manifattura Cinematografica Italiana.

"Le Lion" Cinematographes Company. Paris, France. Made films under the trademark of a rampant lion mauling a roll of film.

"Lion's Head" Film. Made by Cricks & Martin, London.

Lubin Manufacturing Company. Philadelphia, Pennsylvania. Made films under the trademark of the Liberty Bell. Siegmund Lubin, an optician, was an early entrant in the American motion picture industry. Later, he owned a string of theatres in Philadelphia. His first film, *Horse Eating Hay*, was released in 1896.

Lux Film Manufacturing Company, Paris, France.

Manifattura Cinematograficia Italia. 77 Via Appia, Nouva, Rome Italy. Made pictures under the "Latium Film" trademark.

Georges Melies. A French pioneer in the film industry, Melies maintained an office in New York City and produced films under the "Star" trademark. Licensed by the Patents Company. His 1902 science fiction film, *A Trip to the Moon*, became famous in the annals of filmdom.

Motion Picture Distributing and Sales Company. 111 East 14th Street, New York City. Acted as selling agents for a number of American and foreign manufacturers, including Eclair, Imp, Yankee, Bison, Powers, Thanhouser, Ambrosio, Atlas, Champion, Nestor, Italia, Defender, Lux, Cines, Solax, Great Northern, Columbia, Capitol, and Reliance. Usually referred to simply as "Sales Company" on posters and in the trade journals. Rival of the Patents Company.

Motion Picture Patents Company of America. 10 Fifth Avenue, New York City. This company was organized to control the Edison, Biograph, Armat, and Vitagraph patents pertaining to the motion picture industry and to squelch competition. The following companies were licensed to manufacture film under these patents: American Mutoscope & Biograph Company, Edison Manufacturing Company, Essanay Company, Kalem Company, Lubin Manufacturing Company, Pathe Freres, Selig Polyscope Company, Vitagraph Company of America, and G. Melies. In addition, Pathe Freres was licensed to import from their factories in France, and George Kleine was licensed to import Gaumont and Urban-Eclipse films. What was envisioned as a stranglehold on the film industry was broken when Carl Laemmle and William Swanson mounted strong competition as independents and encouraged other film exchanges and distributors to do the same, setting up the Sales Company in competition.

Mutual Film Corporation. Distributed films made by Thanhouser, American, Majestic, and Reliance.

National Film Manufacturing & Leasing, 12 East 15th Street, New York City. A manufacturing and leasing company which operated independently of the Patents Company and the Sales Company.

Navone Film. Torino, Italy.

"Nestor" Films. Made by David Horsley, New York City.

New York Motion Picture Company. Offices and studios in New York City. Offices in 1911 at the Lincoln Building, One Union Square. United States importing agents for Ambrosio and Itala Films. Made its own films under the "Bison" trademark, which was derived from the animal portrait on a contemporary $10 currency note. Distributed through the Sales Company. The firm was formed in 1909 by Adam Kessel, Charles Bauman, Fred Balshofer, Louis Burston, and others. The first film was *A True Indian's Heart*, produced in Coytesville, New Jersey.

Paragon Bioscope Company, Ltd. London, England.

Paramount Pictures Corporation. Formed in 1914 to release films made by Famous Players Film Company. The principals were Adolph Zukor and Jesse Lasky.

Pathe Freres. Home office in Paris. American offices in New York, Chicago and San Francisco. American studio and factory at Bound Brook, New York. Produced films under the "Red Rooster" trademark. Many films were colored. Licensed by the Patents Company. A famous Pathe production was the *Perils of Pauline*, a serial featuring Pauline White, introduced in 1914.

Powers Company, The. 241st Street and Richardson Avenue, New York City. Made motion pictures under the trademark of "Powers Picture Playes." Distribution through the Sales Company. Formed in 1909 by Patrick A. Powers, who opened a studio on Mount Vernon, New York. Not to be confused with the Nicholas Power Company, a leading manufacturer of projecting equipment, including the Cameragraph. The Powers Company plant was destroyed by fire on June 5, 1911.

"Reliance" trademark was used by the Carlton Motion Picture Laboratories.

Revier Motion Picture Company. Majestic Theatre Building, Salt Lake City, Utah. H. Revier, president. The trademark was a picture of a temple with the word "Revier."

Rex Film Company Formed in 1909 by Edwin S. Porter, Joseph Engel, and William Swanson. The trademark was a jeweled crown. The first production was *A Heroine of '76.* "It was a dramatic story about an innkeeper's daughter who accidentally learned of a plot to take the life of George Washington while he was staying at her father's inn. The daughter shows Washington to a different room then the one he was supposed to occupy and takes his room herself, with the result that she is badly wounded. Washington learns the identity of the plotters, thereby insuring a happy ending," recalled Arthur C. Miller in his book, *One Reel a Week* (written with Fred J. Balshofer).

Selig Polyscope Company, Chicago, Illinois. Made pictures under the "Diamond S" trademark. Distribution through the Patents Company. Formed by William L. Selig. In 1910, Selig launched the career of Tom Mix, who that year starred in his first film, *Ranch Life in the Great Southwest.* In the same year, Selig staged *Roosevelt in Africa*, using actors in his Chicago studio. Showing the former president on an African safari, the film had the greatest advance sale of any picture made up to that time. Few in the audience realized that Theodore Roosevelt was portrayed by an actor.

Sicania Film Factory. Palermo, Italy. Made films under the "Sicania" trademark.

Societe Cines. Made films with the trademark of the "Wolf and Babes." Office in Paris. Studios in France and Italy.

Solax Company. 147 Fourth Avenue, New York City. Factory and studio at Flushing, Long Island. Made films under the "Solax" name. Distributed through the Sales Company.

Sunny South Film Company. Rhodes Building, Atlanta, Georgia.

Thanhouser Company. New Rochelle, New York. Distribution through the Sales Company. Used a trademark of the letter T superimposed on a smaller "CO."

Tyler Film Company, Ltd. London, England. Made film under the "TFC" trademark.

Unitas Film Manufacturing Company. Torino, Italy.

Universal Film Manufacturing Company. Formed in 1912 by Carl Laemmle to release Imp, Eclair, Rex, Powers, Victor, and Nestor films.

Charles Urban Trading Company. London, England. Issued "Urban" and "Urban-Eclipse" black and white films and "Urban Smith" color pictures.

Vitagraph Company of America, The. 116 Nassau Street, New York City. Studios in Long Island. Used the letter V trademark surmounted by an eagle with spread wings. Distribution through the Patents Company. Formed in 1896 by J. Stuart Blackton, Albert Smith, and William T. Rock, Vitagraph was a strong early entry in the American industry. The firm continued in business until 1925. An early star was John Bunny, who joined Vitagraph in 1910 and became a famous film comedian.

Warwick Film Trading Company, Ltd. London, England.

"Wrench" Films. 50 Gray's Inn Road, London, England.

Yankee Film Company. 344 East 32nd Street, New York City. Made pictures under the trademark of "Uncle Sam Films" and the sign of Uncle Sam in costume holding a white letter Y. Distribution through the Sales Company. The firm was formed in 1909.

CHAPLIN SAYS

I am with the Mutual

Because this Gigantic Organization is in the best position to serve every exhibitor.

Ask any one of their 68 exchanges.

Mutually yours,

Charles Chaplin

MUTUAL FILM CORPORATION
JOHN R. FREULER, PRESIDENT

Charles Chaplin, better known as Charlie, was America's best known and best paid film comedian during the 'teens. ABOVE: The Rex Theatre in Ogden, Utah, featured Chaplin's portrait on a banner with a notation "I'm Here." LEFT: A March 1916 advertisement notes that Chaplin was with the Mutual Film Corporation at the time, one of many involvements Chaplin had over the years. BELOW: Movie making was tough work, but somebody had to do it, and that included Charlie Chaplin, who is shown cavorting with four lovely "wood nymphs," obviously a tiresome task! "Charlie is clearly quite oblivious of everything but the beauty of the springtime and the enchanting company in which he finds himself," noted the original caption to the picture.

ABOVE: Opening night at the Rex Theater, Hannibal, Missouri, April 4, 1912.

BELOW: Grand opening of the New Bijou, Lowville, New York, February 2, 1914.

ABOVE LEFT: Charles Chaplin in a scene in "Charlie's New Job," an Essanay picture. The seated comedian is Ben Turpin, with Chaplin to the right.

ABOVE: An advertisement for Chaplin's last stage appearance, at the Empress Theatre, Los Angeles, November 1913. Chaplin is shown third from the top in the left column and at the bottom center.

LEFT: Mary Pickford, "America's Sweetheart," shown in a 1916 pose.

BELOW: A scene from "The Violin Maker of Cremona," Mary Pickford's second motion picture, produced by David W. Griffith and released by Biograph on July 7, 1909. Shown standing in the center is David Miles, the leading man.

In the meantime, slides continued their popularity in conjunction with moving pictures. While sing-along slides were most often used, others told of coming attractions, of news events, or furnished admonitions in a comic way such as: "REMEMBER THE JOHNSTOWN FLOOD—Don't spit on the floor!"

Terminology was evolving in the industry. The shooting of moving pictures, earlier called kinephotography by some, was in 1910 known in some quarters as motography. In later years, cinematography became the standard name.

In 1910 the average film was a strip of celluloid one and three-eighths inches wide. Pictures were taken at the average rate of 16 frames per second, but in practice the speed was apt to vary considerably. It was not at all unusual to have the action speed up on one part of the film and diminish to slow motion in another part of the same episode. The standard reel length was maintained at 1,000 feet, although sometimes film was spliced together to achieve a length of 2,000 or even 3,000 feet without intermission, although the use of such large reels was discouraged because of the fire hazard of having so much celluloid in one space. Indeed, fires were probably the greatest hazard confronting the early nickelodeon operator. Many were the stories that told of conflagrations in projection booths, and occasional deaths resulted.

In 1910, it was estimated that 50 to 75% of the new projectors being made were motor driven, with the remainder being hand-cranked. Writing in 1910, F.H. Richardson, in the *Motion Picture Handbook*, noted that hand-cranked projectors had the advantage that they could be regulated to increase or decrease the speed of the action on the screen as called for, something that many models of motorized projectors could not do, although the more expensive ones were equipped with speed regulators. Illumination was provided by a brilliant carbon arc lamp. The carbons required ventilation and insulation and had to be replaced as they wore out. A typical projector was equipped with heavy metal cases for the film and take-up spool and asbestos insulation in the lamp housing in order to minimize the fire hazard. In the later years of the nickelodeon era, projection booths were often made of sheet metal or asbestos sheeting to conform with later building codes.

Gradually, the star system came into being. In earlier times, viewers were content to learn from a poster that an "Essanay Film," a "Biograph Feature," or some other picture was being shown, or that the topic was "Fight Action." By 1910, actors and actresses were being mentioned by name, and before long a number of them came into nationwide, then worldwide prominence. Mary Pickford, who became known as "America's Sweetheart," moved in 1910 from the Carl Laemmle company to the Reliance-Majestic film group for $275 per week. Subsequently, she went to Biograph, where she had been earlier. Before she reached the age of 20, she was making $20,000 per year, then $100,000 per year, then $500,000, then $675,000!

Charlie Chaplin, "discovered" while working with an English vaudeville act in 1913, joined a movie company at $150 per week and went to California to make pictures with Mack Sennett. After his one-year contract had expired, Essanay signed him up for $1,000 per week for the 1915 year, after which he went to the Mutual Film Corporation for $10,000 per week, which amounted to $520,000 per year! The star system was in full swing, and before long many of the leading personalities had their fingers in many pies—not only in acting but in film production and distribution as well.

While most films were apt to illustrate fictitious plots or else were travelogues or documentaries, some provided records of current events. In 1910, the Chicago offices of the Selig Polyscope Company hosted the newspapermen of that city and invited them to see for the first time a moving picture which used actors to simulate ex-president Theodore Roosevelt in Africa, a preview of a film scheduled to be released on April 18th. Roosevelt was shown in various activities, including planting a tree in front of the office of the Bomba Trading Company, examing a gun to be presented to one of the Zulu chiefs, and with various people and animals. The film promised to be a nickelodeon theatre success.

Around the same time, *The Billboard* ran the following editorial:

"Once more the motion picture has shown its intrinsic value; this time to establish with unerring accuracy the perpetration of crime. It so happened that Russian photographic film makers were on the scene in Korea when the great Prince Ito, Japan's foremost statesman, was assassinated by a fanatical Korean. With every detail, the crime was recorded on the film, fixing the facts and definitely locating the responsibility.

"The Japanese government at once possessed itself of the film and is holding the record for use in the courts. This is but another instance of the substantial, practical value of motion pictures, and not a week passes which fails to further testify to the illimitable field which is opening up for film manufacturers. Every branch of art, science, and nature is paying tribute to the merits of the great discovery, the fringes of the usefulness of which have yet been barely touched."

On July 4, 1910, the celebrated Jeffries-Johnson boxing match was staged at Reno, Nevada. The right to film the event was acquired by the *New York Herald*, which sent a motion picture photographer. The sparring contest, which pitted a white man against a black, and which saw Jeffries, the white contender, lose, caused nationwide attention. On July 23, 1910, the Georgia Senate passed a bill prohibiting exhibition anywhere within the state of moving pictures of prize fights between members of different races. Violation was made punishable by fine or imprisonment. Elsewhere, different communities and individuals took stands, as printed in newspapers of the day, either for or against the showing of such films. With nationwide interest aroused, the Jeffries-Johnson fight sequences became a prime box office hit. However, only the *New York Herald* and its licensees had the originals. Undaunted, several other film makers staged reproductions, employ-

ing actors to re-enact the fight blow by blow! Most audiences never knew the difference.

As new theatres opened, *The Billboard* duly reported their debut. For example, in the May 28, 1910 issue the following notice appeared:

"Perhaps one of the safest, prettiest, and most convenient nickelodeons in Chicago was recently opened on the corner of Berwin Avenue and North Clark Street by John H. Adams. The house was constructed solely for the purpose of the theatre, and consequently gave the builders every opportunity to take care of the details which are so essential to the convenience and enjoyment of the patrons. The interior is flanked on each side by a row of seats with a wide aisle running down the center and two exits on either end. The color scheme of its decorations is very pretty and the modern air purifiers make the theatre sanitary. About 2,000 feet of film are shown, furnished by the Theatre Film Service; an illustrated song is also sung. Although no vaudeville is given, the house is furnished with two well-appointed dressing rooms. The seating capacity of the Berwin Theatre is 226."

In the same issue it was noted that in Clarksville, Texas, a new open-air motion picture show, an airdome, was being operated by Burton and Anderson and would have seats for 1,000 people. Still, there were many areas that didn't have a nickelodeon theatre, with a certain Wisconsin town apparently being one of them, as mentioned in this September 3, 1910 advertisement:

"I have the hall, 30 by 90 feet, in a small town of 500, and fine country around. No picture show in town. Would go partners with a good fellow and try it for the season. Write me. George L. Reed. Darien, Wisconsin."

In the same September 3, 1910 of *The Billboard* there appeared a listing of motion picture theatres in principal cities across America. A listing of a few of the names typifies popular titles of the era: Apollo, Arcade, Bijou, Bijou Dream, Black Cat, Bluebell, Blue Mouse, Bon Ton, Broadway, Cameraphone, Casino, Cineograph, Columbia, Comic, Crescent, Criterion, Crown, Crystal Palace, Cupid, Daisy, Dixie, Dreamland, Eagle, Edisonia, Electric, Elektra, Elite, Empire, Fairyland, Family, Gaity, Gem, Grand, Happy Hour, Harmonia, Hippodrome, Ideal, Idle Hour, Isis, Joy Land, Keystone, Leader, Liberty, Luna, Lyric, Majestic, Motion World, Nickelette, Novelty, Odeon, Onlysho, Old Homestead, Olympic, Oreo, Palace, Paradise, Pastime, Pearl, Picture Land, Pleasant Hour, Queen, Rainbow, Red Mill, Red Moon, Royal, Royal Nickelodeon, Semaphore, Star, Superba, Teddy Bear, Temple, Theatorium, Tivoli, Try It, Unique, Union, Variety, Vaudette, White Eagle, Wide Awake, Wonder, and Zenicorn.

In the early years, motion picture studios were nearly all situated on the East Coast, in such locations as Bound Brook and Fort Lee, New Jersey, in various areas of New York City, in New Rochelle (New York), and elsewhere. Around 1910, production companies sent equipment westward, filming on location cowboy and "Wild West" action.

Also influencing the migration was the desire of independents to be as distant as possible from the detectives of the Patents Company, who harassed those who used unauthorized cameras. The first permanent facility in Hollywood was opened by the Centaur Film Company in 1911 and was known as the Nestor Studio. Gradually, the appeal of California's climate was realized, and within a few years Hollywood became known as the film capital of the world. Production facilities expanded, with many companies setting up elaborate stages and sets as well as owning ranches of vast acreage for the shooting of outdoor scenes. In time, the majority of production was shifted to the West Coast.

Moving Picture Theatres Come of Age

By 1912, motion picture theatres were grabbing the lion's share of the American entertainment dollar. Many nickelodeons, in contradiction to their name, were charging 10c or even 15c. Vaudeville houses experienced reduced profits but were still a major force in larger cities such as New York, Chicago, and San Francisco. Stage productions of classic plays and operas were falling upon hard times, as we read in an article in *The Saturday Evening Post*, by Henry W. Savage:

"Just now the theatre is between the devil and the deep blue sea. It is a many-horned dilemma. Destructive agents have been closing in upon it for the last ten years. The most attractive of these are the automobile, the moving-picture show, and the vaudeville house... It was reported that more than $300 million was spent last year for new automobiles and parts in the United States alone. When you consider the maintenance of machines, you may see readily that over a million dollars a day is spent in this way, and by the class of people that formerly bought the best seats in the theatre. The theatre season used to be 40 weeks long. The automobile has cut this down to 30. The minute the warm weather comes, out goes the machine. The man who owns it already has money invested in an amusement plant of his own. Furthermore, he takes his friend for a motor ride instead of to the theatre... On the other extreme, the moving-picture shows afford an hour and a half of entertainment from 5c to 20c, according to the seats. They have made terrific inroads on the cheapest portion of the theatres. Between these two extremes comes vaudeville. Even if the attraction offered by the high-class theatres is of the best character, we can get an evening's distraction at a vaudeville house for half the price or at the moving picture show for vastly less. True, he gets more for his money in the theatre, since he has practically three hours of solid amusement; but perhaps an hour at a moving picture show is all he wants. He buys his amusement as he does coal—in small quantities."

By that time the trend had been recognized by everyone in the vaudeville and stage theatre business. A notice printed in *The Billboard* a year earlier is typical:

"Beginning June 5, 1911, vaudeville was discontinued at the Empire Theatre, New London, Connecticut and will not be replaced during the summer months. The billing

Edna Mayo, who starred for Essanay.

Swanson's Theatre, located at 39th Street and Cottage Grove Avenue, Chicago, offered many attractions including "Swanson's Marvelous Talking Pictures" and singers Virginia Hayden and Virginia Rankin. From the very inception of moving pictures, many attempts were made to synchronize sound with the films. Nearly all employed phonograph records timed to play with the screen action. It was not until the late 1920s that sound synchronized with films became successful, after which time "talkies" were the rage and silent features disappeared.

Many schools and correspondence courses were set up to instruct students in the art of film projection, theatre operation, acting, and theatre management. Taylor's Method offered classroom teaching as well as instruction by mail.

ABOVE: In Greene, Iowa, the Crystal Theatre was playing "Extravagance," a Universal Gold Seal Feature starring Cleo Madison and Hobart Henley.

Mary Pickford, who in later years became America's highest-paid actress of the silent movie era, starred in "The Eagle's Mate," a Famous Players Film Company release. Pickford, who often played ingenue parts, captured the affection of millions. A 1913 popularity poll showed her as an also-ran, but within a few years that changed, and her name was known the world over.

ABOVE: The front of the Star Theatre was a sign painter's dream. Continuous performance was offered, and patrons, paying a nickel or a dime, were invited to walk in.

BELOW: In 1918, when this picture was taken in La Junta, Colorado, the nickelodeon era had ended in most places, but not here, for the Electric Theatre still offered shows for five cents, including "Historical Visit to Versailles" and "They Robbed the Chief of Police," plus an illustrated song, "I Dreamed My Dear Old Mother Was a Queen."

LEADING ESSANAY PLAYERS

WALLACE BEERY

RAPLEY HOLMES

E.H. CALVERT

FRANK DAYTON

Each motion picture production company had its own stable of actors and actresses. Here are shown some Essanay players of 1914. The fortunes of such stars were apt to fade rapidly, and few players active in the early days of production were seen in films in later times. An exception was Wallace Beery (1885-1949), who became a Hollywood fixture, winning an Academy Award for his performance in "The Champ" (1931).

The Imp. Theatre, also spelled the I.M.P. (on the light globes), is believed to have been located in Minnesota. The place was billed as "The Coolest Spot In Town."

View of the Elite Theatre, Kalamazoo, Michigan, circa 1912. Current and coming attractions included "A Disappointed Momma" (a Biograph film), "A Railroad Lochinvar," "The Great Drought," "Father's Hot Toddy" (comedy), "The Martyrs" (a western drama), "Cashmere," "The Green-Eyed Monster," "As Fate Would Have It," and an illustrated song, "The Boy Tenor."

107

presently consists of motion pictures and illustrated songs by Harry Shuberts. This change affects the attendance very little, and the house upholds its past record for capacity business in the excellent manner in which it caters to the public."

An editorial in the February 24, 1912 issue of *Moving Picture World* indicated the dominance of film over vaudeville at that time. Roles were reversed from a decade earlier, when vaudevillians were fond of saying that films were of little value other than a filler:

"By the sheer weight of its own superior quality the motion picture is ousting its undesirable companion, the cheap act of vaudeville. Audiences are more and more made to realize the howling absurdity of freak vaudeville following in the wake of superb picture films. Take, for instance, a picture like *Brutus*, a fair type of hundreds like it. The action on the screen tells a story of great dramatic power; we see masterly acting, a display of consummate art in the setting of the scenes and in the elaboration of every detail that goes to make a play perfect, then while our hearts are still in the grip of the finely developed climax, some 'silly kid' act or ancient 'musical melange,' or raucous 'sister team' rushes upon the stage and begins to do its usual worst. The best vaudeville in small doses is all the intelligent public will stand in connection with motion picture of superior quality."

Comedy films were particularly attractive to the public. As an example, *Smith's Marmalade,* filmed by Powers, was described as:

"A very amusing comedy, made all the more amusing by being set among royalty. The king has passed an edict condemning everyone to death who eats marmalade. His servants, as well as the queen, are fond of it, and are caught eating it. They are brought before the king for trial, but the king appeals to a higher authority before settling upon their punishment. The story runs on through several amusing incidents, and finally closes with the acquittal of the guilty parties. The acting is very good."

Another film, *The New Congressman,* was billed as: "A very amusing farce and one which is well played on stage. Being a comedy, there is very little of the plot, most humor being in the way it is acted. A farmer is sent to Washington as a representative from his district and promises to bust every trust in the country. The home folks are not satisfied with the busting he has accomplished after he has been away a few weeks and send a committee to investigate. The committee is given a royal treatment by the congressman and some of his associates, and, very much intoxicated, both with spirits and viewing beautiful women, they return home to report the congressman is a royal good fellow. The scenes at the reception in Washington are well acted and very funny."

Melodramas and detective stories were likewise popular, as typified by *Hotel Thieves,* a Great Northern film, billed as a full-length detective story:

"In this film a series of incidents connected with the capture of two hotel thieves by Sherlock Holmes are pictured. There is not much plot to this story, the methods of the thieves and Sherlock Holmes being items of interest. The acting is done in the rapid jerky way, probably very true to life, the style in which most Great Northern films are played. The antagonism between parties is very well carried out, it being almost possible to hear the different characters growl."

"Rapid jerky" acting was more the rule than the exception at the time, when actors had little in the way of scripts to follow and relied upon spur of the moment decisions, impromptu movements, and spontaneity. The name of the game was to turn out 1,000 feet of film, often at the rate of a reel each week. Emphasis was on action—the more the better. Subtleties for the most part were overlooked. While the public was often satisfied with whatever was thrown on the screen, reviewers were apt to have minds of their own. Take, for example, *The Feud,* a Lubin drama released on June 5, 1911, somewhat incongruously combined with *The Sardine Industry* on the same reel in order to bring the length up to about 1,000 feet. A reviewer was somewhat disenchanted:

"This little western story succeeds in getting off the track somehow early in the start. The plot is entirely lost, and any source of amusement in the film falls to the beauty of the scenery or people, which is lacking in both. When an actor gets into a cowboy costume he seems to be so enthused with the effect of the costume that he forgets, or the director forgets, to add anything to his makeup which will distinguish him from the other men in the cast. This difficulty, added to the fact that very few explanations are given during the course of the film, succeeds in making the plot unintelligible."

Happily, the accompanying film, *The Sardine Industry,* apparently was more entertaining:

"A good idea is given in this film of the manner in which sardines are caught, cooked and canned. The route of the fish is traced from start to finish, and it is well photographed."

Perhaps conveying a moral was *The Sheriff's Mistake,* a Nestor film, which was thus reviewed:

"Tom Hanson has been out of work for months and now his supplies have run out. Should he fail to bring home money by night, his wife and little one would go supperless to bed. Passing a saloon, he paused to watch a game between a group of men. Suddenly John Hawley declared that he had been robbed. Sheriff Williams orders the doors locked and every man to be searched. Then, to the utter consternation of everyone present, the empty wallet was found in Tom's pocket. In vain did the unfortunate man declare his innocence, but the sheriff would not listen to reason; so, determining to at least make a fight for his liberty, Tom shot out the light, and in the confusion which followed makes his escape. Then came the exciting chase to Tom's shack, which he won, although he was badly wounded. The sheriff, declaring that Tom would soon be starved out, posted his men around the place and galloped away for supplies. Ere night had fallen, the feverish condition of her husband made it imperative that they have water at once. Opening the door, she held up her

Ask Your Theater Manager to Show These Photoplays

THE POWER OF A HYMN.—Depicting the results of a mother's early teaching.

Motion picture companies believed in advertising to the general public. In this 1913 notice the Kalem Company encouraged the public to "Ask your theatre manager to show these photoplays." For twenty-five cents, ten postal card pictures of Kalem players could be purchased.

The 101 Ranch, headquartered in Bliss, Oklahoma, was a traveling show consisting of cowboys, Indians, and other performers plus moving picture features. For many years the 101 Ranch traveled across America. The above picture shows a crowd rushing into the Princess Theatre to see the show.

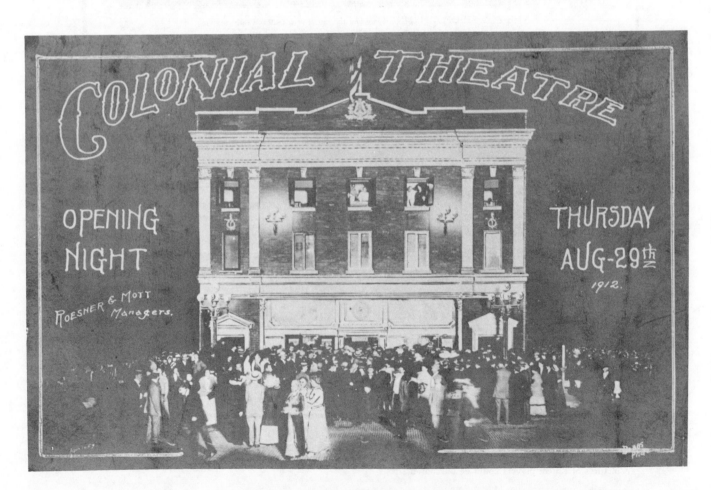

Located on Main Street, Winona, Minnesota, the Colonial Theatre had its opening night on Thursday, August 29, 1912.

The Palace Theatre, Hamilton, New York, was in a rather plain building and appeared anything but palatial. Displayed in the center window were advertisements for two films, "Creation" and "Love and the Leopard," the latter a Selig feature.

The Arcade Theatre, Camden, New York, managed by Tommy Gaffy, offered a varied selection of films, including Marguerite Clark in the Paramount picture "Bab's Diary," Theda Bara starring in "The Darling of Paris," Harry Morey in the Vitagraph picture "The King of Diamonds," William Farnum in the Fox film "Hoodman Blind," and Lawrence Semon in the interestingly named Vitagraph film "Bathing Beauties and Big Boobs," the "boobs" referring to clumsy gentlemen bystanders. Coming attractions included "The Blue Pearl," a Republic Film Corporation feature which asked the question, "Who stole the blue pearl?" and offered "mystery" and "thrills" and was further billed as "fascinating" and "gripping." Also on deck was Charlie Chaplin and a Pathe news feature. Music was provided by a five-piece orchestra. For regular patrons, Episode No. 8 of "The Yawning Abyss" promised entertainment.

By the early 1920s, when the above photograph of the New York Theatre, Merchantville, New Jersey, was taken, the nickelodeon era was over, but some nickelodeon stars, such as Mary Pickford, were still going strong. Posters shown above feature Mary Pickford in "Suds" and Elsie Ferguson in "Lady Rose's Daughter" (a Paramount picture presented by Adolph Zukor).

The above picture, reproduced from a photographic postcard, is dated November 17, 1915 and inscribed on the back: "This is a real town. they have a moving picture show here." Posters advertise "Salomy Jane," a California Motion Picture Corporation film staring Beatriz Michelena, and an episode of "The Perils of Pauline," a dramatic serial illustrating the misadventures of actress Pearl White. This inspired such serials as "The Exploits of Elaine" and "The Hazards of Helen."

EVA TANGUAY

refused moving picture offers, so that a photoplay of her could not be released, that would be detrimental to her career, (as this has happened to so many).

Eva Tanguay

made the five reeler

"ENERGETIC EVA"

for herself, and now that she has decided to release it, you may be assured of satisfaction.

Address all communications to

Eva Tanguay Films

LONGACRE BLDG.　　　NEW YORK CITY

Telephone, Bryant 235.

Stage star Eva Tanguay's entry into films, July 1916.

The Saxe Theatre, in Minneapolis, Minnesota, designed by the architectural firm of Chapman & Magney, is typical of the early "palace" style theatres which gained favor as the nickelodeon era faded, especially beginning around 1912. By that time, movies were here to stay, theatre owners felt, and large and imposing edifices, often constructed at a cost of several hundred thousand dollars, were built to entertain film patrons. The bet was usually hedged, however, and the typical large theatre was apt to have facilities such as dressing rooms, a fly loft, and stage lights for live performances. In practice, the entertainment was apt to include a varied program of stage acts and films. On the day that the above photograph was taken, the featured film was "The Wolf." Several musical acts were also on the program. A dime admission was charged. The picture is from a book, "Theatres and Picture Houses," by Arthur S. Meloy, 1916. It was noted that: "There are about 25,000 picture houses in this country alone, representing an investment of about $175,000,000, with an average daily attendance of about 6 million people." The author explained the reason for growth in the field: "Very few people are able to travel the world over on account of the time and expense required, but it is within the reach of everybody to see the scenes gathered from all over the world and displayed on the screen at a low cost while he sits in comfort. Pictures offer one of the best kinds of entertainment today, and will continue until someone can invent something better for the same admission fee."

little one, then, as the watchers lowered their guns, she fell fainting at their feet. As the men were bathing Tom's wound, the sheriff dashed up with the glad tidings that Pinto Pete, a halfbreed, confessed to stealing the money from Hawley's pocket and dropped the empty wallet into Tom's coat. The men gladly made up a purse for the destitute family, and later saw that Tom had work."

Pretty girls attracted moviegoers, and each studio had its retinue of actresses, many of them in their teens. In March 1912, *Moving Picture World* carried this notice about the Eclair Film Company: "You may have an ability and know all about acting, but you stand a slim chance of an engagement with Eclair directors if you don't wear a pretty face. Out in Fort Lee [New Jersey], where the big Eclair establishment is located, they believe in beautiful girls and handsome men as magnets to attract the public. Girls with dimples are given first choice at all times. Of course, all applicants must possess acting ability along with beauty and form.

"Eclair boasts of nine 'stunners' and stands ready to wager a good dinner for the entire party if any other firm can produce an equal number of prettier girls. What either of the nine contestants would do to the judges in the event of a decision could be imagined. Just the same, Eclair dotes on pretty girls, from the management down to the office help."

In 1912, one of Eclair's beauties was Muriel Ostriche, born in New York in 1897, who started her career when she was barely a teenager. She went on to appear in dozens of movies. Three Florences—Lawrence (the Biograph Girl), Turner, and LaBadie—turned their share of viewer's heads, as did Clara Kimball Young, Dorothy and Lillian Gish, Mary Pickford, Princess Mona Darkfeather, and dozens of other screen beauties.

The years from 1912 through 1915 marked the gradual passing of the nickelodeon era. While a few scattered new houses, the immense Paris Theatre in Denver being an example, still charged a nickel admission, by and large the five-cent admission was an anachronism in many areas. By this time, motion pictures were no longer viewed as a novelty or passing fad. They were here to stay, and theatre owners realized it. Financial commitments were made to raise large and impressive structures, movie houses which rivaled in cost and opulence the stage and vaudeville theatres of earlier times. Happenings on the Chicago scene were typical:

Beginning in 1914, a number of large and impressive motion picture theatres were put up. Three circuits came into being, owned or leased by the Ascher brothers, Alfred Hamburger, and Lubliner & Trinz. The Aschers owned the Oakland Square, Columbus, Terminal, Calo, Lane, President, Frolic, and Cosmopolitan. The Oakland Square seated 1,525 and cost $200,000, while the other theatres typically seated 1,000 each and cost from $150,000 to $200,000. "Organs and five-piece orchestras are installed in all of the Ascher theatres, and appropriate music accompanies the pictures," reported *Moving Picture World*.

The Alfred Hamburger circuit leased the following

theatres: Twentieth Century (1,000 seats), Prairie (1,000), Willard (1,200), Speedway (800), Albany Park (1,100), Pine Grove (800) and Ardmore (800). In addition, seven smaller units were on the circuit. "Each of the larger houses has an orchestra and an organ."

The Lubliner & Trinz circuit controlled the following houses in Chicago, each seating 1,000 people and each with a pipe organ and an eight-piece orchestra: Biograph, Vitagraph, Knickerbocker, and South Shore.

The February 28, 1914 issue of *Moving Picture World* carried an article by W. Stephen Bush, a regular columnist, titled "Is the 'Nickel Show' on the Wane?" Bush noted that five years earlier the nickel was the keystone of the film industry. "The motion picture and the nickel were so intimately associated as inseparable and conjunctive entities in the public mind that it was hard to think of one without making the other vibrate in the memory. To suggest to some exhibitors, even by whisper, that they ought to raise the price of admission to ten cents was regarded by them as a counsel of destruction," he continued.

"Many amusing recollections linger in my mind of the heroic attempts made in those days to divorce the motion picture from the nickel. I recall how, in one small city in the East, the two proprietors of the only shows in town met in friendly conversation and deplored the small returns from their investment. It was suggested by the writer that they add another reel to their program, pay a little more for quality, and then announce an increase in the admission, telling the public the reasons therefor in perfectly candid fashion. The idea seemed to take root. There were deliberations and conferences and at last a solemn covenant was entered into by which both parties bound themselves by every consideration and every earthly advantage to raise the prise of admission to a dime beginning the coming Saturday. I confess that I was considerably elated over the action of my exhibiting friends and waited around the theatres, which were in close proximity to each other, to watch the ten-cent sign go up. Alas for the cold feet of my friends. The ten-cent sign had indeed been painted, but it was never displayed. Instead, the time worn legend, 'Admission Five Cents' was reigning in both temples of art with unabated supremacy.

"There are to this day people who sincerely believe that he who strikes at the nickel strikes at the foundations of the industry. These men, quite well meaning of course, are not satisfied to have the higher-priced motion picture theatre succeed. They believe with a steadfastness which is sweetly impervious to reason that the moment the price is raised from five cents to ten the exhibiting branch of the industry is doomed to early extinction and the producers will have to retire to their palaces to live on returns of the past.

"All of us are agreed, I think, that there will always be well-conducted and prosperous motion picture entertainment with no higher admission than five cents and a possible raise in the price on Saturdays and Sundays. There is an emphatic dissent from this view by some men who in their way are quite as dogmatic as the worshipper of the nickel. It is, however, extremely probable that the number of five cent theatres is going to diminish."

By 1914, multiple-reel films, which had taken hold in a big way beginning in 1911, were very popular with the public, although some (such as Biograph) resisted the trend. The increased cost of theatre construction, the rise of large and ornate houses, and the added expense of showing multiple-reel films dictated that the nickel was to be short lived after 1914. "If there be any doubters as to the situation in all its present aspects, let them look across the water," W. Stephen Bush continued in his "Nickel Show" article. "The quality of kinematography on the other side is not higher than ours, but it is improving more rapidly and it bids fair to beat us if we cannot readjust our prices. Even in the poorest countries of Europe, such as Italy and Spain, it is rare to find a house charging less than ten cents."

By 1916, when Arthur S. Meloy's book, *Theatres and Motion Picture Houses*, appeared, there were at that time about 25,000 picture houses representing an investment of about $175,000,000, with an average daily attendance estimated at about six million people. The nickelodeon era was over, theatres were charging higher admissions, and new enterprises, far from being storefronts with kitchen chairs on the inside, were often designed by architects specializing in the field.

Melloy gave as a rule for estimating the approximate seating capacity of a theatre the square foot area of the auditorium divided by six. For the balcony area, one divided the square footage by seven. "The average capacity for large houses is from 1,200 to 1,800 seats and for *small* houses from 400 to 1,000," he informed readers.

Writing in *The Tibia*, in 1955, Roy Gorish observed:

"The year 1915 is notable as when the silent movie entered its Golden Age, for in this year D.W. Griffith released the film *The Birth of a Nation*, which became widely acclaimed as the world's greatest silent motion picture. This famous 12-reel epic doomed the nickelodeon, as the early movie houses with their two-reelers were called, and established the 'feature picture.' Motion pictures were nationally accepted as the preferred medium of entertainment by this time, vaudeville houses were feeling the effect of the shift, and legitimate theatres were being rented for these feature productions. The time was right for the advent of the 'movie palace.' " From that time onward the days of the hastily conceived, carelessly directed, and amateurishly acted one-reeler were numbered.

In San Francisco, a restaurant which had been convert-

ed to a nickelodeon was converted back to a restaurant, while in Chicago one nickelodeon became a men's clothing store and another was fitted out with shelves for selling hardware. By 1916, in most cases the nickelodeon theatre was but a memory, and for some, a vague one at that. An issue of *Moving Picture World* noted that the old timers in the field had differing versions of who did what and what happened first. It didn't make too much difference, for few people cared. The quaint storefront nickelodeon had spawned a string of palaces across the land, Charlie Chaplin and Mary Pickford were being driven around Hollywood in chauffeured limousines, and the profits of motion picture studios were being counted in the millions of dollars, something that would not have been possible at the earlier rate of a nickel a show.

Eventually, the Bijou Dream, the Big Nickel, and the Electric were replaced by the Roxy, the Paramount, and the Fox. The nickelodeon theatre was all but forgotten, by the public and even by historians. Today, when one speaks of the "golden age of the movie theatre," or "an acre of seats in a palace of splendor," one refers not to the Silver Palace on Market Street, San Francisco, offering shows for a nickel, but to the Radio City Music Hall or one of its contemporaries. Opulent and palatial they might not have been, but still nickelodeon theatres possessed their own charm. Whether there were 8,000, 10,000, or 15,000 of them will probably never be known with certainty, for often a storefront was the Gem one year, the Bijou the next year, and perhaps the Crescent the following year—or perhaps it opened its doors for a few weeks, and then closed them, not living long enough to be recorded in any directories or to be noticed by *The Billboard*, *Moving Picture World*, or other trade publications.

What happened to Snark No. 1 and Snark No. 2 in Kansas, for example? The same question could be asked concerning the thousands of other nickelodeon theatres across the country. These questions may never be answered, and perhaps that makes the history of such theatres all the more interesting. It is only through the medium of old photographs, vintage film footage, and a few surviving descriptions that we can recall the days in which the nickel provided a passport to a wonderful world of entertainment, a trip to Niagara Falls, a visit to a president's home in Ohio, or a journey to the South Seas islands.

To borrow the words of T.S. Eliot, the nickelodeon era ended not with a bang but with a whimper. It quietly slipped away, and few noticed it was gone.

Ornamental Theatres

PLASTER RELIEF DECORATIONS

Theatres Designed Everywhere

Write for Illustrated Theatre Catalog
Send Us Sizes of Theatre for Special Designs

The Decorators Supply Co.

Archer Ave., Chicago, Ill.

Advertising in "The Billboard," trade journal of the amusement business, The Decorators Supply Company, Chicago, invited those interested to write for an illustrated catalogue of theatre fronts. A 1910 catalogue noted: "The motion picture show places have become a fixed institution in this country, they have found a permanent place as American enterprises and are here to stay. Recognizing this fact, we have assembled in this catalogue a few illustrations showing the beautiful effects obtained by using our ornamentation for the enrichment of exteriors and interiors of said theatres. Of the many hundreds of places we have furnished the ornamental work for in different cities, we have reproduced here a few characteristic ones. We want to interest you, prospective theatre builder, in the fact that only through the medium of our class of ornamentation can you hope to have your place rank in beauty and attraction with the best in the country. The time is past when a cheaply fixed up place will pay. You must make a strong effort to get a fine showplace to make money." Illustrated in the above advertisement is the Lyceum Theatre, 39th Street and Cottage Grove Avenue, Chicago.

COPYRIGHTED 1910
BY THE DECORATORS SUPPLY CO.

LEFT: The Bijou Dream Theatre, located on State Street, Chicago, offered upstairs seats for a nickel and downstairs seats for a dime. Continuous performances were given from 9 a.m. until 11 p.m.

FACING PAGE: Caryatids and other ornamental figures suitable for theatre use, as described in a 1910 catalogue issued by The Decorators Supply Company. The central figure, measuring 96 inches high, including base and top, sold for $15 in plaster for interior use or $17 in cement or composition for exterior application. Prices of the other items, for exterior use, were as follows, going clockwise from No. 3606 at the upper left: 3606 $50, 3632 $35, 3631 $35, 3605 $60, 3660 $17, and 3636 $75. 3636 was described as a "Modern Figure."

3606

50½"

7 3/4" SQU.

43"

19"

7½"
3632

19"

50½"

7½"
3631

7¾"X7¾"

3605

43"

16½"

8½

28"

96"

10¾"SQU.

36½"

3636

7" DIAM

3625

1'2¼"

7"

31"

3660

7½

7½"

10¾"X10¾"

The Gem Theatre, shown in a 1909 photograph, was located at 312 State Street, Chicago and had an entrance which measured 22 feet wide by 10 feet deep by 22 feet high. Ornamentation was by The Decorators Supply Company. The program included vaudeville and stage acts, the "Gemophone," and "Fireside Reminiscences."

View of the Liberty Theatre, 1909, located at 135 South Halsted Street, Chicago. The entrance measured 22 feet wide by 12 feet deep by 13 feet high. The ornamentation, ordered from The Decorators Supply Company of the same city, cost $450. The theatre, a nickelodeon, offered a change of pictures each day and boasted: "You Must Acknowledge That We Have the Best 5c Show on the Street."

The Family Theatre, Bristol, Pennsylvania, was showing "St. Elmo," a Thanhouser film, when this snapshot was taken.

Entry to the Normal Theatre, 6850 Halsted Street, Chicago, as shown in a 1909 photograph. The ornamentation cost $300 and was purchased from The Decorators Supply Company, Chicago. To the left is an exhibit of shoes for sale, probably a showcase leased to a local merchant.

Exterior of Sittner's Theatre, North Avenue and Robey Street, Chicago. Sittner's combined stage performances with film features.

The porticoed entrance to Sittner's Theatre, Chicago, featured columns with Ionic capitals. In keeping with a common practice of the day, the theatre name was spelled out in mosaic tiles on the entrance floor. Currently showing when this picture was taken, in 1909, was the stage act of Gilday & Fox, with the following week's attractions noted as "Woodford's Animals" and "Counsel the Second." The bill included film features as well.

The Royal Theatre, a nickelodeon located at 296 State Street, Chicago, earlier was home to another business, as the PENNY AR-CADE lettering in the floor tile in front of the ticket booth shows. The feature subject, "A Gambler's Life," was billed as "Never Equaled," "Interesting," and "Exciting."

The Boston Theatre, located in Chicago at 116 East Madison Street, offered "The Latest and Best Moving Pictures." Showing at the time this picture was taken, circa 1910, was "Levy's Insurance Policy - A Life's Convict." Earlier, the theatre had been a leading Chicago vaudeville house.

Reel II
THEATRE MUSIC

Don't Shoot the Piano Player

"Don't shoot the piano player, he's doing the best he can!" This piece of American wit is appropriate to early nickelodeon theatre music. During the early days of film exhibition in America, music wasn't important. The novelty of the action on the screen—workers leaving the Lumiere factory, ice floes in the Hudson River, horse-drawn carriages crossing the Brooklyn Bridge, or the spectacle of a pie in the face of a surprised lover—was satisfying in itself. Since many if not most pioneer exhibitions of films to paying audiences took place in vaudeville and stage theatres (most of which were equipped with pianos or had musicians on hand) it could have been that music was played to accompany films at an early date. When the first accompaniment occurred has not been recorded, but by the early part of the present century, the addition of a pianist, sometimes with a drummer, a singer, or a violinist in accompaniment, was viewed as a good drawing card.

The musical performance was apt to be amateurish or worse. In *The Art of the Motion Picture*, by Vachel Lindsay (better known as a poet but also a well known motion picture commentator), suggestions were given for the conduct of photoplay audiences. Lindsay didn't care much for music in nickelodeon theatres, for he noted that while "every motion picture theatre has its orchestra, pianist, or mechanical piano, the *perfect* photoplay gathering place would have no sound but the hum of the conversing audience. If this is too ruthless of a theory, let the music be played at intervals between programs, while the advertisements are being flung upon the screen, the lights are on, and the people coming in.

"Unfortunately, the local moving picture managers think it necessary to have orchestras," Lindsay continued. "The musicians they can secure make tunes that are most squalid and horrible. With fathomless imbecility, hootchy kootchy strains are on the air while heroes are dying. The *Miserere* is in our ears while the lovers are reconciled. Ragtime is imposed upon us while the old mother prays for her lost boy. Sometimes the musician with this variety of sympathy abandons himself to thrilling improvisation."

The same writer went on to cite a particularly unfortunate instance in which a film, *The Battle Hymn of the Republic,* was scored not by playing the song of the same name but, rather, by playing *In the Shade of the Old Apple Tree* over and over while the pictures flashed on the screen. When the theatre pianist, a young lady, was asked why she didn't play the *Battle Hymn* she replied that she couldn't locate a copy of the music! Apparently, *In the Shade of the Old Apple Tree* was the only melody she knew.

Lindsay also had his opinions concerning what type of pictures should or should not be shown. When "we come to the picture that is actually insulting, we are up in arms indeed. I was trying to convert a talented and noble friend to the films. The first time we went there was a prize fight between a black and a white man, not advertised, used for a filler." Perhaps this refers to the famous Jeffries-Johnson fight staged in Reno in 1910, a pugilistic encounter which stirred many intense reactions across America. "I said it was queer and would not happen again," Lindsay concluded.

Obviously a well-read individual, Lindsay was insulted time and time again by what he considered to be inept portrayal of literary classics on the screen. Motion pictures were not a complete loss to Lindsay, however, for he noted in a special chapter, "The Substitute for the Saloon," that "often when a moving picture house is set up, the saloon on the right hand or the left declares bankruptcy."

It's not that the industry wasn't aware of the right way

At a time before the photoplayer made its appearance and before the theatre organ became popular, music was apt to be provided by a piano placed down front near the screen. ABOVE: The Normal Theatre, 6850 Halsted Street, Chicago, had music provided by a pianist and drummer. (1909 photograph) BELOW: The New Eagle Theatre, Red Granite, Wisconsin, June 1911, was content with a pianist alone.

to do things musically. *Moving Picture World* contained many articles on the subject. One, "Suggestions for Pianists," offered the following:

"Conscientious and thorough planning of one's music is necessary to the best picture playing. An unplanned program may prove satisfactory, for in this work the same as in anything else there are those for whom the rules do not apply; but the average pianist can do no better than plan his music. There are in every picture a few situations which stand out above all others in importance. These should be singled out for special treatment. The public, always ready to detect incongruities between music and picture, will forgive small errors of judgment if leading situations are played to skillfully.

"To illustrate this point, consider the Biograph subject *A String of Pearls*. The story begins happily with faint suggestions of romance, for which the music should be graceful and pretty on the order of Massenet's *Aragonaise* (Century edition). Then all of a sudden there is a drop. The young man comes home ill, to all appearances the victim of tuberculosis. Despair is in every heart, the future looks forlorn indeed. This the music must reflect and at the same time transform and make sweet. Kate Vaunali's *Goodbye Sweet Day* has all the qualities for this purpose. Then later when the gorgeous social function is on at the millionaire's home, some brilliant piece like Gottschalk's concert valse *Radieuse* is necessary.

"Soon the invalid returns well and happy while the millionaire's wife in striking contrast falls ill and dies. These two situations will bear the most varied treatment. Perhaps the best that can be done is to play the lively *Flower Song* from Faust for the one and *Ase's Death* (Grieg) for the other. Of course more music will be needed for the picture than just what is named here. The point the writer wishes to make, though, is that a great deal will have been done toward a musical interpretation if a few important situations such as these are properly handled.

"How well the people like the old tunes! This was forcibly illustrated on playing for Kalem's *A Spartan Mother*. A song like *Old Folks at Home* with variations can still make a very good impression. In one part of the picture the Union Army is seen driving the Confederates from the field. Carlos Tryor's paraphrase of the *Star Spangled Banner* will sound magnificently here; then without modulating into another key and with the same variations the pianist can play *Dixie* as the Confederates regain their ground in the defeat of the panic-stricken youth. The piano should actually roar in these battle scenes.

"Lubin's *A Mexican Courtship* requires quite a number of Mexican and Spanish pieces. There are several lively Spanish airs in the *Rose of Panama*, a musical comedy that recently held the boards in New York. *Senora* waltzes by Nathan are old, but they have a good swing. Neither should we despise the *Toreador Song* from *Carmen*. It is good to close the picture with *Gypsy Love Song* from the *Fortune Teller*. A most beautiful effect can be obtained by playing this song in the higher register of the piano entirely with arpeggios."

In the same issue of *Moving Picture World* another writer amplified the subject:

"The lively interest in the character of music to be used with pictures is surely a herald of progress. The writer has recently visited motion picture shows in four different states, and in many—yes, most places—found that the idea that it made much difference what was being played did not seem to have entered the pianist's mind.

"How often was the pleasure of seeing a stately military picture marred by the playing of a waltz or a ragtime selection; or the picture of some pathetic scene, by the playing of *Steamboat Bill*. I could mention other innumerable incongruities!

"The music may—nay, should always—be in accord with the spirit of the picture. Some are doing this in a most commendable manner, and these are the ones in demand by all wide awake managers. True, the player who does this has a great and valuable work before him and will receive credit more and more as people awaken to the difference between playing and harmony with the picture or in discord with it.

"Let us not 'censure him for so wasting his genius in a picture theatre,' but give him a cheer and let the world know that we consider the picture theatre deserves the best that can be had."

What may have been a record for theatre piano playing endurance took place at the Lincoln Theatre in Bridgeport, Connecticut, when Nettie M. Hubbell played for 64 continuous hours! In a contest against J.M. Waterbury, who was the regular piano player for the Lenox Theatre in the same city, Miss Hubbell "gave an intelligent and pleasing performance, while Waterbury frequently rested for a few moments at a time and during most of the time did little more than drum on his instrument. Miss Hubbell never left her seat during the entire performance and what nourishment she took was fed to her without interfering with her playing. Thousands of people passed in and out of the theatre during the contest, which attracted great attention throughout the city and surrounding towns."

The *Cyclopedia of Motion Picture Work*, 1911, provided a suggestion for theatre owners who may have had difficulty obtaining a pianist, or who wanted to save on the salary of such an individual:

"An automatic piano may be rented or bought—$800 will usually buy one—and the perforated strip music [music rolls] may be obtained from a music exchange or 'library' with daily or weekly change at a price of $1 to $2.50 per month. The automatic piano may furnish the only music for an 'all picture' show or may be used early and late in the evenings to make the pianist's hours shorter and reduce the expense, besides being ready always to furnish music for a full evening when the pianist fails to appear."

Automatic Instruments

Automatic pianos, electrically operated and using perforated paper rolls, such rolls usually containing a program of ten tunes, were sold by the thousands to

The Majestic Theatre, Memphis, Tennessee, under the management of Frank Montgomery, featured a Wurlitzer Style 17 PianOrchestra, an early model with a set of glockenspiel bars on the front, on a balcony overlooking the street. Presumably, its music reverberated a long distance from the ticket booth and helped to draw patrons to see such features as "Beauty and the Beast" and "Heating Powder."

LEFT: A 1910 Wurlitzer advertisement invites theatre owners to investigate the PianOrchestra, noting that "the leading nickelodeons are putting in this marvelous Automatic Orchestra. It furnishes better music than a regular orchestra of of 5 to 25 pieces, is always 'on the job' and cuts out the enormous expense of musicians." A 96-page catalogue and testimonial booklet showing PianOrchestras in use in nickelodeons was offered.

BELOW: The Sextrola, an attractive orchestrion in a mission-style case, was billed as useful for moving picture theatres, dance halls, fine ice cream parlors, and cafes. So that mail of the North Tonawanda Musical Instrument Works would not be delivered in error to the nearby Rudolph Wurlitzer Company, the ad carefully pointed out: "Be sure and get the address correct."

nickelodeon theatres. Typically, the theatre owner would place the piano down in the front, to the left or the right of the screen, flip a switch, and let it play nonstop from morning until night. The musical program had nothing to do with the character of the film being shown. No attempt was made to cue the melodies to the screen. In other instances, phonographs were employed. Due to their low volume of sound output, they were not as satisfactory as automatic pianos, but their low cost gave them a sales advantage. The Victor Auxetophone, a phonograph which employed compressed air to amplify the music, was used by some to overcome the volume problem, but still the machine was not a substitute for the piano, as B.J. Horgan, a Bostonian, may have found out. His classified ad in *Moving Picture World* indicates there may have been a problem: "I have several Victor Auxetophones for sale. Only used six weeks. These machines will fill your house. Also 1,000 new records."

Apart from numerous attempts to use phonographs to provide sound tracks for movies, the primary use of the record player was to attract patrons into the theatre. Thousands of nickelodeons had phonographs in the projection booth, with the horn projecting out through a wall into the street, playing through an opening usually above the ticket booth. The music thus provided was loud enough to attract passers by directly in front of the theatre but not sufficiently loud that merchants would complain up and down the street.

Much louder, and often employed in downtown areas, were immense orchestrions, or automatic orchestras played by paper rolls, furnished by Wurlitzer, Welte, and others. Typically, such units consisted of an automatic piano, several ranks of pipes, xylophone, bells, drums, and other effects, all enclosed in a tall and imposing cabinet with ornate decorations. Some, such as the popular Wurlitzer PianOrchestra, of which hundreds were sold to theatres, featured an automatic roll-changing mechanism, whereby a program of 30 or more tunes could be played without repetition. Undoubtedly the lunch counter, haberdashery, or grocery across the street was grateful for this, for the strains of music from such instruments drowned out just about every other noise on the street, save perhaps for the clanging of trolley cars. On the other hand, such music often became tiring after the novelty wore off. Some cities passed ordinances regulating music played on or into the streets.

Surviving photographs indicate that a wide variety of automatic musical instruments saw use on the outside of theatres. The Pianolin, a 44-note cabinet-style piano with violin pipes, made by the North Tonawanda Musical Instrument Works, located not far from the Wurlitzer factory in North Tonawanda, New York, was popular for smaller theatres. Large Welte instruments, including those in the Brass Band Orchestrion series, saw service, as did numerous Welte Brisgovia orchestrions. In addition to its immensely successful PianOrchestra, Wurlitzer sold many other styles of coin pianos and orchestrions to theatres. The Wurlitzer Paganini, which was an automatic instrument consisting of a piano and several ranks of violin-

toned organ pipes, was used in theatres, as was the aptly-named Bijou Orchestra, a rather raucous-sounding instrument containing an abbreviated 44-note piano, violin pipes, xylophone, and percussion. In general, the rule seems to have been "the louder, the better"—so long as neighbors didn't call the police!

Inside the theatre, many different types of instruments were used. In addition to simple electric pianos with paper rolls, more elaborate instruments featured pipes, drums, and other effects. In Chicago, the J.P. Seeburg Piano Company found that its large orchestrions, particularly styles G and H, were popular with theatre owners. Lyon & Healy, of the same city, marketed a line of theatre instruments, including a piano with bells, and another instrument containing drums below the keyboard. An idea of some of the equipment, including musical devices, used in theatres in Jacksonville, Florida, can be gained from an advertisement of used items offered by the Montgomery Amusement Company of that city:

"I have the following equipment for sale at a greatly reduced price, all in fine condition. If you are in the market for such equipment and live within a reasonable distance of Jacksonville, it will pay you to run over and investigate the material: two Resotone Grand automatic pianos [actually an automatic chrysoglott consisting of metal bars, with resonators beneath each, struck by felt hammers], two Edengraph moving picture machines, one Motograph machine, 500 opera chairs, one Welte orchestrion, one soda fountain, and a pair of A.C. flaming arc lamps."

Photoplayers

Around 1912, a new breed of instrument, the *photoplayer,* became popular. No longer was the musical program left to chance. The photoplayer could be controlled by an operator, so that the marching troops could step to "hurry up" music, while lovers embraced with the strains of a romantic ballad drifting through the air.

Basically, a photoplayer was an orchestrion or automatic orchestra in disguise. Specifically designed for theatre use to accompany films and to provide sound effects, photoplayers were built in a wide and low format, for installation in the orchestra pit just below the movie screen. Some in the trade called them *pit organs.* Unlike the typical coin-operated orchestrion, the photoplayer was equipped with pedals, buttons, and other controls to enable the operator to supplement the music roll by adding extra effects as desired. Typically, a piano roll was employed, or a specially-scored orchestrion roll was used, which provided the music and turned ranks of pipes on and off and actuated the drums and percussion. Such novelty effects as the bird whistle, crockery smash, horses' hooves, tom-tom, fire alarm, auto horn, steamboat whistle, and the like were activated by the photoplayer operator, who pushed buttons, stepped on pedals, or tugged on rope pulls.

The two leaders in the photoplayer field were the Ru-

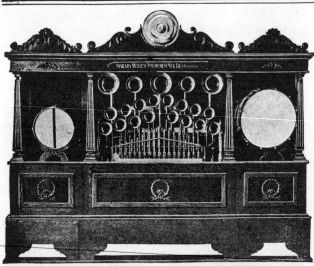

The Niagara Musical Instrument Manufacturing Company, which was one of several firms doing business in North Tonawanda, New York, was active during the 1910-1911 years and featured several varieties of theatre instruments, including the En-Symphonie, which consisted of ranks of pipes played by 65-note home player piano rolls.

In Lancaster, Pennsylvania, the Electric Vaudeville Palace, a nickelodeon which proudly proclaimed in electric lights its 5c admission charge, did business for a brief time next door to the Intelligencer newspaper office. Enticing patrons into the lobby, and presumably providing a diversion for nearby journalists, was a Pianolin 44-note electric piano with violin pipes, shown to the right of the ticket booth. This device was made by the North Tonawanda Musical Instrument Works. At the time this picture was snapped, film features included "Fountain of Youth," "Ghost Story," and "Tommy Atkins Minds The Baby."

The Peerless Orchestrion

Specially designed and created for Photo-Play
Theatres on account of its dimensions

Model "Arcadian"

The name PEERLESS has come to be synonymous with Automatic Pianos and Orchestrions.

Fifteen years of concentration, organization and close study of the needs of a buying public have been the means by which this end has been accomplished.

The instrument shown in this advertisement depicts our latest endeavor, and is one of the most successful styles of the year on account of its adaptability to fit in any place where good music is desired.

Made by

PEERLESS PIANO PLAYER COMPANY
(F. Engelhardt & Sons, Proprietors)

Factories and General Offices: St. JOHNSVILLE, NEW YORK

NEW YORK
14-16 East 33d Street

CHICAGO
316-138 South Wabash Avenue

Advertisement for the Peerless "Arcadian" orchestrion, 1914.

As used in picture theatres

ABOVE: A catalogue issued by M. Welte & Sons, circa 1910, featured orchestrions in the "Brisgovia" series in use in theatres. This was in the day when music - any music - helped attract patrons to the theatre, and such units were turned on and played continuously during the screen feature, with no attempt being made to fit the music to the film action. Often a theatre was a candidate for two large orchestrions, one on the inside to amuse patrons as the film was shown, and another on the outside to draw people in from the street.

A Welte Style C "Brisgovia" orchestrion in a moving picture theatre, in this instance a rather plush one with upholstered seats, carpeting, and an ornate ceiling. "They produce music, not noise," Welte noted.

STYLE "H"

HEIGHT, 7 FT. 3 IN. WIDTH, 6 FT. 4 IN. DEPTH, 2 FT. 10 IN.

A retouched photograph of a Seeburg Style H orchestrion from a 1911 portfolio sent to a West Coast distributor. Although most instruments of this style were used in restaurants, taverns, and hotels, many were employed in theatres as well. The instrument used a type H roll, the same as used on Seeburg photoplayers.

THE WURLITZER
PIANORCHESTRA
"Automatic Orchestra"
Shown on Pages Following.

THE PIANORCHESTRA is without question the most remarkable musical instrument ever built. It represents a combination of the different instruments used in a large orchestra, assembled in a single magnificent case and arranged to play in solo and concert just like a human orchestra.

It is a hopeless task to do the PianOrchestra justice in cold type. The many handsome cases must be seen and the music heard to obtain a fair conception of their appearance and musical possibilities.

Some idea of what the PianOrchestra does musically may be had from the lists of instruments they represent as printed in connection with each style in this catalog.

All the instruments listed are represented in the PianOrchestra and are perfectly regulated by automatic stops which control their playing in much the same manner as an orchestra leader directs his players by the wave of his baton.

In hotels, cafes, theatres, and the better class of public places, where the PianOrchestra is played as a substitute for a human orchestra, it never fails to prove a great drawing card, both because of the fine grade of music it furnishes and its novelty.

In places where a number of coin slot boxes can be distributed, connected with the instrument, so that it may be played from any part of the house by dropping a coin, the PianOrchestra will pay its own way besides increasing patronage.

The PianOrchestra is operated by electricity—a small electric motor being placed inside the case. It plays from paper music rolls which contain from one to six selections. The rolls can be changed in a few seconds.

The Wurlitzer Automatic Roll Changer

All PianOrchestras now come equipped with the Wurlitzer Automatic Roll Changer described on page 9 of this catalog.

This wonderful invention recently perfected by us carries six music rolls at a time and automatically rewinds and changes the music after each piece is played through.

A musical program of an hour and a half to three hours is thus provided without repetition or bother.

The mechanism is constructed with the care and precision of a fine watch, is practically trouble proof and will wear a life time.

The Case Designs

The PianOrchestra cases are magnificent, no finer combined example of the artist designer and master cabinet maker's art are to be found anywhere.

The woods are carefully chosen from the markets of the world—are beautifully carved with the most original designs and embellished with rich decorations of gold leaf and brass in combination with striking art glass panels, beveled French mirrors and showy inlaid wood effects.

The interiors light up while playing and show the artistic art glass effects.

Some of the Wurlitzer PianOrchestras have the most original motion picture effects in front. The center panels are in the shape of translucent oil paintings. When the interiors light up the arrangement is such that a vivid motion picture is produced.

Fountains ripple and overflow their basins; mountain streams flow and waterfalls tumble in the most picturesque cascades; aeroplanes race with steamboats, and so on.

To give all the variety possible and make each PianOrchestra exclusive, the case designs are constantly being changed and in this way only a few of any particular style are sent out exactly alike—slight variations are made in the cases that practically give every purchaser an exclusive, different style of case.

Wurlitzer's Advertising Department had a field day describing the PianOrchestra orchestrion. According to the text, the instrument could "play in solo and concert just like a human orchestra." While the Automatic Roll Changer was billed as a "wonderful invention recently perfected by us," in actuality it was made in Germany by J. D. Philipps & Sons, and imported by Wurlitzer. Advertising claims aside, the PianOrchestra was one of the most popular large orchestrion types sold in the United States, and well over 1,000 were used in various establishments, including theatres, where they were particular favorites.

Wurlitzer PianOrchestra—Style 16
With Wurlitzer Automatic Roll Changer
Instrumentation:

Piano   Orchestration of 42 Violin and Violoncello Pipes
Chimes   Bass, Snare and Kettle Drums, Cymbals and Mandolin Attachment.
Xylophone   Tambourine   Castanets

Height over all, 8 ft. 8 in. Height without Globes, 7 ft. 10 in. Width, 5 ft. 10½ in.
Depth, 2 ft. 11 in. Shipping weight, 1600 lbs.

Price, with Electric Motor and 6 Music Rolls..................**$2,200**

The Style 16 Wurlitzer PianOrchestra was one of several dozen styles sold to theatres, dance halls, hotels, restaurants, and other locations. The Wurlitzer Automatic Roll Changer stored six paper rolls, usually containing five tunes each, permitting a program of over one hour in length without repetition.

Majestic Theater, San Francisco, Cal.

Popular Photoplay House Managed by Henry F. Slater for Seven Years—Success from Start.

ONE of the most interesting of the moving picture houses in the south of Market street district of San Francisco is the Majestic theater, conducted by Henry F. Slater, at 365 Third street. Before the great fire of 1906 this part of the city was thickly populated, but following the catastrophe thousands made their home in the Mission district and the downtown section was given over largely to factories and business enterprises. However, in the vicinity of Third street and around Rincon Hill quite a colony sprang up and several moving picture houses were opened, among these being the Majestic.

This house is popularly known as the "House of Universal pictures" and above each entrance in the large lobby appears the Universal trademark in colors. Mr. Slater was in a reminiscent mood when he told of his first connection with the house seven years ago and of his early experience in the business. When he first entered the field as an exhibitor there were but three film exchanges in San Francisco, the one conducted by Turner & Dahnken, that of Miles Bros. and the one of Morris L. Markowitz on Seventh street. At first he showed the so-called "trust" pictures and tells how the

Majestic Theater, San Francisco, Cal.

first run pictures of this kind were given to a competitor when a larger and finer house was opened in the neighborhood. Immediately after the opening of this new house he canceled his service and commenced showing the independent releases handled by Mr. Markowitz, who is now manager of the California Film Exchange. The manner in which this exchange co-operated with him at the time made a lasting impression on Mr. Slater and he expresses the opinion that its policy of square dealing has done as much to make it successful as the quality of its pictures.

The Majestic theater is conducted along lines a little different from those of most theaters in this locality. There are no matinees, except on Sunday, when the house is opened at 1 o'clock, the performances commencing at 5 o'clock on week days. The regular price of admission is 5 cents, but when serials are shown 10 cents is charged and the house is usually crowded. Univeral pictures are shown principally but other makes are booked whenever they appeal to Mr. Slater. All of the Universal serials have been shown here. The "Mysteries of Myra" is also being offered here, it having been found advisable to have two serial nights a week, and this has started off in fine shape, being assisted by a great advertising campaign. The Hearst-International News pictures are also being shown. A complete change of program is made each day and the lobby is used for publicity purposes.

Since Mr. Slater entered the field here he has had no less than five competitors and has made a success where others have failed. His motto is to give the people what they want and to give the business his personal and undivided attention.

The Majestic theater has a seating capacity of about 400 and has two large exits on a side street, making it a safe house. Edison machines are used in the projection room and music is furnished by a Wurlitzer player. The location of the theater is about midway between the business center of the city and the Southern Pacific depot, and transient trade is depended upon but little.

ABOVE: Hundreds of Wurlitzer PianOrchestra orchestrions were sold for use in theatres, on the inside to provide continuous music and on the outside, such as shown in the Oriental Theatre, above, to attract patrons from the streets. Such instruments were apt to play nonstop from ten or eleven in the morning until late at night.

LEFT: The story of the Majestic Theatre, San Francisco, as related in a 1916 issue of "The Moving Picture World." The last paragraph notes that "music is furnished by a Wurlitzer player," probably a photoplayer.

BELOW: A sketch, circa 1910, of a New York City rooftop studio of the Vitagraph Company. The entire apparatus was mounted on wheels so that it could be pivoted to best catch the sun's illumination at various times of day. The enclosed structure contained the camera and could be moved closer or more distant by means of wheels on a track.

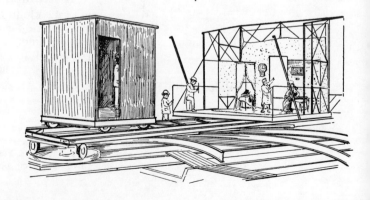

Lyon & Healy's Empress
Bell Electric Pianos

The newest, finest and most effective musical instrument for

Motion Picture Theatres

Operator not necessary, but may also be played by hand.

Good Music Pays

The Rolls which operate this piano give the bell part the effect of artistic hand playing

Contains 24 Sheffield Steel Orchestra Bell Bars Also Mandolin Attachment

Write for Catalog and Special Terms

World's Largest Music House
Chicago

The Empress Electric "Bell Piano" utilized a special Style O orchestrion roll which played solo melodies on a set of 24 steel orchestra bells, giving "the effect of artistic hand playing." This particular style of instrument was widely advertised for theatre use.

dolph Wurlitzer Manufacturing Company, North Tonawanda, New York, which entered the field in a big way in 1912, and the American Photo Player Company of Berkeley, California, which got its start about the same time. The American Photo Player Company later evolved into the Robert-Morton Organ Company. Other entrants included Seeburg, Berry-Wood, Operators Piano Company, Peerless, Link, and Marquette, among others. The writer estimates that during the period from 1912 to 1930, between 6,000 and 8,000 photoplayers were sold in the United States, primarily to small and medium-size theatres. Larger houses were candidates for pipe organs.

Wurlitzer alone made nearly 2,500 photoplayers, many of which were marketed under the "One Man Orchestra" label. In its simplest form, a Wurlitzer photoplayer consisted of a piano unit with a few extra effects added. An example is the Wurlitzer Style G Duplex Orchestra, which comprised a keyboard piano with mandolin effect and two ranks of pipes (imitating violin and flute). Music was provided automatically by means of Wurlitzer "Automatic Player Piano" rolls—the same rolls used on small and medium-sized coin-operated pianos and orchestrions. In a brochure, Wurlitzer noted that the Style G was recommended for a theatre of 150 seats and that "This is an ideal instrument for a very small house where drums might be too loud. It has flute and violin pipes, yet takes up no more space than a good-sized upright piano. It is an instrument built by us particularly for professional work—built to stand the wear and tear that instruments get in public places."

Wear and tear such instruments indeed did get. Oswald Wurdeman, who used to sell and service photoplayers in the Minneapolis area, related to the author that such units were usually played non-stop from early in the morning until late at night. The typical photoplayer was apt to wear out after a few years of use! The serviceman had to be called frequently, for valves would stick, lines would clog, and components would break. Repairing such units was a distasteful job, for it had to be done late at night or in the wee hours of the morning, often in dim light and in an area of the theatre which the cleaning lady didn't visit often. If the theatre had mice, chances were good that they made the photoplayer their home. Cleaning out match covers, candy wrappers, ticket stubs, and other debris carted in by mice was a regular chore for the photoplayer repairman.

A similar sentiment was echoed by Louis J. Schoenstein, whose *Memoirs of a San Francisco Organ Builder* told of photoplayers and theatre organs in that city in the early years:

"As a person who was never particularly enthusiastic about the theatre organ, or, better said, about the working conditions that prevailed about the theatres and their organs, I could never get any joy out of working, invariably after 11 p.m., when other people were enjoying their night's sleep, in the dark, smelly theatres where no ray of sunlight had ever entered the building since they were constructed; crawling around in dusty organ chambers, orchestra pits, basement and backstage, which often seemed not to belong to the theatre so far as the janitori-

al service was concerned... These [photoplayers and organs] were put under terrific strain, being played uninterruptedly, often from 11 a.m. to 11 p.m., making the life of a new theatre organ only about seven years."

Oswald Wurdeman, the Minneapolis repairman, recalled that if repairs weren't completed by the first morning's show, the instrument had to be put together as quickly as possible, even if it wasn't completely working, used for the day, and then disassembled again after the last patrons filed out that evening. Theatre instruments of all kinds had very short operating lives. Wurdeman noted that large Wurlitzer PianOrchestras, used in theatre lobbies or out front to attract patrons, would wear out after several years of virtually continuous use and were fit only for the scrap heap. It was cheaper to buy a new orchestrion than to rebuild an old one.

While many Wurlitzer Style G photoplayers of small size were sold, the typical Wurlitzer unit was apt to be a larger instrument with a center piano flanked by two large side chests containing pipes, drums, and other effects. The center or "console" part usually consisted of an upright piano with one or two keyboards. Two-keyboard models employed the lower one for the piano (and sometimes for an organ as well) and the upper for organ only. The console also contained the roll mechanism or, as was often the case, two roll mechanisms. The twin-roll format had the advantage of permitting continuous music. One roll could play while the other was being rewound. It was common practice to put two different types of music on the rolls, perhaps one roll having snappy march or ragtime selections, with the other roll containing romantic interludes. In that way the operator could quickly switch from one to another to approximately fit the action on the screen.

Seated on a bench in front of the instrument, the photoplayer operator controlled the sound effects—such as the fire gong, telephone bell, locomotive whistle, or bird call—while the roll provided the musical notes. By the end of the day, after the feature film had been seen a half dozen or more times, the typical operator knew just when a pistol shot, telegraph key click, policeman's whistle, or other effect should be interjected. But, the next day was apt to bring a new film, and those attending the theatre early in the morning were apt to hear many miscues by the photoplayer operator. In the meantime, the piano and accompanying ranks of pipes produced a generous amount of music and often turned in a performance worthy of a small orchestra, especially if the unit played well-arranged music rolls.

The Wurlitzer name was pre-eminent in the field of theatre music in America during the early part of the present century. In addition to the nearly 2,500 photoplayers turned out by the firm, over 2,000 theatre organs were made. It is a testimonial to the selling ability of the dozens of Wurlitzer field representatives that one of the most popular photoplayer models was also one of the most expensive, the Style K, which at one time sold for $4,500 or more. At the time this was about twice the price of the average residential home in America! Week after week in

ABOVE: Part of the Photoplayer Division at the North Tonawanda (New York) plant of the Wurlitzer Company. Note the foot pedals on the photoplayer console above right. Such pedals were used to operate various novelty sound effects.

The Royal Theatre, Lima, Ohio, had not one but two Wurlitzer automatic instruments. At the left rear of the gallery is a PianOrchestra orchestrion, a rather small model in a series known for large sizes. Centered is a Mandolin Sextette (incorrectly spelled "sextet" in the picture caption), a device incorporating a piano played upon by wooden hammers actuated by a rotating shaft, giving a fanciful imitation of the sound of mandolins, with the accompaniment of a rank of pipes. Apparently, the instruments played at different times, possibly to provide music of two different tonal characters. The units played continuously using rolls not related to the mood of the films being shown.

141

WURLITZER

Wurlitzer Orchestra, Style G, in the "Photoplay," Columbus, O.

THE above picture—from a photograph, says as plainly as words could that business is rushing at the "Photoplay." Although competition is active, this theatre is doing finely, much better than any other in its section of the town. One thing is sure if you have Wurlitzer music and the other fellow hasn't, you win hands down.

A Wurlitzer Style G photoplayer in use, circa 1912.

Building photoplayers at Wurlitzer's North Tonawanda (New York) factory, 1917.

A Wurlitzer advertisement, circa 1914, for photoplayers. Note that the Olympic Theatre, Chicago, installed its Style H (or K) up on the stage, a very unusual location. Typically, such devices were placed in the orchestra pit, as in the Lyric and Oriole photographs.

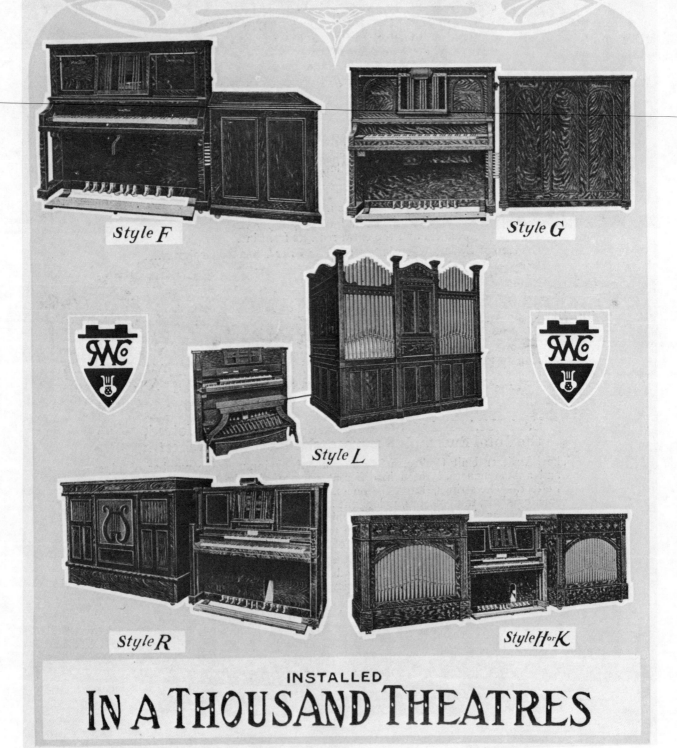

THE FINEST
THEATRE ORCHESTRAS
are built by
WURLITZER

Style F

Style G

Style L

Style R

Style H or K

INSTALLED
IN A THOUSAND THEATRES

Advertisement for Wurlitzer photoplayers, circa 1913-1914. The installations "in a thousand theatres" undoubtedly included PianOrchestras and other Wurlitzer automatic musical instruments.

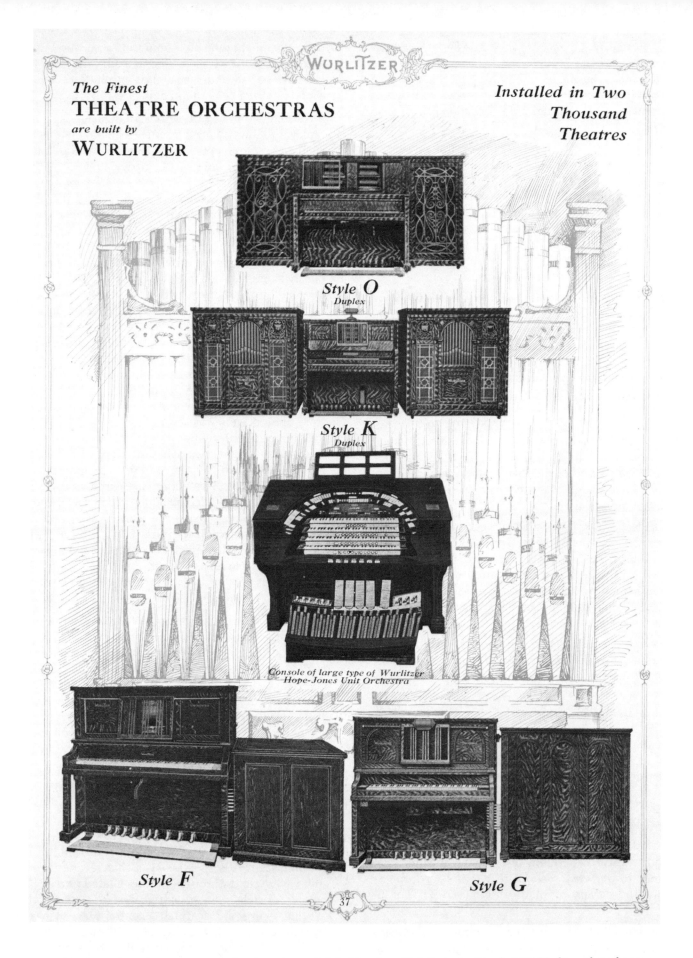

The Finest
THEATRE ORCHESTRAS
are built by
WURLITZER

Installed in Two
Thousand
Theatres

Style **O**
Duplex

Style **K**
Duplex

Console of large type of Wurlitzer
Hope-Jones Unit Orchestra

Style **F**

Style **G**

37

Wurlitzer advertisement, circa 1914, for photoplayers and the Hope-Jones Unit Orchestra. Nearly 2,500 Wurlitzer photoplayers of various kinds were sold, but only a few dozen still survive. Of the more than 2,000 Unit Orchestras made, hundreds still exist.

Moving Picture World, readers in 1915 saw large advertisements for the Style K and were told that it was equal to a full orchestra, or, in one instance, that Clarence Eddy, a well-known organist, used a Style K to play the entire musical score for a grand production of Handel's *Messiah.*

Wurlitzer theatre photoplayers employed two types of orchestrated rolls, depending on the model. Smaller units such as styles F, G, and O used regular 10-tune long-frame Wurlitzer "Automatic Player Piano" rolls—the same rolls that were used on most keyboard-style Wurlitzer coin pianos and orchestrions. Larger models, such as styles H, K, and L, used Wurlitzer Concert PianOrchestra rolls—the same as used on the immense orchestrions of like name.

One of the most popular units in the line was the Style O photoplayer, which incorporated a piano with two side chests. Two ranks of pipes furnished violin, viola, flute, and bass effects, while percussion devices included bass drum, snare drum, triangle, and fire gong. The production statistics of the Style O give an indication of the years in which photoplayers achieved their greatest popularity: 1915 (82 made), 1916 (78), 1917 (36), 1918 (34), 1919 (49), 1920 (91), 1921 (52), 1922 (19), 1923 (15), 1924 (7), 1926 (2), and 1927 (1). Undoubtedly, Wurlitzer would have made more photoplayers in the later years had it not been for the immense success of their larger and vastly more expensive theatre organs. Many theatre owners were "talked up" to the more elaborate units.

The largest regular production model photoplayer in the Wurlitzer line was the immense Style K, which measured 15 feet, four inches wide, about five feet high, and four feet deep—and presented a very imposing appearance when placed in the orchestra pit, just below the screen. This $4,500 unit used Concert PianOrchestra rolls. A Wurlitzer catalogue, circa 1915, noted:

"This style can be played by a pianist or with the paper music roll. It was the first instrument put on the market that fully met the requirements of the motion picture theatre.

"In the accompanying of varied pictures, the many different musical effects, with the quick changes possible, lend a charm and effectiveness to the performance otherwise impossible, even with an expensive orchestra composed of fine musicians. The effects are simply marvelous, and the instrument must be heard to be really appreciated.

"Their success has been demonstrated, and our proposition on this instrument has worked for both the financial and musical betterment of so many theatres that assurance to our customers of results is based on experience under every condition and in every kind of locality."

It was noted that the instrumentation consisted of: "piano, violins, cornet, oboe, cellos, church organ, double flutes, double flute stopped bass, bass drum, snare drum, kettle drums, cymbals, extended glockenspiel, triangle, castanets, Indian drum, train effect, fire gong, tambou-rine, steamboat whistle, horse trot, auto horn, vox humana, cathedral chimes, electric bell, and xylophone," stated to be "all under absolute control—can be used in every conceivable combination."

A listing of production figures for the large Style K photoplayer follows about the same trend as the previously-cited Style O, except that the Style K made its market debut earlier, in 1913: 1913 (42 made), 1914 (67), 1915 (43), 1916 (40), 1917 (12), 1918 (13), 1919 (32), 1920 (21), 1921 (10), 1922 (5), 1923 (2), 1924 (4), and 1927 (1). It is interesting to note that of the 292 Style K photoplayers made, only one example is known to collectors today—a unit rescued by the author from the Pastime Theatre, Coshocton, Ohio, where it was originally installed in 1915. That these glorious instruments—capable of exciting laughter or producing tears in the audiences they served—were discarded is a sad commentary on the American penchant for overlooking the glories of yesteryear, and then, after it is too late, recognizing the loss. On the other hand, it is probably safe to say that by the end of the silent movie era in the late 1920s, most Wurlitzer photoplayers were simply worn out and were not fit to use for anything. The generation of collectors who would appreciate and carefully restore photoplayers was several decades away, and in the meantime the surviving instruments fell victim to just about every hazard imaginable, including fires, floods, termites, and, in particular, the scrap heap. Some survived, however. In Victor, West Virginia, a Wurlitzer Style O was unceremoniously hauled off and stored in a feed and grain depot. In the 1960s a collector learned of it, and later it went into the collection of Murray Clark, who subsequently restored it. In the same era, a collector poking around in a theatre in Riverside, California, discovered another Style O, this one hidden in a storeroom behind the stage. It too was sold to a collector.

In Miamisburg, Ohio, a large Wurlitzer Style U photoplayer, an instrument which originally used 88-note player piano rolls, fared worse. After stripping out the "interesting" components—the drums, bells, sound effects gadgets, and the like—an early owner of the theatre extended a wooden stage over it, using the photoplayer case for structural support. When discovered by collectors in the 1960s, about all that could be saved were the roll mechanism, some pipes and chests, and a few other stray parts.

Giving Wurlitzer a run for its money in the early days was the American Photo Player Company, with manufacturing facilities in Berkeley and (beginning in 1917) Van Nuys, California. This firm produced a wide variety of pit instruments, ranging from small Fotopianos to larger instruments trademarked as Fotoplayers. From the 'teens through the 1920s, it is believed that several thousand units were sold throughout the United States. Most Fotoplayer styles were of simpler designs than the ornate Wurlitzer cases and featured a central piano flanked by two side chests, with the cases of most being made of light golden oak arranged in rectangular strips and panels. Although others were made, the most popular Fotoplayer models were Styles 20, 25 (probably *the* most popular), 35, 40, 45, and 50. Prices for these ranged from about

Wurlitzer Motion Picture Orchestra
Style H

This style can be played by a pianist or with the paper music roll. It was the first instrument put on the market that fully met the requirements of the Motion Picture Theatre. In illustrating varied pictures, the many different musical effects, with the quick changes possible, lend a charm and effectiveness to the performance otherwise impossible, even with an expensive orchestra composed of fine musicians. The effects are simply marvelous and the instrument must be heard to be really appreciated. Their success has been demonstrated and our proposition on this instrument has worked for both the financial and musical betterment of so many theatres that assurance to our customers for results is based on experience under every condition in any kind of locality.

Piano May be Played Separately if Desired

Instrumentation
Besides many others it includes:

Piano	Violins	Cornet	Oboe	Cellos	Church Organ
Double Flutes	Double Flute	Stopped Bass		Bass Drum	
Snare Drum	Kettle Drums	Cymbal	Glockenspiel		Triangle
Cow Bell	Tambourine	Steamboat Whistle		Horse Trot	
Auto Horn	Cathedral Chimes		Electric Bell		

All under absolute control—can be used in every conceivable combination

Height over all, 5 ft. 2 in.   Width, 15 ft. 4 in.   Depth, 3 ft. 3 in.
Shipping Weight, 3600 lbs.

**Style K—same as style H with addition of Vox Humana Pipes
and Xylophone**

One of several case variations of the Style H and K Wurlitzer Motion Picture Orchestra, a photoplayer billed as the Pipe Organ Orchestra.

In Pennsylvania the Bijou Dream nickelodeon boasted ceilings an incredible 75 feet high and noted that it was "The most complete and finest picture theatre in Pittsburgh." Music was provided by: "Wurlitzer's Wonderful Electric Organ, the finest musical instrument known to musical science." The instrument was a PianOrchestra.

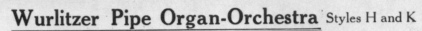

Wurlitzer Pipe Organ-Orchestra Styles H and K

PRICE, STYLE H — Single Roll System, $3,500   PRICE, STYLE K — Single Roll System, $4,500

PRICE, STYLE H — Duplex Roll System, $3,850   PRICE, STYLE K — Duplex Roll System, $4,850

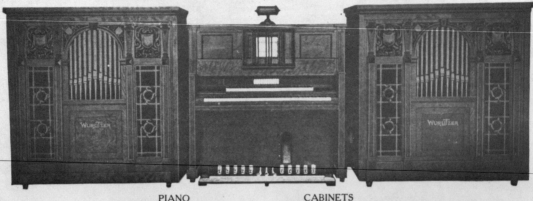

PIANO
Height over all, 5 ft.
Length, 15 ft. 4 in.

CABINETS
Depth, 2 ft. 9 in.
Shipping weight, about 4,000 lbs.

14

Description of **Wurlitzer Motion Picture Pipe Organ-Orchestra** Styles H and K

Played by hand or by roll. Rolls cut especially for motion picture accompaniment.

Has high-grade Concert Piano, built for hard, professional usage. Mandolin attachment. Plays cathedral chimes, vox humana (human voice effect), horns, flutes, violins, cellos, stop diapason, xylophone and glockenspiel; snare drum, bass drum, kettle drum, tom toms, castanets, fire gong, train effect, steamboat and bird whistles, auto horn, tambourines, and electric bell, horse trot triangle, cymbal. Has adjustable tremulant, and swell pedal for tone control and expression, all of which, in their various registrations, and when unified, represent:

Church pipe organ of 10 combinations, Orchestra of 16 combinations, and Snare Drums, Bass Drums and 12 Motion Picture Effects.

The wind is provided by patent, electric combination blower, which is separate from the instrument, and movable. Has high-grade, automatic playing device, built for theatrical usage. Is self-registering, bringing on and throwing off the pipe organ, orchestra and drum sections without hand manipulation.

Style H same as Style K, with the exception that it does not have the Xylophone or Vox Humana (Human Voice) stops. This instrument also equipped with Duplex Roll System. For illustration and description, see pages 18 and 19.

15

Sold under the "Pipe Organ Orchestra" name, Wurlitzer photoplayers were made in a wide variety of styles, the largest standard model of which was the Style K, which in 1915 cost $4,850 if equipped with the duplex roll system. Wurlitzer Concert PianOrchestra orchestrion rolls, with piano, pipe, and percussion orchestration, were employed to follow the action on the screen. Novelty effects were operated by means of a row of foot pedals located on the central piano unit. Hundreds of these expensive instruments were sold. Several different case variations were produced, of which the above represents a model in use in the year 1915.

Wurlitzer Motion Picture Orchestra
Style J

This style is designed to furnish music in motion picture houses requiring an orchestra of ten to fifteen men. All the orchestral effects can be obtained. It is played either by hand by a single musician or by the perforated paper music roll.

It will be noticed that this instrument is built in two parts or sections, one part being a regular piano with a double keyboard, one set of keys for the orchestral and organ effects and the other set for the regular piano playing. The other part contains the orchestral parts such as *Trumpets, Flutes, Piccolos, Strings, Tuba, Glockenspiel, Xylophone, Cathedral Chimes, Bass and Snare Drums, Cymbals and Church Organ.*

All the different instruments can be played either as solo effects or in various combinations, ranging from a fine violin solo accompanied by the piano up to the full orchestral effects of an orchestra of ten to fifteen men.

The action of the instrument is electric throughout. One electric motor supplies the power to run both the electric current generator and a blower which furnishes the wind required for the pipes.

The expression is controlled by eleven swell shutters operated by the player at the console. The player has absolute control over the expression and different instrumental effects and can vary the music instantly to follow the changes of pictures. In this respect the instrument is far superior to any human orchestra, because the various changes can be so quickly made, whereas the human orchestra has to follow the written score.

There is no limit to the great variety of musical effects the player can produce. Any good pianist with a little practice can play this instrument and produce all the various changes to suit the various shifting scene of the pictures.

This instrument will give excellent satisfaction in the better class motion picture theatres where real orchestral music is required.

Part One	Part Two
Height, 4 ft. 11 in. Width, 5 ft. Depth, 4 ft.	Height, 11 ft. Width, 10 ft. Depth, 5 ft.

Shipping Weight 9000 lbs.

ABOVE: The Wurlitzer Motion Picture Orchestra, Style J, and the somewhat similar Style L, used Wurlitzer Concert PianOrchestra rolls to control the piano, ranks, pipes, and percussion effects. Novelty sound effects were controlled by the photoplayer operator. Unlike most photoplayers, they used electrical connections between the piano and the pipe unit. The Style J was popular from 1912 through 1915, while the Style L was primarily sold from 1913 to 1916. BELOW: The Wurlitzer factory at North Tonawanda, New York, circa 1915.

$3,000 to $10,000, with a discount of nearly 50% allowed to music stores and other sales agents. Without exception to the writer's knowledge, the music system of Fotoplayer units employed regular 88-note player piano rolls. In addition, special "Picturolls" were made for Fotoplayers by the Los Angeles Film Music Company. These rolls, while of the standard 88-note home player piano scale, had thematic arrangements to suit various moods and were labeled "romantic," "sneaky," or given one or another of many characteristics.

Fotoplayers were well instrumented. For example, the popular Style 25 contained an upright piano, pipes producing violin, flute, violoncello, and bass effects, a set of 31 orchestra bells, and various sound effects as follows: bass drum, snare drum, cymbal, Chinese crash cymbal, tom-tom, tympani or thunder effect, wind siren, tambourine, doorbell or telephone bell, steamboat or locomotive whistle, castanets, pistol crack, klaxon, bird whistle, and a single cathedral chime.

As the 88-note player piano rolls played piano music only (without scoring or controls for turning on and off ranks of pipes or operating the drums and other percussion effects), it was left to the operator to bring the Fotoplayer's potential into play as needed. Indeed, in Chicago the musical merchandising firm of Lyon & Healy conducted a school specifically for Fotoplayer operators. Seated at the piano, the operator scored the film by touching a series of buttons and tilting tablets, with some of the sound effects manually operated by tugging on a series of rope pulls dangling from the piano console and which, by means of pulleys, were connected to the various effects. The dangling knobs caused this type of unit to be known as the "cow photoplayer" in the trade, according to the recollections of Oswald Wurdeman, who used to service many of them.

When, for example, the siren effect was desired, a strong pull on the siren rope caused a bellows to collapse and wind to exit through the siren whistle. By varying the strength and duration of the pull, the pitch could be made to rise and fall or to operate with expression.

Fotoplayer units were equipped with two roll mechanisms, one above the other. By means of the duplex mechanism, the operator could change the top roll while the bottom roll was playing, or vice versa. It was a common practice to program the music for a given film by selecting a dozen or two rolls. These would be placed on top of the piano and changed alternately on the roll mechanism as the action on the screen dictated. So that the audience would not tire of a particular tune, the operator often made pencil notations on the roll box indicating the dates that the music had been used. In that way close repetition could be avoided.

During the early years the American Photo Player Company produced many unusual styles, some examples of which were sold under the "American Orchestra" label. Still other models were built in very tall cases in the manner of a large orchestrion. Too high to fit under a music screen, these were undoubtedly employed to the side, with the operator turning to the left or the right to see

what action was occurring.

In later years, the firm's business was dominated by its wholly-owned subsidiary, the Robert-Morton Organ Company. Early in 1925 the Berkeley plant was closed, and operations were consolidated in Van Nuys. The Photo Player name was discontinued (the "American" part of the name having been dropped in 1923), after which the Robert Morton Organ Company name (without hyphenation in later years) was used exclusively.

As was the case with photoplayers of other makes, products of the American Photo Player Company saw hard use and rapidly wore out. Many were scrapped after literally being worked to death. Some survived, including a Style 25 Fotoplayer shipped sometime around 1927 or 1928 from a theatre in Ephrata, Pennsylvania to a theatre in Philipsburg in the same state. Before it was uncrated, the owners realized that the new sound movies were here to stay. Finally, in the 1960s, the theatre proprietor decided that it was of no further use. It was happily hauled away, still in its shipping crates, by Harvey Roehl, who restored it and who subsequently featured it among other instruments in the Vestal Press Collection. Less happy was a situation related to the author by Arthur Reblitz. A serviceman he knew, I.C. Sausa, who moved to Denver in 1912 after learning techniques of piano repair in the East, used to take care of many different Fotoplayers in the Denver area and came into the possession of these once their usefulness had ended. Storing them in a warehouse until sometime in the 1950s, he finally decided that they would never have any value, so he brought them home and disassembled them, keeping boxes of small parts and selling pipes, chests and other components to local organ technicians. By the time Art Reblitz met Mr. Sausa in the early 1970s, all that was left were front panels and other side chest cabinet parts from at least six Fotoplayers—Styles 35, 40, 45 and 50—as well as two different Wurlitzer Style Ks and one Style U. Also remaining were boxes of small parts such as valves, stop tabs, etc., one set of xylophone bars, a set of orchestra bells and a few sound effects.

In another instance, a large Style 50 Fotoplayer, originally sold by the Darrow Music Company of Denver, turned up in a New Mexico storage warehouse around 1970. The author acquired it and subsequently offered it for sale. Purchased by Alan Fox, a California collector, the immense unit was restored by Ron Cappel. Later it was resold to the Brown Collection in Indiana. Still another Fotoplayer, a Style 45, was obtained by Herb Shriner, a well-known entertainer in the 1950s and 1960s. Later it went into the Gilson Collection. A further Style 45 was located by Hathaway & Bowers and sold to Gordon Lipe. Later it was acquired by Roger Dayton, a Chicago collector.

In the early days, another major contender in the photoplayer field was the J.P. Seeburg Piano Company, a large and well-known Chicago coin piano and orchestrion firm. Beginning about 1913, Seeburg jumped into the market with both feet. From then through the early 1920s, over a dozen different photoplayer styles, most of large format, were marketed. These ranged from compact units con-

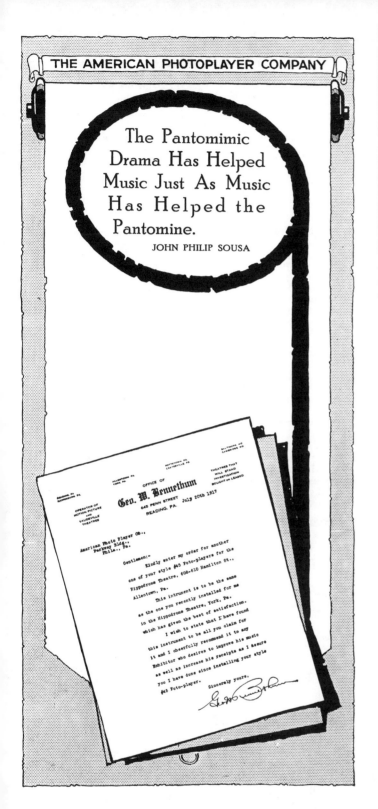

> The Pantomimic Drama Has Helped Music Just As Music Has Helped the Pantomine.
>
> JOHN PHILIP SOUSA

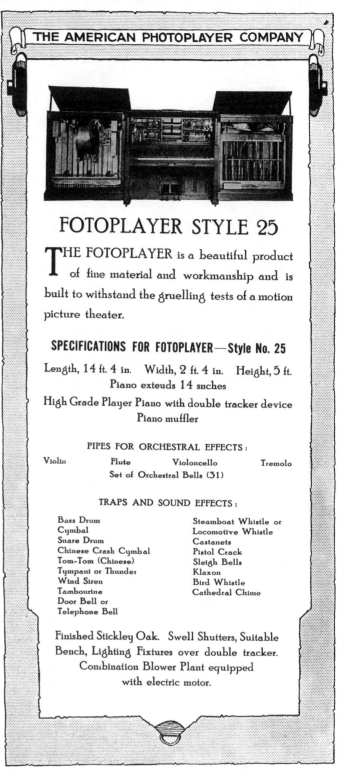

FOTOPLAYER STYLE 25

THE FOTOPLAYER is a beautiful product of fine material and workmanship and is built to withstand the gruelling tests of a motion picture theater.

SPECIFICATIONS FOR FOTOPLAYER—Style No. 25

Length, 14 ft. 4 in.   Width, 2 ft. 4 in.   Height, 5 ft.
Piano exteuds 14 snches

High Grade Player Piano with double tracker device
Piano muffler

PIPES FOR ORCHESTRAL EFFECTS:

Violin   Flute   Violoncello   Tremolo
Set of Orchestral Bells (31)

TRAPS AND SOUND EFFECTS:

Bass Drum	Steamboat Whistle or
Cymbal	Locomotive Whistle
Snare Drum	Castanets
Chinese Crash Cymbal	Pistol Crack
Tom-Tom (Chinese)	Sleigh Bells
Tympani or Thunder	Klaxon
Wind Siren	Bird Whistle
Tambourine	Cathedral Chime
Door Bell or	
Telephone Bell	

Finished Stickley Oak. Swell Shutters, Suitable Bench, Lighting Fixtures over double tracker. Combination Blower Plant equipped with electric motor.

Of all Fotoplayer models, the Style 25 was probably the most popular. Containing a piano, violin and flute pipes, orchestra bells, drums, and a large complement of novelty sound effects, the Style 25 was sold by the hundreds. Like other instruments made by the American Photo Player Company, the Style 25 used two 88-note home player piano rolls, one above the other. This configuration permitted one to rewind or be changed while the other was playing, thus providing uninterrupted music. Often, music of two different characters would be placed on each roll, perhaps the top roll having a march or ragtime tune and the bottom having a classical number. During the course of the film, the music could be played from one roll or the other at a moment's notice.

In the 1960s, Harvey and Marion Roehl, owners of The Vestal Press, obtained one of these in its original factory shipping crates from a Philipsburg, Pennsylvania theatre. Restored, the instrument has since entertained many collectors and enthusiasts.

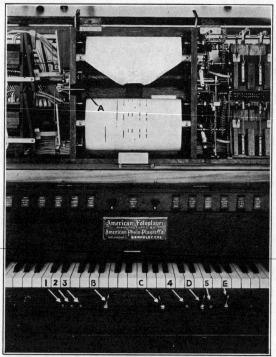

DOUBLE TRACKER DEVICE and CONTROL LEVERS

KEY TO ILLUSTRATION

(a) Double tracker shifting lever. (d) Lower rewind lever.
(b) Piano expression or choker.   (e) Upper rewind lever.
(c) Tempo lever for either roll.

(1) Sustaining pedal.
(2) Soft bass.
(3) Soft treble.
(4) Supplies vacuum direct to lower motor for rewinding.
(5) Supplies vacuum direct to upper motor for rewinding. The last two named are also used for running the music rolls forward silently.

EXPLANATION FOR OPERATING DOUBLE TRACKER

The view shows the instrument with shifting lever (a) at neutral point.

By pressing button (5) upper roll will come into position for playing.

By shifting lever (a) downward and lever (c) to the proper tempo, the lower roll will be brought into action.

To change to the upper roll, merely shift lever (a) as far up as it will go.

To rewind lower roll, shift lever (d), press button (4).

To rewind upper roll, shift lever (e), press button (5).

When placing tune sheets on take-up rolls, have levers (d) and (e) perpendicular, which will throw take-up rolls out of gear. If gears do not mesh readily do not force them. The trouble can be remedied by a quick touch of (4) or (5), as the case may be.

Page from an instruction booklet furnished to an owner of an American Fotoplayer. Made by the American Photo Player Company, such units used regular 88-note home player piano rolls without orchestration. Ranks of pipes, xylophone, and bells could be turned on and off by the tilting tablets shown in a row above the "American Fotoplayer" plaque.

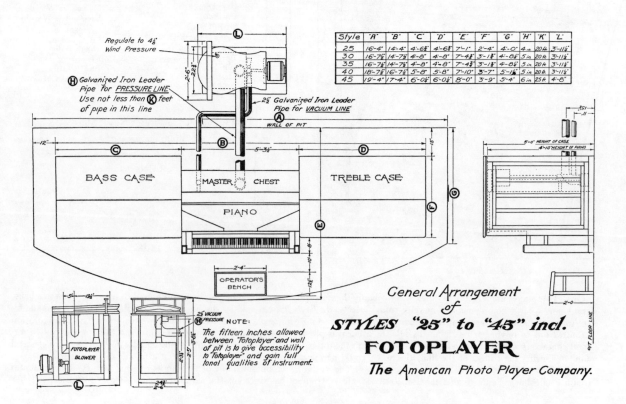

A technical diagram showing suggested installation arrangements and specifications of various Fotoplayer units from Style 25 through Style 45.

Selection of Standard Rolls Cued for *Fotoplayer* Use
with Moving Pictures

HEAVY MUSIC.

Fights, fires, riots, storms, etc.

Concerto D Minor—Beethoven,
Revolutionary Etude,
Rhapsodie Mignonne,
Jolly Robbers,
Semiramide,
Concerto—Op. No. 25,
Phedre Overture,
William Tell—2nd and 4th movements and finale,
Flying Dutchman—by Wagner,
Staccato—Etude—Rubenstein,
The Storm—by Stradel,
Light Cavalry Overture.

WALTZES.

Naughty-Waltz,
Hawaiian Moonlight,
Dreaming,
Dream of Heaven,
Blue Danube,
Amourette,
Destiny,
Mon Reve,
Glorious Dream,
Song De Automne,
Carolina Sunshine,
Melody Waltz,
Waltz of the Season.

PATHETIC.

Largo—Handel,
Barcarolle, Love Tales of Hoffman,
Apple Blossoms,
Heart Throbs,
Dreams—Pascal,
Elegie—Massenet,
Broken Blossoms,
Fifth Nocturne.

ORIENTAL.

Vision of Salome,
Moment Musical,
Amina Serenade,
Nadja,
Naila,
Dardanella,
Out of the East,
Soko,
Turkish Patrol
Passing of Salome,
King Henry VIII Dances.

NOVELETTES.

Inter mezzi, caprices, polkas, minuets, etc.

Tulips,
Butterfly of Fashion,
Amerinda,
Under the Stars,
Silhouettes,
Al Fresco,
Laces and Graces,
Butterflies,
Shades of Night,
Birds and Butterflies,
Dance of Song Birds,
Poppyland,
Ghost Dance,
Danse Grotesque,
Goster Good Bye,
Chrysanthemums.

PATRIOTIC.

America,
Star-Spangled Banner,
Dixie,
America, I Love You,
Over There,
1863 March Melody.

GALLOPS.

Under the Tent,
Midnight Fire Alarm,
Mazeppa,
Dance of Demons,
Ventre a Terre,
Galop de Concert,
Chasse au Lion,
The Race,
Fire, Fire, Fire.

MARCHES.

Sousa Medley,
Holzman Medley,
Boy Scouts—Sousa,
Seventh Regiment,
Semper Fideles,
Funeral March—Chopin,
Wedding March—Mendelssohn,
Arrival of the Elks,
The Diplomat,
Charge of the Light Brigade,
Pryor Medley,
Honeymoon March,
Gen. Pershing.

OPERATIC.

Sextette from Lucia,
Poet and Peasant,
Evening Star,
Cavalleria Rusticana,
Toreador "Carmen,"
Pagliacci—Prologue,
Quartette from Rigoletto,
Favorite Strains from Pagliacci,
Anvil Chorus,
Serenade—Shubert,
Manow Lescant Selection,
Grand Opera Bits,
Cupid's Patrol,
Dream Song "La Tosca."

SENTIMENTAL.

Sunshine of Your Smile,
Just A-wearying for You,
The End of a Perfect Day,
Mighty Lak a Rose,
O Dry Those Tears,
Dear Old Pal of Mine,
Let the Rest of the World Go By,
Jean,
Forever Is a Long, Long Time,
Good Bye, Good Luck, God Bless You,
Whispering.

DRAMATIC.

Melo-Dramatic and Tragi-Pathetic.
Song of the Soul,
Martha Selection,
Song of Songs,
Melody of Spring,
Moonlight,
Serenade d'Amour,
Barcarolle in G Minor by Tschaikowsky, etc.,
Romance Rubenstein,
Concerto Op. 11 by Chopin,
Nocturne Op. 48, No. 1—Chopin,
Prelude C Sharp Minor,
Nocturne—Grieg,
El Canto del Prisonew,
Chopin's Preludes,
El King,
Pique Dame Overture,
Okay.

AGITATO.

Mysterioso, intrigue, burglar, etc.
March of the Dwarfs by Grieg,
March of the Marionette,
Beethoven Sonata, Op. 27—No. 2,
Hungarian Rhapsody No. 2,
Hungarian Rhapsody No. 8—Liszt,
Hall of the Mountain King,
Misterioso,
Rondo Caprioccoso,
Ziegerneweisen—Sarasate,
Moonlight Sonata.

PASTORAL.

The Nightingale,
Day in Venice,
The Palms,
High Mass,
Nightingale and Frogs.

WESTERN ALLEGROS.

Al Fresco,
Moonlight Dance,
Silver Heels.

SONG.

Among the Roses,
Oh What a Pal Was Mary,
Longing, My Sweetheart, for You,
Daddy, You've Been a Mother to Me,
Rosary,
Ave Maria.

The American Photo Player Company printed this suggested list of standard 88-note home player piano rolls adaptable to various screen action. In general, the idea was to provide background music - not songs with themes so prominent that they would override the screen happenings. Typically, a Fotoplayer operator kept a large selection of rolls on hand, making notations on the roll boxes, stating the dates the rolls were used - so as to avoid repetition. The Filmusic Company, Los Angeles, produced "Picturolls" for the Fotoplayer, "indexed as to dramatic and emotional character." A catalog noted, "The right music gives the punch to every scene. The audience is in a state of mind which responds to the action on the screen. It goes away, saying, 'That's a wonderful picture.' "

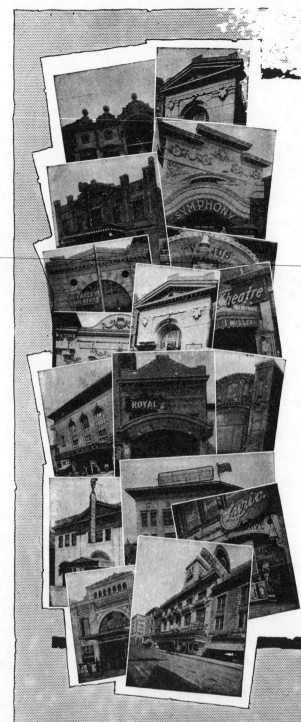

THE theatre-going public of this city for the past few months has had the opportunity to compare the quality of music rendered on the Fotoplayer with that of the regular theatrical orchestra. The result might be expressed in the slang phrase "there is nothing to it." Since the installation we have the best music in town.

The Maynard Theatre, Waltham, Mass.

I HAVE found it possible to adapt both its tone and expression to every conceivable emotional situation depicted on the screen. Its response to the operator's touch is nothing short of marvelous; whilst its simplicity enables any one with any ear of sound to acquire the necessary technique for Fotoplayer manipulation.

Fountain Theatre, Los Angeles

WE are incapable of expressing to you our appreciation of the wonderful and beautiful tones produced by the FOTOPLAYER, we can simply say they are magnificent.

Theatre Louisiana, Baton Rouge

THE Fotoplayer which you installed in the Park Theatre is a great success. The writer made a most exhaustive investigation before we installed the Fotoplayer which ranks far ahead of others.

The Park Theatre, Phila., Pa.

OUR business has shown a steady increase since the installation of the Fotoplayer and we hear nothing but complimentary remarks about the instrument. Many of our regular patrons tell us they come especially to hear the music and these people usually occupy the front seats which we were never able to fill when we had an orchestra

The most gratifying of the whole proposition, however, is the great saving in the cost of music.

Starland Theatre, St. Paul

Fotoplay Your Pictures

Most manufacturers of photoplayers featured in their advertisements the testimonials of satisfied customers. The American Photo Player Company, Berkeley, California, maker of the Fotoplayer, was no exception. In later years the firm became part of the Robert-Morton Organ Company, which was second only to Wurlitzer in terms of the number of unified pipe organs sold to theatres.

sisting of a piano with a single side chest to very large photoplayers with two chests containing many ranks of pipes and elaborate percussion effects. The grandest model of all, the Style A Deluxe, had an external rank of bass pipes operated by an electromagnetic action. Beyond photoplayers, Seeburg installed a number of theatre pipe organs under the Seeburg-Smith trade name. An early Seeburg entry into the photoplayer field was the Style M Motion Picture Player, advertised extensively to the trade in 1914 and featured (along with two large orchestrions) at a New York trade show in June. In October 1914, *Moving Picture World* reported:

"In order to be able to demonstrate to exhibitors the possibility of this new Motion Picture Player in a small theatre, the J. P. Seeburg Piano Company of Chicago, has opened a picture house at 5056 Broadway [Chicago], called the Carmen Theatre. Exhibitors everywhere are invited by the company to call and see the instrument in operation.

"The western representative of *Moving Picture World* went one evening to see Mr. Seeburg's demonstrating theatre and found a pretty well-equipped house, seating 288, and charging admission to the public of ten cents. The auditorium, which is rather long and narrow, is tastefully decorated in pink and gray and lighted by the indirect lighting system. When we entered, an Essanay two-reeler was on the screen, well projected, but what engaged our attention most was the soothing flow of melodious music that came from the orchestra pit where the new Seeburg Motion Picture Player had been installed. It is quite remarkable what one of these instruments can do and how well adapted it is to moving pictures.

"The writer was particularly well pleased with the organ part of the player, which John H. Bunte, the congenial and energetic sales manager of the Seeburg Piano Company, told him consisted of 104 pipes, a set of cathedral chimes and automatic attachments for bass and treble. The instrument has two keyboards, one a regular 88-note piano and the other a 58-note organ. Either can be played separately or both together. It can also be played automatically with music rolls which are of considerable length, each containing ten selections. The rolls are made especially for the Seeburg Motion Picture Player.

"In addition to the piano and organ part of the player are a number of other instruments which can be played separately or in combination with others. These are: xylophone, bass drum, snare drum, cymbal, triangle and castanets, and for sound effects, a cow bell, fire gong, steamboat whistle, locomotive whistle, thunder effects, wind siren, tom-tom, crash cymbal, bird call, baby cry, telephone and doorbell, horse trot, automobile horn, etc. These instruments and effects are operated by buttons and pedals.

"Motion picture exhibitors these days invest considerable money in church organs. The organ of the Seeburg Motion Picture Player is, of course, not as big and comprehensive as the $10,000 church organ, but in tone quality it compares most favorably with any organ the writer has ever heard in a picture show. The cost of the Seeburg Motion Picture Player is much less, and besides it has all

the instruments and sound effects for playing up a picture."

Separately, a *Moving Picture World* reporter was told that the J. P. Seeburg Piano Company had started manufacturing its own instruments in 1909, and during that year the factory capacity was three electric pianos per week. Since that time, large orchestrions, including the Style G and Style H had been added to the line, followed by the recent Motion Picture Player.

Nearly all Seeburg photoplayers used standard orchestrion rolls. Styles P, Q, and W used regular Seeburg G orchestrion rolls, a style made in quantity for the popular Seeburg G orchestrion—one of the firm's best sellers. Larger styles such as the M, R, S, T, V, W, and A Deluxe used type H orchestrion or MSR organ rolls interchangeably. Most H rolls were fully orchestrated with bass drum, tympani, castanets, snare drum, and other effects, while MSR rolls had the same general tracker bar layout but featured organ-type arrangements with extended perforations for sustaining pipe tones.

Seeburg produced a brochure, *The Soul of the Film*, which described its photoplayers, called Pipe-Organ Orchestras. Interspersed among descriptions were such forgettable rhymes as "Seeburg music full of life—instant change from drum to fife," "Seeburg's value quickly seen—as music changes with the screen," and the rather curious "Seeburg players do not fail—Seeburg music don't get stale."

From Savannah, Georgia, the owner of two theatres wrote to say: "We take pleasure in stating that both the Style R Pipe Organ Orchestra installed in our Odeon Theatre, as well as the Style S installed in our Folly Theatre, have given us complete satisfaction in every way. We were at first quite dubious about making the switch from orchestra to Seeburg player, however the two Seeburg instruments have so far exceeded our expectations that we would not think of going back to the old regimen."

In the mind of a copywriter employed by Seeburg, there wasn't much difference between listening to a Seeburg Pipe Organ Orchestra and hearing a real musician:

"World famous artists make master records for Seeburg music rolls. The pianist's composition is recorded by means of electric wires connected with the recorder placed behind the piano. When you consider that the celebrated artists who make these records are paid hundreds of dollars for recording a single composition, and that the Seeburg music rolls are reproduced from such records, you will then get an adequate idea as to the artistic results which can be obtained from the Seeburg pipe organ and self-playing orchestras in connection with which these artists' music rolls are used. The result is similar to listening to a phonograph record by Kreisler, the great violinist, or Caruso, the wonderful tenor." Actually, Seeburg H and MSR roll masters were orchestrated from QRS 88-note player piano roll masters which were recorded by some of the finest popular pianists of the day, including Pete Wendling, Zez Confrey and others. H and MSR rolls were

Phenomenal Success
Has Come to the
SEEBURG LINE
Because
the Variety Increases Constantly

As the importance of the automatic industry increases, and our knowledge of the business and its possibilities develops, so does our realization grow that a great variety of requirements must be met.

In view of this we have added three wonderful new instruments, prominent among which is

The New Style "M" Seeburg Photoplayer.

An instrument that represents the very highest attainment in musical merit for the moving picture theatres.

The instrument, Mr. Dealer, which you have been wanting to supply a long felt want with.

Get aquainted with this and the other varieties of our wonderful line by sending for our new "Art Catalog."

J. P. Seeburg Piano Company
Manufacturers of
SEEBURG AUTOMATIC PIANOS, ORCHESTRIONS AND PHOTOPLAYERS

Office and Warerooms
900 Republic Bldg., State and Adams Streets

CHICAGO

Factory
913 W. Van Buren Street

An advertisement for the Seeburg Style M photoplayer as featured in "The Presto," a musical trade publication, issue of February 19, 1914.

Seeburg ~ Photo Player ~

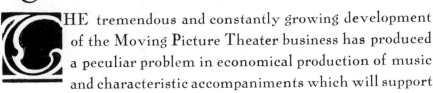

Successfully Solves the Theater Music Problem

THE tremendous and constantly growing development of the Moving Picture Theater business has produced a peculiar problem in economical production of music and characteristic accompaniments which will support and lend character and action to the pictures shown. This problem is perfectly solved in the Seeburg Photo Player. This problem involved the production of an instrument which would not only supply perfect music of a high quality, but which would also make it possible to produce sound effects to emphasize and bring out the action of the play, and at the same time to accomplish this by individual operation in order that economy might be achieved.

It is manifest that unless these effects can be so accurately controlled that they may be always brought in at the right time, that they would better be dispensed with entirely, while —if properly produced both as to time and accuracy of sound— they add tremendously to the effect of the entertainment.

Good Music Plus Dramatic Effects

One of the great difficulties experienced in producing an instrument of this character, has been to combine the production of high quality piano and organ tone with the mechanical results necessary for the special effects such as automobile horns, drums, telephone bells and similar sounds. This result has been perfectly worked out in the Seeburg Photo Player so that a perfect quality of piano and organ music is produced, with full opportunity of the use of special effects at exactly the right instant of time.

Absolute Command of Operation

The arrangement of the Seeburg Photo Player is such that the music roll, containing ten selections, is directly before the operator, and can be instantly moved by him forward or back, to a suitable selection for each picture presented. The various accessory of effects are produced by pressure of buttons and foot pedals.

In quality of musical tone, of simplicity and accuracy of operation in assurance of accurate timing, adjustment of all effects, the Seeburg Photo Player renders perfect results.

The Seeburg Photo Player as described in a catalogue issued by the J. P. Seeburg Piano Company, circa 1912-1914.

Seeburg Pipe-Organ Orchestra, Style "R"

This style has a greater tonal range than Style T, and is exceptionally pleasing; it is one of our most popular styles. It has two manuals, organ and piano. However, by means of a new Seeburg device, consisting of a lever to the right of the piano keyboard, the organ can be coupled to the piano, thereby bringing into play the double acting Seeburg piano keyboard. This makes any pianist an organist without previous practice on the organ.

Equipped with an orchestrated music roll which is specially arranged to bring out the manifold tone combinations of the instrument—covering the organ, piano and orchestral tones, including a magnificent set of **twenty chimes,** also drums, etc., which makes the instrument superior to a human orchestra. The Seeburg **SOLO** music rolls are hand interpreted (hand played) so that they actually reproduce the playing of world-famous pianists and organists. The Seeburg Shutter (swell) for tone and expression control is a vastly superior device compared with the usual "swell." It reduces the tone to a mere murmur or pianissimo and increases it to an immense fortissimo and the varying degrees of expression between these extremes.

Built with one or two rolls. Double veneered hardwood case finished in dull mission oak. Equipped with the Seeburg **SOLO**-effect features and hand arranged rolls containing three to ten selections. Height 5 feet 3 inches. Width 3 feet 9 inches. Length 13 feet 4 inches. Weight, boxed for shipment about 2500 pounds.

INSTRUMENTATION

Two Manuals—Piano and Organ

Violin	Castanets
Flute	Tambourine
Piccolo	Mandolin
Cello	Tom-Tom
Saxophone	Steamboat Whistle
Bass Melodia	Locomotive Whistle
Echo Clarinet	Bird Whistle
Vox Humana (human voice)	Baby Cry
20 Cathedral Chimes	Wind Siren
Organ Swell	Thunder Effect
Tremolo	Telephone Bell
Bass Drum	Door Bell
Snare Drum	Fire Gong
Kettle Drum Effect	Horse Trot
Cymbal	Locomotive Exhaust
Triangle	Tug-boat Exhaust
Scotch Bag-pipe Effect	Tympani
Crash Cymbal	Cuckoo Effect
Xylophone	Pig Grunt

*"SEEBURG music full of life—
instant change from drum to fife"*

One of the most popular Seeburg photoplayer models, circa 1914, was the Pipe Organ Orchestra Style R. Using Style H orchestrion rolls, the unit contained several ranks of pipes and a wide variety of novelty effects, including "tug boat exhaust," "cuckoo effect," "Scotch bagpipe effect," and what must have been a noise used only infrequently, the "pig grunt." A contemporary Seeburg catalogue set the mood: "It is Tuesday night and you are showing a 5-reel feature of undoubted merit; but it is more than a film which has filled your theatre to the last row. With an orchestra at his finger ends, your piano player sits at his keyboard and watches the film flit across the screen. He is only a single person, an individual, mind you, and yet he has at his instant command the resources of a pipe organ with its wonderful variety of stops, the tender, true tones of a violin, the brisk notes of a xylophone, the gay click of the castanets, the silver rattle of the tambourine and the syncopated beats of the drum. There is no descriptive demand which a film story can make but he is able to meet it—no episode in movie land that he cannot make more thrilling, more touching, more enjoyable to the audience. As his fingers run over the keyboard he is master of every situation. He is the living interpreter of every shade of emotion registered by the silent players. He can express the sorrow of the life stories enacted there in the heart-searching melodies of that great organ's voice; or he can add zest and life to a comedy film with an instrumental accompaniment which puts a new bustle and spirit into the funmaking of the screen comedians. The silent audience sitting there with eyes glued on the screen as yard after yard of film unwinds may not be conscious that this one man holds their emotions in the hollow of his hand. They may not realize that it is his perfectly fitting accompaniment which make a photo play in your theatre twice as enjoyable as in the movie house across the street, but when the final 'close up' of the lovers clasped in each other's arms fades away with the sweet pianissimo tones of the organ giving the scene new meaning, then they turn to one another and say 'What perfect music!' "

Mary Pickford's first screen appearance was in "The Lonely Villa," produced by David W. Griffith for Biograph in 1909. Shown in this scene is Marion Leonard at the telephone, with young Mary Pickford to her right. This small part, followed by an appearance in "The Violin Maker of Cremona" (released by Biograph on June 7, 1909), launched Mary Pickford on her unparalleled career of screen success. A decade later, she was America's best paid and most famous movie actress.

SEEBURG GUARANTEES RESULTS

PIPE ORGANS and SELF-PLAYING ORCHESTRAS
100% SATISFACTORY
ASK ANY OWNER

Rosewood Theatre
Montrose Ave. and Lincoln St.

One of the handsomest theaters and biggest money makers in the United States—Wanted the best pipe organ—**it has a Seeburg.** Hundreds of the most successful theaters are using **Seeburg organs.**

Styles and prices suitable for any size theater.
Valuable information on request.
Address nearest branch.

J. P. SEEBURG PIANO COMPANY
Manufacturers
1004 REPUBLIC BUILDING, CHICAGO

BOSTON	NEW YORK	PHILADELPHIA	PITTSBURGH	ATLANTA
162 Boylston St.	729 Seventh Ave.	923 Walnut St.	791 Penn St.	65 N. Pryor St.
MINNEAPOLIS	BEAUMONT, TEXAS	FARGO, N. D.	ST. LOUIS	SAN FRANCISCO
80 So. 8th St.	702 Pearl St.	Stone Bldg.	602 Princess Theatre Bldg.	52 Turk St.

Seeburg theatre organ advertisement, 1916.

MYRTLE THEATRE, LEWISTOWN, MONT.

PENN THEATRE, PITTSBURGH, PA.

The Myrtle Theatre

JOHN B. RITCH, MANAGER

Lewistown, Montana

December 8, 1915.

J. P. Seeburg Piano Co.
209 S. State Street, Chicago.

Gentlemen:-

I purchased one of your Style "M" Seeburg Pipe Organ a little more than one year ago, and have used it daily in the Myrtle Theatre ever since. The instrument has an exceptionally fine tone, has stood the work surprisingly well, and has not given me more than ordinary expense to keep it in condition to render the service required of it.

The tone of my Seeburg is more pleasing than that of other much higher priced instruments of other makes in use in this city.

Yours very truly,

John B. Ritch

Penn Theatre

WALTER E. ARTZBERGER, MANAGER

Pittsburgh, Pa.,
Dec. 2, 1915.

J. P. Seeburg Piano Co.
209 S. State St., Chicago.

Dear Sirs:-

The Style R Pipe Organ Orchestra that I purchased from you last August has been giving me perfect satisfaction in every way. It increased my business. This I know as a lot of my patrons told me that they come to hear the music. I have been in the motion picture business for over ten years, and in my four theatres this is the only instrument that has proved absolutely satisfactory. I have used several other makes of instruments, and none pleased me as well as the Seeburg. You have my heartiest co-operation in the way of recommendation for your instrument.

Thanking you for the attentions and courtesies extended to me, wishing you success, I beg to remain

Respectfully yours,

Walter E. Artzberger

WEA/C

Two testimonials from a 1916 Seeburg booklet, "The Soul of the Film," tell of successful installations of Seeburg Pipe Organ Orchestra photoplayers, one a Style M and the other a Style R. Although many hundreds of Seeburg photoplayers were sold, just a few survive today. Most of the larger style units using type H orchestrion rolls were marketed prior to 1920. By the time that sound movies became popular toward the end of the 1920s, most Seeburg photoplayers had worn out and were consigned to the scrap heap. In Spencer, West Virginia, a Style R held forth in the Robey Theatre, and remained until the 1960s, although by that time it had long since lapsed into silence.

160

numbered from 1 to over 1,000, with nearly 10,000 musical selections made over the years.

Similarly, Wurlitzer advertisements noted that its PianOrchestra rolls were arranged by the leader of a famous metropolitan symphony orchestra. When queried on the subject years later, Farny Wurlitzer said with a smile, "That was just advertising—everyone was very competitive in the old days." Seeburg, Wurlitzer, and most other rolls used on photoplayers of the era were mechanically laid out on a roll-arranging board, although in some instances the piano score alone was taken from a recorded human performance. In actuality, mechanically-arranged music rolls had many advantages, for while a pianist is limited to his hands and feet, the drafting-board arranger could insert solos, percussion novelties, and other effects to great advantage.

Following their introduction, Seeburg photoplayers achieved a wide acceptance and popularity. It is estimated that production of the larger models approached the 1,000 mark, quite a remarkable performance. Like other instruments of the genre, Seeburg photoplayers saw long and hard use. Several testimonials printed in 1926 tell of instruments purchased in an earlier era and bear this out:

"Just want to say that we have been using a Seeburg organ for the last 15 years, and it is still giving us entire satisfaction. It is the best instrument of its kind I have ever heard. I would not trade it for any other self-playing instrument I know of. It is a bit ancient, but still going good"—Princess and Dixie Theatres, Mayfield, Kentucky.

"I used the Style T Seeburg for six years in the Grand Theatre, and during the six years it was not touched by a mechanic. It was only tuned three times. Having used the Seeburg so long, I have created a library of 300 music rolls."—Gem and Grand Theatres, Cooper, Texas. (Author's note: one cannot help but feel sorry for the Grand Theatre patrons who had to listen to a piano used daily but tuned only once every two years!)

"We are using three Seeburg pianos and one Seeburg organ," noted the proprietor of the Capitol and Creighton theatres, Fort Wayne, Indiana. "Your Seeburg organ has been in operation for the past 11 years, an average of about six to 11 hours per day."

In the 1960s, the author located in Spencer, West Virginia the large Style R photoplayer used years earlier in the Robey Theatre in that town. Another Seeburg Style R turned up in a rural Illinois location.

If Wurlitzer and the American Photo Player Company were the two leaders in the photoplayer field, Seeburg probably was third, at least in terms of larger units, with the Operators Piano Company coming closely behind (or even edging ahead in terms of compact units, such as the Reproduco).

The Operators Piano Company of Chicago, founded in 1904 or 1905 (depending upon which advertisement you read), aggressively marketed its Coinola line of coin pianos and orchestrions during the 'teens. For theatres, the Reproduco, consisting of a piano with the accompaniment of two or three ranks of pipes, all mounted in a large console with two keyboards, achieved success, with one advertising pamphlet listing some 700 theatres that used them. Certain larger models such as the Super Reproduco and the Super Junior Reproduco were equipped with attached side chests and had more extensive pipework, with some models being equipped with a xylophone as well. These used type OS (for Organ Series) and NOS (for New Organ Series) rolls, usually of 10-tune length. Such rolls were equipped for changing pipe registration and playing piano and pipe notes, but no drums or traps were scored on them, nor did standard Reproducos contain novelty sound effects.

A large model in a horseshoe-type console, the Unified Reproduco, used a special roll. By means of elaborate pneumatic cross-connections, the instrument was "unified" much in the same manner as a theatre pipe organ. While most theatre instruments made by the Operator's Piano Company were marketed toward the late 'teens and 1920s, a few were sold in the period prior to 1915. In addition to the Reproduco instruments, certain Coinola pianos and orchestrions were equipped with extra foot pedals and were sold for theatre use. Some of these were marketed under the "Multitone" label by M. Welte & Sons. Still others were sold by Lyon & Healy, the leading Chicago musical merchandising firm. Most of the Multitone and related theatre instruments used type O orchestrion rolls such as used on Coinola instruments. These provided music for the piano, a solo section of 24 notes, and percussion effects. The Empress Bell Piano, extensively advertised for theatre use by Lyon & Healy, also used this type of roll.

In the Midwest, Dan Barton was an early entry in the field of movie theatre music. His "Bartola" attachments to upright pianos provided organ and percussion effects and were very popular. These were hand-played, not roll-operated.

A number of other firms entered the photoplayer market as well. In 1913 the Berry-Wood Piano Player Company, of Kansas City, Missouri, announced that it would soon be adding photoplayers to its line of coin-operated pianos and orchestrions, the latter sold under the Auto Orchestra name. Apparently, few Berry-Wood photoplayers were ever made. David Junchen, the theatre pipe organ historian, discovered that at least two organ blowers were shipped to Berry-Wood; one in 1912 and the other in 1915, indicating that at least two organs or large photoplayers were installed.

Another entry of which little is known today is "The Harmo," a theatre instrument described in 1915 as "a perfect powerful cathedral pipe organ played from the piano keyboard. Three in one—organ alone—piano alone—or both together. Fills the needs of the modern theatre. Has the refined orchestral effects, such as drums, cymbals, chimes, etc. Five models to fit any size house with capacity of 300 to 5,000." The seller was The Harmo Electric Company, Chicago.

The Automatic Musical Company of Binghamton, New York, name later changed (c. 1913) to the Link Piano Company and still later to the Link Piano & Organ Company

Colonel William N. Selig, who operated the Selig Polyscope Company studios in Chicago, desired to accompany former president Theodore Roosevelt on a 1909 expedition to Africa. Rebuffed in his attempt, Selig, undaunted, set up jungle scenes in his Chicago plant. Soon, movie audiences all across America were treated to "Theodore Roosevelt" hunting big game.

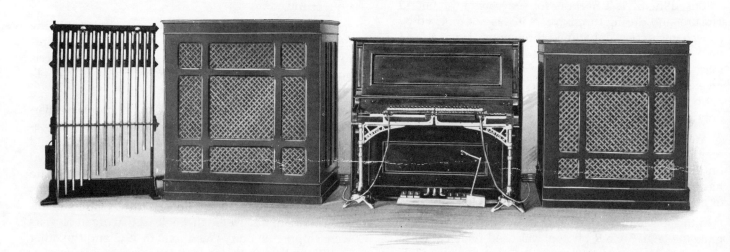

The Bartola Musical Instrument Company, Oshkosh, Wisconsin, managed by its founder, Daniel W. Barton, introduced the Bartola Orchestra, a version of which is shown above. The unit consisted of two side chests and other devices which could be attached to an ordinary upright piano. Auxiliary keyboards and a foot board connected to the piano operated the various effects. A human player was required; no roll-operated units were ever made. The Bartola Junior, consisting of a xylophone, marimba, bass drum, snare drum, cymbal, and "storm effect," was housed in a single case and cost just $850. Larger was Style No. 1, housed in two cases, offered at $1,850. Still larger were the Style A ($2,200), Style A Special ($2,650), Style AA ($3,050), and the Bartola Grand ($3,750). These units were immensely popular during the 1910-1915 era, and it was all that Daniel Barton and his associates could do to keep pace with the incoming stream of orders. Soon, so many Bartolas were sold that difficulty was experienced in locating operators to play them. Eventually, a training school was set up, and this solved the problem.

ABOVE: A factory photograph of a large photoplayer unit made by the North Tonawanda Musical Instrument Works. Note the richly figured quartered oak case, a popular finish used on photoplayers and orchestrions of many different manufacturers. Two paper rolls, mounted side by side, were behind the sliding doors above the keyboard. At the bottom of the piano various foot pedals provided for the operation of the novelty sound effects.

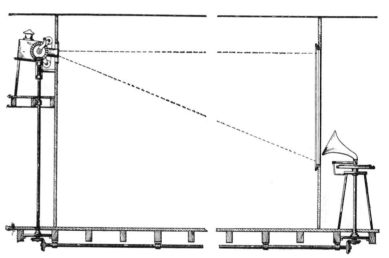

Talking Picture Reproduction by Two Reproducers Driven from a Long Power Shaft

Many different devices for synchronizing sound to motion pictures were proposed. The one shown here is a particularly cumbersome contrivance and shows a disc phonograph linked directly to a projector by means of a long power shaft extending under the theatre floor.

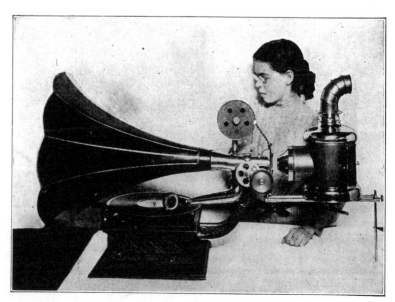

The Photophone.   A Unitary Talking-Picture Machine

A simpler method of providing sound for movies was the Photophone, a device which incorporated the projector and phonograph into a single unit. It appears that the picture image was projected through the phonograph horn!

produced numerous theatre instruments, including unified pipe organs. Coin pianos, orchestrions, and theatre photoplayers, most of which were produced after 1915, employed an endless roll system. One variety of photoplayer consisted of a piano with pipes and, sometimes, an extra cabinet with additional pipe ranks. The operation was automatic. A separate cabinet held four endless-type Link organ rolls. By means of pushbuttons in his booth, the projectionist could switch instantly from one roll to another. By giving each of the four rolls a separate character of music—snappy marches on one, romantic interludes on another, fox trots on another, and classical selections on the fourth—a creditable musical accompaniment to the scenes on the screen could be produced. The majority of such Link instruments were marketed in the early 1920s.

Still another entry in the photoplayer competition was the Marquette Piano Company, a Chicago firm which sold orchestrions and photoplayers under the Cremona trademark. The Style M3 and Style O were their most popular photoplayer types. Each could be purchased in the buyer's choice of several formats: (1) with a single roll mechanism which used special 134-note "S" rolls, (2) with a duplex roll mechanism which used two Style S rolls side by side, (3) with a duplex roll mechanism which used a Style S roll on one side and a regular 88-note home player piano roll on the other; or (4) with two Style M orchestrion rolls controlled by selector mechanisms.

An interesting *Instructions for Care of Instruments With Pipes* leaflet issued by Marquette was furnished to photoplayer buyers. It reads, in part:

"The different climates have different effects on wooden pipes. In order to obtain the best results the following suggestions should be observed.

"Sudden changes in temperature and humidity will naturally affect any wooden pipes, and a little care will improve the service and materially reduce the number of tunings necessary.

"In the Gulf states, Arkansas, Eastern Oklahoma, and the Pacific Northwest, where the rainfall is heavy and where a great many damp, foggy days occur, it is essential that an electric lamp be placed in each compartment of the instrument during the wet season.

"Care should be taken that the lights should not be burned in the pipe cabinet longer than necessary to overcome the excessive humidity, as continual burning is apt to produce trouble from too great warmth or from too much dryness.

"In dry climates or during dry seasons the burning of lamps and instruments should be guarded against as the instrument is apt to be dried out too much thereby. In certain localities such as Western Texas, Western Oklahoma, Colorado, New Mexico, and Arizona, it is necessary to place a small vessel containing water in each pipe cabinet and in the bottom of the piano, otherwise the instrument will dry out too much, getting the pipes out of tune as well as creating a tendency for leaks in the pneumatic system. The drum cabinet requires the same attention as the pipe cabinet, as damp weather slackens the drum heads."

Production of these units, sold as Cremona Theatre Orchestras, was probably primarily in the late 'teens. The writer estimates that not more than 100 were sold, and even this figure may be liberal.

A minor entry in the field of automatic music for theatres was the Mills Novelty Company, a Chicago manufacturer of slot machines and amusement devices. Its primary success in the field of automatic musical instruments was the Violano-Virtuoso, a violin-playing machine, of which approximately 5,000 were made from about 1910 to 1930 and primarily sold to restaurants, taverns, and candy kitchens. Two different adaptations of this machine were made specifically for theatre use. The first was a mechanism, called the Four Feeder, which contained four different Violano-Virtuoso rolls. By means of a remote control panel the projectionist could select from his choice of rolls—in the same manner as the Link four-roll unit mentioned earlier. The music was played on a regular Violano-Virtuoso instrument with one or two real violins accompanied by a 44-note electric piano.

The second theatre device was known as the Mills Melody Violin. By means of this unit, any number of violins could be played remotely from a keyboard. Mills noted: "The musician sits at the console, touches the keys, and plays the violins. He can draw out of the instruments any amount, any variety of real violin music. He can play all four strings at once, hold notes for any length of time, and perform a score of feats that even the most skillful musician cannot do. For the moving picture house or legitimate theatre, this is the perfect instrument to be used in conjunction with the organ or piano."

Although descriptions of these curious Mills instruments make interesting reading today, it is unlikely that many were ever sold for theatre use.

Another Chicago firm, the Nelson-Wiggen Piano Company, which was a latecomer to the automatic musical instrument business and whose activity was mainly confined to the 1920-1930 decade, produced several varieties of theatre instruments, including the Selectra Duplex Organ billed as "a small automatic organ suitable for chapels, lodge halls and moving picture houses. Contains eight-foot organ bass, four-foot flute and four-foot quintadena. Full-size piano and specially arranged organ roll with ten pieces, playing without rewind."

The Niagara Musical Instrument Manufacturing Company, of North Tonawanda, New York, was active for a short time in the 1910-1912 era. Several instruments were offered to theatre owners, including the En-Symphonie, which was essentially a pipe organ playing from home player piano rolls. Several dozen examples were sold, including one shipped on April 15, 1911 to the Brice Moving Picture Show of Homestead, Connecticut, according to the factory records.

The North Tonawanda Musical Instrument Works, located in the same town as Niagara, was formed around 1906 by employees who left Eugene DeKleist, the entre-

164

THE "SYMPHONY" AUTOMATIC ORCHESTRA
MADE IN ANY SIZE DESIRED.

PLAYED BY HAND OR AUTOMATICALLY WITH PERFORATED ROLL.
Especially designed for MOVING PICTURE HOUSES, THEATERS, and other Places of Amusement.

The Piano Player Manufacturing Company of Covington, Kentucky, advertised the Symphony Automatic Orchestra theatre instruments. The style shown above is an artist's conception and employs two stock retouched photographs of Welte Brisgovia orchestrions flanking the stage, with a piano below the screen.

CAN BE PLAYED BY OPERATOR OR AUTOMATICALLY.

WHY NOT
PREPARE FOR THE WINTER SEASON NOW?

And have your patronage established when it arrives. You can do this by giving your patrons good music with the films. Your business depends on their attendance—**increase it.**

SHOW THEM THAT THE BEST IS NONE TOO GOOD
YOU CAN DO ALL THIS AND MORE BY INSTALLING
A SYMPHONY ORCHESTRA PLAYER

Style G is shown above. 224 organ pipes, bass, flute, cello, violin, piccolo and vox humana. All the necessary effects. A complete instrument. Other styles in catalog. Write for same—price and easy terms.

THE SYMPHONY PLAYER COMPANY
CINCINNATI, U.S.A.
FACTORY AND OFFICE, COVINGTON, KY.

NEW YORK DISPLAY ROOMS
60 West 37th Street

CHICAGO DISPLAY ROOMS
730 N. Franklin Street

preneur who subsequently sold out to Wurlitzer. Several varieties of the Ideal Moving Picture Orchestra were offered by the North Tonawanda Musical Instrument Works in the years before 1920. These ranged from a single piano unit to larger styles with a piano flanked by two side chests. The music was provided by two piano rolls side by side. A human operator sat at the console unit and, by means of pedals and buttons, brought the pipes, bells, drums, and other instruments in and out of play, although rolls containing orchestration were available for larger models.

A December 31, 1914 letter from the North Tonawanda Musical Instruments Works states:

"Enclosed please find a cut of our new Ideal Moving Picture Orchestra. It contains 137 pipes. The perfect balancing of the instrumentation and the specially arranged music places the Ideal Moving Picture Orchestra in advance of any other instrument of its kind on the market. The tremolo, the slurring of the violins (pipes), together with the exquisite shading of expression—the whole instrument is marvelous, the traps being played exactly as a trap drummer would play them.

"There are stops or buttons directly before the operator to be used in shutting off any part of the instrument, so that if he desires musical effects to correspond with any phase of the pictures, he can get just what is needed, whether it be a church organ, a string quartette, country fiddler, straight piano, drum corps, cello solo, violin solo, flute solo (all with piano accompaniment), steamboat whistle, locomotive whistle, doorbell, telephone, and various other imitations of different noises."

The Peerless Piano Player Company, headquartered in St. Johnsville, a small upstate New York town, produced a wide variety of home player pianos, coin-operated pianos, orchestrions, and other automatic musical instruments, particularly during the first 15 years or so of the 20th century. The larger Peerless orchestrions used the type O roll (not to be confused with the similarly-named Coinola O roll, which has different specifications). Extant Peerless rolls mention that they are also for use on the Peerless Photo Orchestra, but apart from this brief notation, the author has no information concerning such units. It is known, however, that certain Peerless instruments were favored in theatre lobbies and on the inside for continuous playing during feature films, in the days before photoplayers became popular. Indeed, around 1910, Peerless orchestrions were among the most popular in the field.

The Piano Player Manufacturing Company, also known as the Symphony Player Company, headquartered in Covington, Kentucky, at the foot of Scott Street, just across the Ohio River from Cincinnati, advertised the Symphony Automatic Orchestra, billed as being "especially designed for moving picture houses, theatres, and other places of amusement." It could be played automatically by means of a perforated roll, according to a notice. Shown in one advertisement was an artist's conception of a two-keyboard piano, below the screen, with two large Welte Style B-1 Brisgovia orchestrions to the left and the right.

A catalogue description noted that the Symphony Automatic Orchestra was made in any size desired and cost from $1,500 to $20,000. It was envisioned that by means of electrical connections, Welte orchestrions could be played from a central keyboard unit. Apparently no such combinations survive today, and whether or not any were ever made is conjectural. At the time, such firms as Welte, Wurlitzer, Seeburg, and others gave deep discounts to piano houses, theatre supply agents, and others who were in a position to sell photoplayers and organs. It could be that the Piano Player Manufacturing Company primarily sold the products of others under its own name, although Symphony Automatic Orchestra styles E and G apparently were made by the firm. Of relatively simple construction, the large Style G, marketed in 1915, was operated by a style "A" coin piano roll mounted in the bottom of the piano under the right side of the keyboard. The roll provided the music. By means of stop tablets and pedals, the photoplayer operator controlled the pipes and other effects housed in two large side cabinets.

The American branch of M. Welte & Sons, a German firm, sold a variety of instruments for theatre use in the days before World War I. The Brisgovia and Brass Band orchestrions in particular were ideal for use on a balcony above the ticket booth to draw passers by into a theatre. Likewise, in the early days such instruments were used inside—where they played continuously, often being situated either at the back of the theatre or to the side of the screen. Some smaller pianos, units purchased from the Operators Piano Company of Chicago and sold under the "Multitone" label by Welte, used type O orchestrion rolls. Larger instruments, such as those in the Brisgovia series, used rolls made by Welte, primarily in its plant in Freiburg, Germany. So far as is known, nearly all large orchestrions sold by the firm were imported by Welte. However, theatre and residence pipe organs were produced in Welte's American plant located in Poughkeepsie, New York.

While most photoplayer activity occurred in the decade from about 1913 to 1923, hundreds of units were sold in later years as well. In the 1920s many hundreds of Reproduco theatre instruments, made by the Operators Piano Company, were sold. In the 1920s, Seeburg introduced several varieties of compact theatre instruments, including the Twin Roll Reproducing Pipe Organ (which made its debut in 1926). Similarly, Wurlitzer had several late entries in the field, including the Style W Orchestra, introduced in 1924 and made through 1930. Also known as the Wurlitzer Organette, this device consisted of a single unit with two keyboards which controlled a piano and pipes.

Of the thousands of photoplayers made over the years, only a few dozen survive today, primarily Wurlitzer, Fotoplayer, and Reproduco models. A number of these have been restored and are proudly displayed by collectors fortunate enough to own them.

A MOST BEAUTIFUL THEATRE
Showing Groups of Pipes in Archways
CHICAGO, Ill.

LEXINGTON THEATRE
MILWAUKEE, WIS.

In 1916, Jerome B. Meyer & Son, organ pipe manufacturers located in Milwaukee, Wisconsin, produced a catalogue telling of the virtues of display (non-functional) organ pipes in a theatre, either separately as decorations or fronting a chamber containing speaking pipes. Above are shown two theatres using Meyer pipes, while below is a Meyer factory scene. The Lexington Theatre, Milwaukee, Wisconsin, treated its patrons to music played on a one-manual tubular pneumatic Schuelke organ installed in 1911. The unit was equipped with a roll player. The dummy organ pipes concealed the fact that the entire functional pipe section was located in a single loft on the left side of the theatre. "Pipes can be placed artistically in any theatre," the catalogue related. "In archways, former door openings, over exit doors, across corners, or against flat walls. Can be easily attached. Anybody can set them in position. Have them put in your theatre—they will give that pipe organ effect." At the same time, the firm of Jerome B. Meyer & Son was a leading manufacturer of real organ pipes for various orchestrion and organ companies.

Showing one Setion of Factory where Organ Pipes are made

Here Is A
FEDERAL ELECTRIC SIGN
You Can Change Every Day

IF you are showing a big feature to-morrow, you want the public to know about it, don't you? That is just what a FEDERAL Simplex Electric Sign will do for your theatre.

It is a combination of permanent sign and a bulletin of information that you can change as often as you wish. Exhibitors all over the country are using FEDERAL Simplex Electric Signs—and their profits show it.

You may be tempted to buy a cheap, ineffective sign, but if you do you are losing money every day you operate it. If you want the crowds, the FEDERAL Electric Sign will get them for you.

Beside the FEDERAL Simplex changeable letter sign, we make electric signs in all sizes and designs for motion picture theatres.

If you are going to get a sign, you had best get a FEDERAL Simplex. We will be glad to send the Federal Theatre Booklet No. 140. Write for it today. There is no obligation whatsoever.

FEDERAL SIGN SYSTEM (Electric)
Lake and Desplaines Streets, Chicago

1790 Broadway
New York

1618 Mission Street
San Francisco, Cal.

4 Factories. Branches in All Large Cities

The Federal Sign System offered the possibility of daily changes of illuminated lettering. Brightly lighted facades were the trademark of nickelodeon and later theatres, with the philosophy being "the brighter, the better."

Weickhardt Pipe Organs

are not stock instruments, but built to order according to the ever varying individual requirements. Result: Wonderful musical effects, such as only a real, complete and genuine MASTER PIPE ORGAN can produce.

WRITE FOR THEATRE ORGAN CATALOG
WANGERIN-WEICKHARDT CO.
···· 112-124 BURRELL STREET ····
MILWAUKEE, WISCONSIN U.S.A.

An advertisement for Weickhardt pipe organs, circa 1915, features theatre instruments and invites prospective clients to write for a catalogue.

The pipe organ in Chicago's Alcazar Theatre, 1908, was one of the earliest, if not the very earliest pipe organ specifically installed in a moving picture house in that city. To the left of the screen is an electric piano similar to those made by Peerless, Berry-Wood, and the Automatic Musical Company.

The Alcazar Theatre

Theatre Pipe Organs

In 1898 a "concert organ" was installed in a Kansas City picture show, according to an early report. In 1905 Thomas L. Tally installed a 4-manual, 47-rank Murray Harris pipe organ in a Los Angeles movie theatre. In 1906 the Austin Organ Company of Hartford, Connecticut, installed for $12,500 a large four-manual organ in the Temple Auditorium in Los Angeles. In 1911 a $5,000 instrument was installed in the New Amsterdam Theatre, New York City, by the same firm. The Estey Organ Company, of Brattleboro, Vermont, recorded such installations as organs in the Mike Gore Theatre, Los Angeles, 1906, and the Star Theatre in Portland (Oregon) in 1910, as well as dozens of later contracts. Most organs installed in places of public amusement prior to 1910 and 1911 were used to provide music for vaudeville acts or stage performances; however many were specifically intended for the accompaniment of motion pictures. Another early installation specifically for movies was the previously-mentioned organ built into the Alcazar Theatre, Chicago, in 1908.

Louis J. Schoenstein, the San Francisco organ builder and repairman, noted in his memoirs that he installed organs in theatres as early as 1912, when an Austin pipe organ of ten stops was put in the Globe Theatre in Portland, Oregon, followed by another Austin with an automatic player unit in a similarly-named house in Salem in the same state. Both of these instruments were church-type or classical-style organs adopted to theatre use and were unlike the so-called unit organs pioneered by Robert Hope-Jones.

What is a *theatre* organ? In general, it is appropriate to designate as a theatre organ any organ that was installed in a theatre, auditorium, or other place of public performance in which the audience was seated while watching films or stage activities. If this definition is used, theatre organs include numerous instruments installed in municipal auditoriums, concert halls, and other locations, not to overlook church meeting rooms and social halls occasionally used for entertainment. By this definition, theatre organs were in wide use during the 19th century. However, for our purposes, a theatre organ is one that saw its primary use to accompany silent films.

In his book, *The Encyclopedia of the American Theatre Organ*, David Junchen states as his requirement that an organ has to meet at least one of the following criteria in order to qualify: (1) It must have been installed in a building called a theatre; (2) It must have been installed in an auditorium where silent films were shown; or (3) It must have been used to play popular music. Under the last category, organs in private residences and radio stations could be included, but these are not within the scope of the present text.

From about 1910 onward, organs installed in theatres and other public locations can be divided into two categories: classic or "straight" organs and, second, theatre organs, particularly those with unified systems, following the devices popularized or invented by Robert Hope-Jones.

Neither definition is exclusive. There were many hybrid instruments built. In general, a church or a straight organ is voiced on relatively low wind pressure. To achieve a needed volume of music, many ranks are used, including mixture ranks consisting of multiple rows of pipes drawn on a single stop or control. Such organs were customarily voiced on several inches of wind or so, up to five or six inches. On the other hand, theatre organs were voiced on higher wind, including pressures of seven and one-half inches, 10 inches, 15 inches, 25 inches, or even more. Thus, fewer pipes were needed to achieve a desired volume of sound.

The unification system, popularized by Robert Hope-Jones, was primarily used in theatre organs, although many church or straight organs employed this scheme as well. By unification, an extended rank of pipes could be played not only from a designated manual or keyboard as on a straight organ, but by means of controls it could be switched from one manual to another or to the pedalboard. Further, different sections or pitches of a given rank could be selected, so that a given keyboard could, if desired, play the same note on a rank of pipes at several different pitches.

The Wurlitzer Hope-Jones Unit Orchestra, the most famous theatre organ style, was imitative of a human orchestra and contained pipes voiced to sound like the clarinet, oboe, violin, flute, and other instruments. Other Hope-Jones innovations included the curved or horseshoe-type console and the use of colored stop tabs to indicate different qualities, such as reeds, flue pipes, and percussion.

Most successful theatre pipe organs, even small ones, had as a basic rank the tibia clausa, a large-scale stopped wooden flute with a heavy tremolo. Indeed, Robert Hope-Jones considered the tibia to be a basic necessity, the foundation of any organ. To control the volume and to add expression, theatre organs were nearly always enclosed in chambers fronted with swell shutters which could be opened partially or entirely, in varying degrees. By contrast, many church organs were built unenclosed, depending upon the addition or subtraction of ranks in use to furnish the desired volume during the playing of a particular selection.

Organs installed in auditoriums were used in connection with the showing of motion pictures during the early days, but it was not until about 1912 that the unification system became popular. Earlier instruments were mostly of the straight variety. Some smaller theatres were even equipped with foot-pumped parlor reed organs made by Estey, Carpenter, Beatty, and other firms.

In October 1914, the Liberty Theatre in Seattle opened its doors and was greeted with crowds extending several city blocks—so many people, in fact, that the police had to be called to control them! Primary credit for this outstanding success was given to the Wurlitzer organ played by Henry Murtagh to accompany the films. From that point on, the success of the Wurlitzer Hope-Jones Unit Orchestra was assured. Soon, other firms jumped into the fray, including established organ builders who added theatre instruments to their line, as well as a number of companies set up specifically to manufacture theatre-style instruments. Most of these copied Wurlitzer in one way or another, and before long the horseshoe-style console, colored stop tabs, and unification became standard throughout the industry. In the period from about 1912 through the 1930s, Wurlitzer was the leading manufacturer of theatre organs, with over 2,000 made, followed by Robert Morton with over 800, and other contenders such as Kimball, Moller, Barton, Marr & Colton, Wicks, Kilgen, Smith, Hilgreen-Lane, Estey, Link, Austin and Page. This listing, according to David L. Junchen's *Encyclopedia of the American Theatre Organ*, covers makers who made more than 100 theatre organs during the time indicated. Some, such as Kimball, Moller, Wicks, Kilgen, Estey, and Austin, were very prominent in the field of church and classical organs, with theatre organs being a sideline.

Theatre organs were prominent in Denver motion picture exhibition in the 'teens. The showing of films in that city began years earlier, however, with the first exclusive motion picture emporium being the Theatorium, opened in June 1906 on 16th Street, opposite the Post Office. Owned by the Moore & Greaves Amusement Company, and managed by G. H. Greaves, the theatre seated 400 people and charged a nickel admission. Soon thereafter, Samuel L. Baxter, a cattleman who also dealt in real estate and who earlier had traveled to Los Angeles to seek a business opportunity, came to Denver to set up a nickelodeon theatre on a side street, spending several hundred dollars in the process. Lanterns were used for lighting, and seating was provided by kitchen chairs. "Mrs. Baxter sold the tickets, trimmed the wicks and hung the posters, while Mr. Baxter operated a projection machine and managed the theatre," noted an early report. "For music he started with a player piano."

The venture prospered, and in 1907 the Denver Theatre, located on 17th Street, opened its doors. Seating 250 persons, it soon provided the funds for still other ventures on the part of its proprietor. Within a short time, Baxter had $22,000 in his bank account, it was reported.

While several nickelodeon theatres on 16th and 17th streets in Denver attracted thousands of patrons who spent a steady stream of nickels, not far away on Curtis Street a half dozen theatres with live performances were doing well with admission charges ranging from a dime to $2. Gradually, patrons drifted away from the more elaborate houses and went to the nickelodeons, often creating long waiting lines in front. S.L. Baxter purchased the Novelty Theatre on Curtis Street, then a vaudeville house. The building with its 600 seats was converted to motion pictures, the first on the street that would later become famous for its picture shows. G. H. Greaves built the Princess Theatre, seating 1200 or more people, on Curtis Street, the first large structure built in Denver for the express purpose of exhibiting films. An account in *The Billboard*, July 1910, mentions that the steel work for "the biggest picture show in the West, which is being erected on Curtis Street, along Theatre Row, by the Princess Amuse-ment Company is about finished. No doubt the house will be ready by early fall. The house will cost about $50,000 and will have a seating capacity of 1,200. It will be known as the Princess."

The Princess was built in the middle of the nickelodeon era, when few suspected that larger establishments would soon capture the business of their storefront progenitors and render the storefront theatres obsolete.

Soon, S.L. Baxter acquired the 1,000-seat Curtis Street Theatre, home of dramatic shows, and converted it to movies, followed in 1913 by the New Isis Theatre (later simply known as the Isis), seating 1,800, at a cost of $115,000.

About the same time, the Paris Theatre, seating 2,200 people and charging a nickel admission, was put up on Curtis Street, while most vaudeville houses in the district changed over to movies. The Paris installed a large Wurlitzer theatre organ, with pipes personally voiced by Robert Hope-Jones. $250,000 was spent to construct and furnish the edifice. "The front of the Paris Theatre is of such exceptionally artistic treatment that it has been copied many times," noted a Wurlitzer catalogue. "The Paris is also noted for having the greatest amount of electricity used in any theatre front. Forty of the prominent organists of Denver voluntarily adopted the following resolution: 'Resolved that the thanks of the musicians of Denver be tendered to the management of the Paris Theatre for introducing into this city an instrument of such great artistic merit—an instrument having a wide range of tone color and well-nigh limitless possibilities.' "

W.A. Roderic, president of the Paris Theatre Company, was equally enthusiastic, and on June 19, 1913 he wrote to the Wurlitzer Company:

"I wish to thank you for the work you planned and have carried out for us in the theatre. We feel that your genius has provided for us an altogether unique attraction. The wonderful instrument planned and installed under your direction is providing a source of interest to the whole city and has materially added to the fame of the Paris as the leading picture theatre of Denver.

"No 30-piece orchestra could accompany the picture so well as the Hope-Jones Unit Orchestra does. Neither would it so completely carry away with enthusiasm the crowds that flock to hear it."

Success spawned more success, and Curtis Street saw a flurry of building activity. Soon, a writer noted "Denver's moving picture row now extends two blocks along Curtis Street, the city's main thoroughfare. Beginning at the east end is the Iris; directly across the street is the Paris and on the same side is the New Isis with the Plaza opposite. In the next block is the Strand with the Princess within a few doors. Across the street is the Colonial. Around the corner on 16th Street is the Lyric which was built on the site of the Theatorium, Denver's first motion picture theatre. Across 16th Street from the Lyric is the Tabor Grand, and on Curtis below 16th is the Rialto. There are other houses in the downtown section on Larimer

Princess Theatre at Night, Denver, Colo.

PARIS THEATRE AT NIGHT, DENVER, COLO.

CURTIS STREET AT NIGHT, DENVER, COLO.

Night views, as reproduced on postcards, of Curtis Street, the "Broadway of the West," in Denver. Among the many theatres on the street the Paris and the Isis achieved fame with their Wurlitzer theatre pipe organ installations. In later years, the ornate movie palaces were bulldozed, to be replaced by plain commercial buildings.

172

Wurlitzer Hope-Jones Unit Orchestra Installed in Paris Theatre, Denver, Colo.

UNQUESTIONABLY the largest theatre in the United States, giving a high-grade program for 5c. Seats 2,200. Represents a capitalization of $250,000, paid up. The front of the theatre is of such exceptionally artistic and elaborate treatment that it has been copied many times. The Paris Theatre also is noted for having the greatest amount of electricity used in any theatre front.

Forty of the prominent organists of Denver voluntarily adopted the following resolution: "Resolved, that the thanks of the musicians of Denver be tendered to the management of the Paris Theatre for introducing into this city an instrument of such great artistic merit — an instrument having wide range of tone color and well-nigh limitless possibilities."

Mr. Robert Hope-Jones, personally, voiced the pipes of the Unit Orchestra installed in this theatre.

The Wurlitzer organ installed in the Paris Theatre, Denver, in 1913 created a sensation and overnight elevated the Paris to a position of pre-eminence in the city. S.L. Baxter, whose Isis Theatre opened nearby on May 1, 1913, soon ordered an even larger Wurlitzer instrument.

NEW ISIS PHOTO-PLAY THEATRE

1724 Curtis Street, Denver, Colorado
Open, May 1st 1913.
* * *

It embodies every principle known to the expert mind to insure the
*   public against Disaster by Fire and Panic.*
Representing an investment of $225,000.
Ventilating System delivers 50,000 cubic ft. of pure air per min-
*   ute--cooled in summer and heated in winter--and takes out all*
*   the impure air at the same time.*
Capacity 2200 Comfortable Seats.
Electric Power and Light 120,000 C.P.
*   S. L. BAXTER, Prop. & Mgr.*

Samuel L. Baxter

The Isis Theatre was opened by Samuel L. Baxter on May 1, 1913. Located at 1724 Curtis Street, Denver, the motion picture house, representing an investment said to have amounted to $225,000, was an immediate attraction. However, Baxter soon realized that the nearby Paris Theatre, with its Wurlitzer Hope-Jones Unit Orchestra pipe organ, was doing even better. Baxter contacted Wurlitzer and arranged to purchase the largest Wurlitzer organ ever installed in a theatre up to that time. In August 1915 the organ made its debut. Subsequently, Wurlitzer noted in a catalogue: "The Wurlitzer Hope-Jones Unit Orchestra installed in the Isis Theatre is the largest musical instrument ever installed in any theatre in the United States. The instrument occupied four freight cars in transit to Denver. In the theatre it extends out over the auditorium, all over the stage, and in many rooms in the basement. The work of installation required three months. The instrument is capable of producing hundreds of different tone effects and musical orchestrations."

A Denver newspaper commented on the Wurlitzer organ in the Isis Theatre: "A feature of the city. Something that every visitor must see at least once, and every citizen will want to hear time after time."

Street—the Joy, the Fun, the Grand, and the Annex, all with small seating capacity and all are five-cent houses."

The success of the Paris Theatre with its organ was not lost on Samuel L. Baxter, who before long placed an order with Wurlitzer for an even larger instrument for his Isis Theatre.

Farny Wurlitzer wrote to Baxter on July 4, 1915:

"As regards distinctive varieties of tone color for each of the various stops, here we feel none will question our supremacy. Beyond dispute, the Unit Orchestra leads and always has led in providing extreme colors. In this connection, we venture to call attention to the fact that the variety of tone an organ yields depends much less upon the number of its stops than on the degree of variance of each from all others."

The contract for the Wurlitzer organ was negotiated on January 11, 1915, with a price established at $40,000. Including alterations to the building, the total expenditure reached $50,000, representing the largest amount ever spent to that date for a motion picture theatre organ.

Henry B. Murtagh, whose performances at the Liberty Theatre, Seattle, caused a sensation earlier, helped with specifications and ideas. The first of three shipments left the Wurlitzer factory in North Tonawanda, New York on May 22, 1915, followed by additional dispatches on June 3rd and 4th, all by railroad car. When completed, the Wurlitzer Hope-Jones Unit Orchestra consisted of a four-manual mahogany console, with 156 stop tablets, situated in the orchestra pit, controlling 28 ranks of pipes installed in six chambers. It far outranked, literally and figuratively, the 13-rank unit in the nearby Paris Theatre.

Writing in 1955, historian Roy Gorish related:

"The organ made its debut [in the Isis] on August 14, 1915. It was a gala affair. Farny Wurlitzer had pursuaded Henry Murtagh to come to Denver for the opening. Carmenza Vander Lezz, employed by the Wurlitzer Company as an official demonstrator, also performed. In the audience were the principals from the Wurlitzer Company, the mayor of Denver, and other local dignitaries. There is a story that the pedal tones caused the fragile electric filaments in the light bulbs to break, plunging the theatre into total darkness for a period.

"Mr. Murtagh apparently remained at the Isis for some time, because early newspaper accounts make reference to his daily recitals. The organ was an important and vitally needed addition to the musical life of Denver at this time. It was acclaimed as a great concert instrument and utilized by the chamber of commerce as an example of one aspect of Denver's cultural life."

A month after the opening, Samuel L. Baxter wrote to Wurlitzer:

"In checking up on the month's business, I feel in the mood to write you the strongest kind of recommendation. We certainly have done business. All the old patrons of the house seem more than pleased, and we are gaining an astonishing volume of new patronage which hereto-fore seemed to take no particular interest in film productions and rarely or ever patronized any of the theatres.

"We give recitals all through the month and after every one get expressions of pleasure from our people. I'm simply delighted with the results all the way through and do not regret a single penny of the cost.

"The Isis seats 2,000, and we often turn them away at night, but this month has been the first time when we have filled regularly at the afternoon shows the way we wanted to. Our business is gaining now for every hour that the Wurlitzer Hope-Jones Unit Orchestra is played, and we have given up everything else in the way of music."

A early Wurlitzer catalogue refers to the Isis installation: "In the theatre it extends out over the auditorium, all over the stage, and in many rooms in the basement. The work of installation required three months. The instrument is capable of producing hundreds of different tone effects and musical orchestrations. There are three sets of vox humana (human voice) pipes located in different parts of the building, producing the most wonderful singing effects, both in solo and chorus. Two large harps, costing $1,000 each, are built in the instrument. Also two mammoth sets of cathedral chimes and drums and crash cymbals. One of the instrument's stops is dedicated entirely to reproducing simply the sound of a bee on a windowpane, and the wind and rain machines are so accurate as to defy detection. It also has an electrical applicance reproducing lightning flashes to accompany thunder. The console or key desk has four manuals of 61 notes, plus the pedal, and two complete semi-circles of stops and couplers to the number of 150. There is a double touch system, by the use of which many individual pipes may be brought out in moderate tone; and when the key is depressed clear down, the tone is made to swell to a great volume, which accentuates or segregates the melody of the selection. A Denver newspaper, commenting on the installation of the Wurlitzer Hope-Jones Unit Orchestra in the Isis Theatre, had the following to say: 'A feature of this city, something that every visitor must see at least once; and every citizen will want to hear time after time.' "

Still another account noted that Baxter started business with a nickelodeon theatre. His business prospered "until finally the crowning triumph of his career was recently realized in the installation of a Wurlitzer Hope-Jones Unit Orchestra. His success, Mr. Baxter frankly states, was due mainly to his ambition to give to his patrons the very best of music. So satisfied has Mr. Baxter been over the success of his Wurlitzer Hope-Jones Unit Orchestra that he has already paid the entire amount, years in advance of the terms of the contract."

Throughout the 1920s, the Isis was filled with movie-goers. With the advent of the Depression, Curtis Street faded, its lights dimmed, and the center of commercial activity expanded toward the east. Modern theatres sprang up, the Isis and its contemporaries were neglected, and soon Curtis Street catered to a less desirable element of society. "The organ was last played in 1939," historian Ray Gorish wrote. "Its swan song was played by a pert little lady by the name of Mary Dobbs Tuttle. Mrs. Tuttle had been with the organ from the very beginning. By 1939, not only the theatre, but the organ itself was merely a shadow of its former being. In an effort to draw patronage, an over-zealous manager decided to present stage shows. However, the Isis had been designed strictly for motion pictures and it had no dressing rooms. Therefore, a junkman was called in, and two of the organ chambers, the organ relay, and the console were literally axed and hammered into scrap to make dressing rooms from the evacuated space. Although the destruction of the organ was a pathetic blunder, yet, needless to say, no bribery could cajole patrons into what had become an unpleasant neighborhood."

In 1955 the Isis Theatre succumbed to the wrecking ball and bulldozer blade. By the 1970s, when this writer visited Curtis Street, all that remained were sterile concrete commercial buildings, a bus station, and other structures which gave no indication of the glory days of the "Broadway of the West," the days when the Isis, Paris, Colonial and other ornate theatres lit up the night with their bright lights and, inside, thrilled crowds with entertaining films and beautiful music.

In the meantime, back in 1915 in Seattle the Liberty Theatre, which had opened to record crowds attracted by the Wurlitzer organ music, continued to please thousands of moviegoers. The house, with a white front three stories high, cost $140,000 to build and on the exterior had a large sign in the shape of the Statue of Liberty measuring 40 feet high, embellished with 1,200 lights in eight different colors. The management claimed to have a daily attendance of 8,000 to 10,000 individuals. The admission charge ranged from 10c to 25c, depending upon the time of day and the seat location.

The success of the Liberty, the Isis, the Paris, and other early Wurlitzer installations engendered enthusiasm, and within the next 20 years approximately 2,000 Wurlitzer theatre pipe organs replaced musicians and orchestras. In addition, many more photoplayers and pit organs did their duty.

Years later, Ben M. Hall, in *The Best Remaining Seats*, wrote:

"Few wonders of the movie palace brought more shivery pleasure to audiences (or caused more breast-beating among crusaders for culture) than the Mighty Wurlitzer. Part one-man band, part symphony orchestra, part sound-effects department, the Wurlitzer was one of the most versatile instruments ever devised by man.

"Of course, there were a score or more manufacturers of theatre organs, but the Wurlitzer basked in the same sweet sunlight of generic familiarity as the Frigidaire, the Victrola, and the Kodak. It might be a Kimball, a Robert-Morton, a Moller, a Page, a Barton, or a Marr & Colton (a few of the better-known makes), but to the average movie goer if it rose up out of the pit at intermission with a roar that made the marrow dance in one's bones, if rows of colored stop-tabs, lit by hidden lights, arched like a rain-bow above the flawless dental work of the keyboards—if it could imitate anything from a brass band to a Ford horn to a choir of angels—gee, Dad, it was a Wurlitzer!"

Hall went on to say that "the Mighty Wurlitzer (and its counterparts) was as much a part of the movie palace as the electric lights that danced around the marquee, or the goldfish that swam in the lobby fountain. Inside the theatre the music seemed to bubble up and soar into the darkness of the balcony. Far below, bathed in a rose spotlight, was the organist perched in the maw of the great golden console. A flick of the finger, and chimes would call Ramona back beside the waterfall; a dramatic sweep of the hand and all would be silenced save for the sobbing of the broken-hearted tibia languishing in the left loft as it was comforted by its mate, the crooning vox humana over on the right, to the tune of *Prisoner of Love*. A quick kick at the crescendo pedal, a lighting jab at the combination pistons, and the mood would change to joy again—all glockenspiel, trumpets, tubas, snare drums, as an invisible MacNamara's Band marched across the balcony."

The Hope-Jones Unit Orchestra

Robert Hope-Jones was born on February 9, 1859 at Hooten Grange, Cheshire, England to a family which eventually consisted of nine children. At an early age he developed musical ability, and by the time he was nine he played for occasional services at a local church. As a teenager he was organist at the Birkenhead School Chapel.

After serving an apprenticeship in electrical engineering, Hope-Jones secured a position with a telephone company, during which time he devised several important innovations. From 1886 until 1892 he was engaged with the help of volunteers in rebuilding the pipe organ installed in St. John's Church in Birkenhead. During the rebuilding process he introduced several innovations, including tablet-style stop controls and a new style of electric action.

He wasn't the first, or even close to the first, to apply electricity to organ mechanisms. The originator may never be known for certain, for as is the case with the invention of the automobile, the steamboat, and a number of other devices, claims proliferate. Many pages of print have been devoted to the achievements of pioneers in the electric organ field. Henry John Gauntlett proposed a system for electrically playing all the organs at the 1851 Great Exhibition from a common console, either separately or simultaneously, and the Exhibition Committee was contacted concerning it. A British patent was taken out on the system in 1852, but no working model was constructed. Had it been, it is likely that the organ would not have functioned properly.

Karl G. Weigle, of Germany, constructed an organ with electric action as early as 1870, followed by another instrument he showed at the Vienna Exhibition in 1873. In the meantime, at the Paris Exhibition of 1855, an organ with

Illustrating Style 3 of Wurlitzer Hope-Jones Unit Orchestra
Specially Designed Case

IN volume and variety it will surpass any twelve-piece orchestra, and because of flexibility and instantaneous responsiveness, is ideal for the cueing and playing of motion pictures. Flexible in tone, brilliant in theatrical voicing and, though orchestral, retains the dignity of church pipe organ. Keyboard is provided with a second touch system, practically converting it into a four manual. Action is elastic, snappy and responsive. All parts quickly accessible to player.

The console or keydesk (in foreground) is detached and movable. Organ proper may be placed at convenient distance from keyboard.

Dimensions and full specifications upon request.

Clara Kimball-Young, famous photoplay actress, is shown playing the instrument.

The Style 3 Wurlitzer Hope-Jones Unit Orchestra pipe organ was one of the most popular models circa 1915. Most were installed in organ chambers, not in a wooden cabinet such as shown here. Seated at the console is Clara Kimball Young, a popular actress of the era. At his North Tonawanda office, Farny Wurlitzer maintained a file of film and stage personalities photographed with Wurlitzer theatre instruments, including one of Mary Pickford and one showing theatre owners Balaban and Katz, who were among Wurlitzer's best customers in the 1920s.

Clara Kimball Young was an accomplished organist and at one time played a concert for the editorial staff of "Motion Picture World," using the instrument pictured here, which was set up in Wurlitzer's New York City showroom.

Circa 1914 advertisement for Wurlitzer theatre organs.

electric action built by Stein was shown, but it was reported that the current was not sufficient to control the larger pallets. Numerous others engaged in the building of electric organ systems met with varying degrees of success. At the 1876 Centennial Exhibition, held in Philadelphia, Schmoelc displayed a large organ with electric action, automatically played by sensing fingers which read perforated cardboard strips. Numerous other organs with electric actions were displayed during the latter part of the 19th century, including the first successful electric organ built in England, the instrument constructed by Bryceson for Her Majesty's Opera Theatre Royal, Drury Lane, which made its public debut in 1868. Organ builders such as Roosevelt and Willis employed electric actions in many installations.

On May 3, 1891, Robert Hope-Jones read a paper before the Royal College of Organists, stating that although the application of electricity to controlling organs was hardly new, his own work was accomplished without the benefit of the knowledge of the activity of others, "for until a few months ago, I had never seen either an electric organ or a sketch of any part of one, save the instrument of my own building in St. John's Church, Birkenhead. The whole of my work in the connection with this subject is entirely original with me, knowing in some details it must doubtlessly be more or less a repetition of what has been done before me.

"One very great advance upon my predecessors, however, I distinctly claim, and that is the fact that the electro-pneumatic action has now become reliable, simple and cheap. I feel confident in asserting that electro-pneumatics will very shortly be the only form of action that organ builders will adopt for large and moderate size instruments."

Hope-Jones went on to discuss the four types of organ actions then in use: mechanical, pneumatic lever, tubular-pneumatic, and electro-pneumatic. He noted that mechanical or tracker actions were cheap and efficient for small instruments, "but the control of very large organs by this means is quite impossible," while the pneumatic lever, a system of amplifying force by bellows and pneumatics, was intricate, costly, complicated, and disadvantageous in many respects. The tubular pneumatic system "never can, never will be perfected. Instantaneous response is an absolute impossibility, for the air being compressible, the impulse resulting from the movement of the key is bound to be transmitted through the tube as a wave. For that reason no tubular pneumatic organ is crisp."

From the 1890s onward Hope-Jones filed many patents concerning pipe organs. One granted in England on September 30, 1890 was from a filing giving an extensive dissertation concerning many different ideas and innovations, including electrical unification of stops, suitable bass, operation of swell shutters, colored key tablets to identify the tonal character of various ranks, and so on. Subsequently the same ideas were incorporated in United States patent No. 522,209 dated July 3, 1894 (application filed September 18, 1891). Additional innovations and ideas were described in a British patent granted on November 20, 1890 and similar American patent No. 514,146 (February 6, 1894; application filed August 8, 1892). The unification system was described in detail in American patent 849,241 dated April 2, 1907 (applied for on April 22, 1904). Numerous other patents were granted to Hope-Jones over a long period of years, including some filed during Hope-Jones' lifetime but granted posthumously.

Having left the field of telephone engineering in 1889, Hope-Jones in the 1890s was a professional organ builder. An early project was the modification of an instrument for J. Martin White, who had a large estate at Balruddery, Dundee, Scotland. White, himself an organist, was impressed with Hope-Jones' work and gave him financial backing to pursue other ideas, including the concept of unification.

Following Hope-Jones' address to the Royal College of Organists in 1891, organists divided themselves into two camps—those who admired Hope-Jones and his innovations, and those who thought he was an infidel tampering with the tradition of generations. So severe did the dislike of certain adversaries become that numerous instances are recorded of his organs being sabotaged.

A businessman Hope-Jones was not, and financial adversities dogged him from the very beginning. A factory established at Battersea in 1897 had difficulty from its inception, as did several other ventures. Grants from benefactors such as J. Martin White helped but were not sufficient to finance his ever-expanding ideas.

In 1895 a Hope-Jones electric organ was set up in St. George's Church, Hanover Square, London, England, and attracted much admiration. However, the fame was quickly cut short by a fire which destroyed the organ and the church tower. Immediately, it was pointed out that the electric action was responsible as the cause of the fire, but it probably was the work of an arsonist. Church officials soon ordered a replacement organ with the same electrical action.

Around the same time, wires in an electric cable of the Hope-Jones organ at Hendon Parish Church, London, were cut, followed by the cutting of the cable connecting the console of the organ he installed in a church in Lancashire. Pipes were stolen from a Hope-Jones organ at the Burton-on-Trent Parish Church.

With his wife Cecil, whom he had married in 1893, Hope-Jones came to America in 1903, leaving behind him two dozen or so organs improved or installed by him. The intention was to visit for a short period of time, but at the instigation of R.P. Elliot, an official of the Austin Organ Company, Hartford, Connecticut, he was persuaded to remain in the United States and join Austin as a vice-president. A year later, he left Austin to form a new company, Hope-Jones & Harrison, which he intended to set up in Bloomfield, New Jersey, but not enough money could be raised to launch the firm, so, after completing only one contract, a rebuild, in New Jersey, he then went to the Ernest M. Skinner Company, Boston, in 1905.

A Skinner contract for the installation of an organ in

the Park Church, Elmira, New York, gave Hope-Jones the opportunity to design an instrument incorporating all of his ideas. The chairman of the church organ committee, Jervis Langdon, was impressed with Hope-Jones and encouraged him to leave Skinner and move to Elmira, which he did in 1907, setting up the Hope-Jones Organ Company there. Langdon served also as the treasurer of the Chamber of Commerce of Elmira and took charge of raising sufficient capital to provide financial backing for the new venture. One of the investors was Mark Twain.

A number of successful organ installations followed, about 40 in all, but Hope-Jones' constant preoccupation with new ideas, innovations, and changes in projects in progress, plus a general lack of business ability, resulted in continuing lawsuits. By 1910, despite acclaim given to his organs and the success in particular of a mammoth installation at the Ocean Grove (New Jersey) Auditorium, a building seating 10,000 people, the Elmira firm came to an end. Even with continuous infusion of capital, losses mounted. The generosity of his backers ended, and operations halted.

Howard Wurlitzer, the business manager of the company bearing his name, was persuaded by his brother Farny to acquire the Hope-Jones patents and remaining assets. This he did, and in 1910 they were transferred to the facilities of the Rudolph Wurlitzer Manufacturing Company in North Tonawanda, New York.

On August 6, 1910, Robert Hope-Jones, pleased with his new connection with the Wurlitzer Company, gave an enthusiastic address to the National Association of Organists in a familiar setting—the immense Auditorium at Ocean Grove, New Jersey. He told the listeners of his many ideas—of unification, of suitable bass, of a new type of swell shutter, of the pizzicato touch, and of other things—stating how these would inevitably be incorporated by others in the field. This philosophy was spread by Wurlitzer, which reprinted the remarks in a small booklet.

At North Tonawanda, Hope-Jones superintended a number of installations, including organs sold to the Baptist Temple (Philadelphia), the Ethical Culture Society (New York), and several theatre installations, including the Vitagraph Theatre (New York), the Crescent Theatre (Brooklyn), the previously-noted Paris Theatre (Denver), the Imperial Theatre (Montreal), and the Pitt Theatre (Pittsburgh), the last of which Hope-Jones considered to be his finest effort, according to George L. Miller in his book, *The Recent Revolution in Organ Building*, 1913.

Despite the enthusiasm of Hope-Jones and the success of his organ installations, the organ division at North Tonawanda ran at a loss from the very outset, a situation which caused much enmity between the two Wurlitzer brothers. Farny and Howard Wurlitzer were not the best of friends anyway, and their business arrangement was one of necessity, not one of choice. Earlier, Farny had dated Grace Keene, Howard's secretary in Cincinnati. After moving to North Tonawanda in early 1909, Farny journeyed back to Cincinnati each weekend to see Grace. Howard learned of the romantic interest and fired Grace on the spot. Grace later became Mrs. Farny Wurlitzer. Howard, perhaps from

fraternal jealousy, seemed to criticize everything that was done at the North Tonawanda plant.

The situation was complicated by Hope-Jones, who continually interfered with the organ production line, making changes and alterations on organs in progress or ready for shipment. The problem became so intense that Hope-Jones was barred from the factory. His contractual salary of $60 per week was still paid, thereby making him an employee of the Wurlitzer Company and preventing him from working elsewhere. He was told that if and when organ manufacturing became profitable he could return. However, during the first two years of operation Wurlitzer lost $200,000 on its organ division.

Still, many organs were made. Opus numbers, or serial numbers, were given to organs beginning in 1911, when two organs were so numbered. In 1912, 15 were produced. Opus No. 18 headed the 1913 listing, which continued until Opus No. 32, the initial entry for 1914. In the meantime, Robert Hope-Jones was becoming increasingly disillusioned. Unable to work on pipe organs, and frustrated with the inability to put in effect many new ideas, he committed suicide in September 1914.

Gradually, the business increased. Opus No. 52, shipped on January 16, 1915, was the first entry for that year and represented an instrument sent to the Panama-Pacific International Exposition in San Francisco. The organ, a Style 3, was displayed at the United States Steel Company exhibit at the fair. Accompanying the instrument were educational exhibits showing the different types of springs, wires, and other steel products used in the organ, as well as an explanation of how the organ operated. A special brochure, *The Evolution of the Organ*, was issued by Wurlitzer for distribution to Exposition visitors.

The last opus entry for 1915 was No. 79. However, more than 79 theatre organs were built in the years before 1916, for the opus list omits some earlier installations. In addition, slightly over 1,000 photoplayers were made in the years prior to 1916, including 13 examples of the Style L, a large instrument with an electropneumatic action, more in the style of a theatre organ than a photoplayer. (The Style L instruments are listed twice in the Wurlitzer records—in the photoplayer lists and catalogues as well as the theatre organ opus list.) Years later, the factory opus list concluded with 2,231, an instrument shipped on November 27, 1939, to South Africa. In 1933, Wurlitzer opened an organ factory in England, in response to a "buy British" campaign mounted by its competitors. Certain components were shipped from North Tonawanda for use in the British organs. Under the direction of Walter Pearce and Major S.J. Wright, the first two organs were installed in the Troxy and Empire theatres, Edmonton.

In comparison to the more than 2,000 organs built by Wurlitzer, the Robert-Morton Organ Company, Wurlitzer's nearest competitor, shipped about 800 theatre organs during its corporate life.

Several years after Hope-Jones' death, pipe organs started bringing in profits to the Wurlitzer Company. By the

ABOVE: Robert Hope-Jones proudly stands with employees of the Hope-Jones Organ Company, Elmira, New York, in this photograph taken shortly before 1910. The firm, despite constant infusions of cash, continually lost money. Subsequently, it was sold to Wurlitzer, and the equipment, many employees, and instruments in process were moved to North Tonawanda, New York.

Robert Hope-Jones

Better music—bigger crowds—greater returns—larger profits

Ocean Grove (N. J.) Auditorium.
Seating 10,000 people.

Superb Baptist Temple,
Philadelphia.

The Paris Theater, Denver.

The Cort Theater, New York.

The Million Dollar Elks' Lodge,
New York.

In Many Famous Theatres and Auditoriums

Everywhere Theaters Are Putting In Wurlitzer Instruments

Look at the newspapers. Watch the announcements of the large theaters being finished. Wurlitzer Music is being installed in all of them. Everywhere the Wurlitzer Orchestra is a success.

The Imperial Theater, at Montreal; the magnificent New Pitt Theater, in Philadelphia—three in Ohio, four in Indiana, two in California, five in New York, etc., etc.—all have installed the wonderful Wurlitzer Orchestra—a complete orchestra, played by one man.

Theater Owners of National Prominence Endorse It

Prominent theater owners, such as WM. A. BRADY, President of the National Association of Theatrical Producing Managers; COHAN AND HARRIS, the well-known New York firm; B. N. SHERWOOD, of the Fitzhugh-Hall Amusement Co., of Rochester, New York; W. A. RODERIC, of the Paris Theater Co., of Denver, and many other theater owners, believe the Wurlitzer instrument to be the theater orchestra of the future. The instruments in the auditoriums shown on this page have performed for thousands of music-loving people and musical critics, and the enthusiasm has been tremendous.

Thirty-three Motion Picture Theaters In Twenty-five Cities
Installed Wurlitzer Music During August Alone

All of the finest, up-to-date Motion Picture Theaters are now beginning to install the Wurlitzer One-Man Orchestra. Thirty-three in thirty days. It must not be overlooked that there are three or four styles specially adapted for their needs. These *vary in cost* according to the size of auditorium and the needs of the theater, but they are all *musically perfect*, a complete orchestra. Because of the variety of musical effects and changes instantly attainable, they alone make a really artistic performance possible. They have attracted large attendance in every theater where they have been installed.

EVERY KNOWN MUSICAL EFFECT ATTAINABLE   **THE RIGHT MUSIC WITH EVERY PICTURE**

TERMS: *The needs of every theatre vary—the conditions in every community are different—our terms are such as to meet them.*

WRITE US TODAY   IT COSTS NOTHING TO INVESTIGATE

The Rudolph Wurlitzer Company

20 BRANCHES   982 Fourth Street, Cincinnati   20 BRANCHES

Wurlitzer advertisement September 1913, in "The Billboard."

Wurlitzer Hope - Jones Unit Orchestra Installed in Germantown Theatre, Germantown, Philadelphia, Pa.

THE Germantown Theatre is recognized as one of the finest picture play houses in Philadelphia, located in Germantown, Philadelphia's most popular suburb. Has a seating capacity of 1,400, and was built at a cost of $12,500. It is devoted to the presentation of Paramount Pictures, and caters to the most fashionable trade in Philadelphia.

Mr. Stuempfig, the Proprietor, has a large collection of letters from people, commenting upon the Unit Orchestra, and requesting special selections. The instrument is featured at every performance by an announcement that a certain selection will be played, and a spot light thrown on the player.

The Wurlitzer organ installed in the Germantown Theatre, Philadelphia, was widely featured in advertisements of the famous organ builder. Presumably, the cost figure of $12,500 given in the above Wurlitzer catalogue description is in error and should have been $125,000. In 1915, the owner of the theatre advised Wurlitzer that vaudeville and other stage acts had been dropped and that entertainment consisted of photoplays and Wurlitzer organ music.

The Wurlitzer Unit Orchestra
Breathes the Very Temperament of the Operator. It Expresses His Every Musical Instinct.

Unlike any other instrument of this character, the tones are effected by the touch of the performers' fingers upon the keys. He can reveal the same sensitive feeling as an artist playing upon a violin, and can control the shades of expression by manipulation of the knee swells, piston pedal and touch upon the action. The artist who plays upon the Wurlitzer Unit Orchestra occupies the same position in the pit of the theatre as the musical director, and so satisfying and realistic is his performance that those sitting out of view of him never question but that it is the playing of a large human orchestra.

Each Unit Being So Wonderfully Tuned and Voiced, the Total Ensemble Represents a Mammoth Orchestra

The Wurlitzer Unit Orchestra is made up of an innumerable number of pipes, stops and appurtenances, located in different parts of the theatre to bring about the desired effect. The strings, flutes, clarionets, etc., are located in the orchestra pit, as are the drums, cymbals, tambourines, xylophone and other so-called percussion instruments. The organ tones are located in another chamber in the theatre; and the harp and larger set of cathedral chimes in still another, the total ensemble giving a majestic foundation of diaphone tones swelling from every side of the proscenium arch.

The instrument is electrically operated by two large motors, and the slightest touch upon the keys causing a pipe no larger than a straw and three-quarters of an inch in length to speak, or pouring an immense pressure of air into the large 32-foot pipes, 32 inches inside diameter. Over two hundred miles of electric wire are used—the whole showing the wonderful magnitude of the Orchestra, and at the same time indicating its simplicity of operation.

PICTURE OF INSIDE OF BEAUTIFUL VITAGRAPH THEATRE
SHOWING POSITION OF THE CONSOLE OF WURLITZER UNIT ORCHESTRA

The Vitagraph Theatre, New York City, made its debut on February 7, 1914, with music provided by a Wurlitzer Hope-Jones Unit Orchestra. A contemporary news account relates that the intended instrument, valued at $35,000, as shown above, was not ready, so a less expensive Style J was substituted temporarily.

W.T ROCK, Prest.

J. STUART BLACKTON, Sec'y.

ALBERT E. SMITH, Treas.

N.Y. OFFICE
MORTON BUILDING
116 NASSAU ST
TEL BEEKMAN 5540

FACTORY:
GENNEVILLIERS
PARIS. FRANCE

FACTORY AND
STUDIOS
E.15TH ST.& LOCUST AVE.
BROOKLYN N.Y.

THE VITAGRAPH COMPANY
OF AMERICA

EXECUTIVE OFFICES
E.15TH ST. & CHESTNUT AVE.
TELEPHONE {6100 / 6101} MIDWOOD.

BRANCHES:
CHICAGO
64 W. RANDOLPH ST.

LONDON. W.C.
15 CECIL COURT
CHARING CROSS ROAD.

PARIS
15. RUE SAINTE - CECILE.

BERLIN
FRIEDRICH STRASSE,236.

CABLE ADDRESS.
"VITAGRAPH"
WESTERN UNION CODE.

Brooklyn, N.Y. April 8th, 1914.

The Rudolph Wurlitzer Co.,
115 - 119 West 40th St.,
New York City.

Gentlemen:-

The wonderful success of the Wurlitzer
Hope-Jones Unit Orchestra, which you installed for
us in the Vitagraph Theatre, Broadway & 44th St.,
New York City, has proven that our judgment was
correct in dispensing with the usual orchestral
accompaniment for Motion Pictures.

We early concluded that an orchestra
could not give the proper atmosphere nor the artistic
accompaniment which we felt our special features demanded. In this instrument, there is no disturbing
element of scratchy string tone or blatant brass
effects, which are usually found in an orchestra.

We have had many favorable comments regarding
the splendid musical accompaniment to suit every action
and mood, whether it be intensely dramatic or comedy.

As the instrument is controlled by one
musician, the effects and changes are made instan-
taneously, which, in our opinion, helps to improve
the picture.

The thanks of the Motion Picture Exhibitor
should be given to the Wurlitzer Company for their in-
itiative and progressiveness in supplying such a wonderful instrument to the public.

Again assuring you of our deep appreciation,
we are,

Yours very truly,

The Vitagraph Company of America

B/B.

VICE-PRESIDENT & SECRETARY

J. Stuart Blackton, a principal of The Vitagraph Company, wrote to Wurlitzer on April 8, 1914, to express appreciation for the Wurlitzer Hope-Jones Unit Orchestra installed in the Vitagraph Theatre.

early 1920s the incoming funds were sufficiently great that the Wurlitzer factory in North Tonawanda was considerably enlarged, and ornately landscaped gardens were planted in front. At the height of the business, Wurlitzer was shipping organs at the rate of nearly one each business day!

Hope-Jones' name was kept in print after his death, and for many years Wurlitzer catalogues referred to the Hope-Jones Unit Orchestra, and organ consoles carried a plate bearing the same inscription. Wurlitzer catalogues paid glowing tributes to his genius, with never a mention of the difficulties which attended the early years of the North Tonawanda operation.

Hope-Jones in History

In the field of pipe organs, the innovations of Robert Hope-Jones lived after him, as did the controversies. By some he was called a charlatan, an imposter, an opportunist, an exploiter of the ideas of others. His admirers considered him to be a genius, the finest mind that the field had ever seen.

"It took over 23 years to accomplish the work that changed the functions of an organ into that of an orchestra, and yet it appears to be very little when we consider for a moment the result," reported *Scientific American* on February 14, 1914. "Thousands have listened to the Wurlitzer Hope-Jones Unit Orchestra night after night at the New York Century Theatre, and the Cort Theatre of Chicago, and in perhaps ten more places in different parts of the country; also orders are said to have been received for many more in a number of states. The inventor of this wonderful instrument is Mr. Robert Hope-Jones, the famous electrician and organ builder of England.

"Mr. Hope-Jones began his experiments as a hobby, and, though it has now become his life work, he still looks upon it with the same fondness as one who does work for sheer pleasure. Naturally, he commenced this work on the organ. He began by placing all the movements in the organ under electrical control. This very soon showed that he could secure an action on the instrument that far exceeded the ordinary movement. But this did not satisfy him. As a musician, he felt that the musical qualities of the organ were not what they might be, and he, therefore, set out to improve them. Very soon he had a new invention that made possible finer quality of tone and larger variety of timbre. This was an apparatus for photographing sound waves in the atmosphere. With photographs of every conceivable instrument and every conceivable variety of tone, it was a comparatively easy matter to reproduce pipes whose notes were, if not exactly identical with those of the original, very near them. And when the percussive instruments that worked in harmony with the organ pipes were added, it enabled the player to absolutely control the expression by hand and foot. It was now possible to reproduce the tones of the very finest musicians, and the control of the instrument and its rapid action permit the operator to produce music such as we associate with the very finest orchestras."

Undoubtedly, many of Hope-Jones' contemporaries in the organ building field were rankled to see him given credit for "placing all the movements in the organ under electrical control," as if no one had thought of it earlier. And, not all organists agreed that the Hope-Jones Unit Orchestra was able to "produce music such as we associate with the very finest orchestras."

Much of the fame given to Hope-Jones in the early days was the result of a book, *The Recent Revolution in Organ Building,* by George Laing Miller. Published in 1909, with a revised edition in 1913, the volume laid credit at Hope-Jones' doorstep for many of the innovations of the era, nearly all of which the author considered to be of great desirability.

Miller had excellent credentials as a classic organist, as a Fellow of the Royal College of Organists, and was vested with numerous other accomplishments, so his words had great impact. Concerning such concepts as unification, the movable console, increased wind pressure, the leathered lip, small-scale strings, and so on, Miller noted:

"Musical men, hearing the new tones and musical effects now produced, realize for the first time the grandeur and refinement and amazing variety of musical effects that the organ is capable of yielding; returning to their own churches they are filled with 'divine discontent,' and they do not rest until the movement for obtaining a new organ, or at least modernizing the old one, is set on foot. The abandonment of old ideas as to limitations of the organ has begun. New ideas are being set up, and a revolution which will sweep the whole country has now obtained firm foothold.

"Until recently, England unquestionably led the development of the organ, and Hope-Jones led England. Now that his genius is at work in this country, who shall set limit to our progress? Even when expressing himself through other friends, his influence entirely altered the standard practice of the leading builders, and now, since direct expression has been obtained, improvements have appeared with even greater rapidity. It is the author's opinion that in the course of the last ten years this country has made such great strides in the art that it may now claim ability to produce organs that are equal to the best of those built in England. And I venture to prophesy that in another ten years American-built organs will be accepted as the world's highest standard.

"At a banquet given in his honor in New York in 1906, the late Alexandre Guilmant complained that no organ he had played in this country possessed majesty of effect. The advent of Hope-Jones has entirely changed the situation. Tertius Noble, late of York Minster, England, who has just come to this country, has searched so that organs can be found here equal to or superior to any built in England, and the celebrated English organist, Edwin Lemare, pronounced the reeds at Ocean Grove, New Jersey, the finest he had ever heard."

In *The Electric Organ,* Reginald Whitworth in 1940 discussed Hope-Jones:

"Few people have received so much blame and so much

The Pitt Theatre, in Pittsburgh, Pennsylvania, was equipped with an early Wurlitzer Hope-Jones Unit Orchestra. Note that the above two advertisements, reproduced from small leaflets, do not mention the Wurlitzer name. The "storm" sequence was undoubtedly inspired by the "Storm Fantasia" which thrilled thousands who came each summer to hear the Hope-Jones Unit Orchestra at the Ocean Grove Municipal Auditorium in New Jersey. The piece showcased the various percussion instruments, bass pipes, and other effects.

The Wurlitzer Hope-Jones Unit Orchestra installation in the Baptist Temple, Philadelphia, Pennsylvania. From a brochure which noted that Wurlitzer: "Invites interested parties to visit its factories at North Tonawanda, N.Y. where the Wurlitzer Hope-Jones organs are built under the direction of the inventor, Mr. Robert Hope-Jones."

praise as Hope-Jones, frequently exaggerated in both directions. Undoubtedly the man was a genius, and in his enthusiasm made some rather wild claims. His many costly experiments cost him and others serious financial loss. In this connection, it is but fair to mention that the late Martin White, of Balruddery, Dundee, came to his assistance on more than one occasion. Undoubtedly, too, in his earlier work he had not sufficient knowledge of the art of organ building proper. He was by profession a telephone engineer, and often the purely electrical part of his action was vastly superior to the pneumatic work. Although some of his organs worked well, and a few are still working well, there were a number of serious defects in this type of action. For instance, the adjustable valve seat was fixed in a wooden block bedded on thick leather, which meant that atmospheric changes upset the action, especially so in view of the fact that the armature valves only worked on a distance of one one-hundredths part of an inch. Then the valves rusted in the 'on' position when the organ was not in use, damp and residual magnetism causing cipherings from time to time; also, the dry cells which were used for the current supply often gave out, rendering the organ dumb."

The work of Robert Hope-Jones elicited sharp criticism from many classic organists as well as organ builders in the traditional idiom. Farny Wurlitzer explained to the author that a large part of this was due to the public's admiration for theatre music:

"A theatre-goer would hear an organist, perhaps one of relatively little training, play the Wurlitzer at a theatre and be impressed with the performance, probably part of the effect being due to watching exciting movies at the same time," Farny Wurlitzer noted. "Then the same movie patron would tell a church organist the following Sunday how much he enjoyed the movie performance at the Bijou. The church organist, who may have had far better training and may have been a far better organist, had his feelings hurt. In that way the Wurlitzer organ gained many enemies. After theatre organs no longer found a ready market, we tried to sell them to churches, but so strong was the feeling against Wurlitzer theatre organs that we were not successful."

This sentiment is evident in many printed sources, including texts published long after the theatre organ era had ended. For example, William Leslie Sumner, in *The Organ*, published in 1953, noted:

"The work of Robert Hope-Jones, a telephone engineer who took up organ building on his own account and later in connection with a number of English and American friends, has been the cause of uncritical encomiums on the one hand and wholesale condemnation on the other. The Hope-Jones organ was a 'one man orchestra' and obviously a poor substitute for muster of orchestral players. New and extreme tone-qualities were added to the instrument, diaphones were used to supply basses of smooth quality and immense power, diapasons were provided with leather lips and blown with high wind pressure so that there was no blend between one rank of pipes and another, and the organ was stripped of the remains of its

crowning glory: its mutations and mixtures." A few pages later in the same book, the author mentions "the evil wrought to the tonal structure of the organ by Robert Hope-Jones on both sides of the Atlantic."

In 1970, William H. Barnes and Edward V. Gammons produced *Two Centuries of American Organ Building,* a book which devoted a chapter to the subject of theatre organs. While a few barbs were directed at Hope-Jones' innovations, the overall tone of the text was positive. "He must be given credit for a great inventive genius because of the astounding number and variety of his contributions to organ building," it was noted. "His work covered tonal as well as mechanical developments. Hope-Jones advocated the use of a limited number of ranks—each one contributing a high measure of power or color to the total organ effect.

"The theatre organ is a collection of powerful, distinctive and colorful voices—almost every one a solo stop. Therefore, chorus and ensemble in the traditional sense are non-existent. Most stops are heavily scaled, and there are seldom mixtures or straight mutations. Ensemble effect in theatre organs is aided by tremulants which help blend widely diverse tone colors... Despite its short lifespan, the theatre organ went through a complete tonal evolution. The very first organs used in theatres were simply 'romantic' church or concert organs combined with the traps and effects found in amusement park band organs. The best of them, the Hope-Jones Unit Orchestra, was the most adaptable to theatre use because it was the most orchestral of the romantic organs used in churches or concert halls and offered the best substitute for the live orchestra in the theatre."

Further, the same authors wrote: "The theatre organ is responsible, at least indirectly, for many valuable and mechanical improvements. When viewed from the standpoint of legitimate tonal organ design, it may be said by some to be a 'total loss'; but, it must be remembered that the theatre organ is not intended to be a church organ, and, therefore, should not be judged in terms of church organ design. Also church organists should keep in mind the fact that undoubtedly many more thousands of people have listened to theatre organs than to church organs. The theatre organ has introduced many people to the joys of organ music who have later developed a taste for the church and concert music. It is a phase of American organ building that is of the past and yet, not quite history to the active present day interests."

Possibly in response to early criticism of Hope-Jones, and certainly as an aid to selling instruments, Wurlitzer solicited the opinions of well-known musicians, many of whom were happy to comply with the request.

In 1914, a Wurlitzer catalogue noted that Hamilton C. MacDougal, professor of music at Wellesley College in Massachusetts, considered Hope-Jones to be "the greatest mind engaged in the art of organ building in this or any other age," while Dr. Varley Roberts, organist of Magdalene College, Oxford, England, stated, "The results Hope-Jones achieves are outstanding."

Walter Henry, a former organist of the Cathedral of St. John the Divine, New York City, stated that a Hope-Jones organ with which he was familiar was "supremely above any other instrument I have ever heard," echoing a somewhat similar statement, "the finest organ in the world—one of the best instruments ever built," given by Madame Schumann-Heink. J.I. Edgewood, a fellow of the Royal Historical Society of Great Britain, stated, "I feel certain that this new instrument will shortly be used in all theatres in place of the usual orchestra," while S. Archer Gibson, a well-known New York society organist, wrote: "I endorse Hope-Jones far and above all the other organ builders." Dr. R. Cresser, organist to His Majesty, the King of England, noted, "your art provides you with the genius of making a small organ contain as much variety as a large cathedral organ."

In the modern era, the factions have made peace with each other, and theatre organs are recognized for what they are—organs imitative of a human orchestra intended to replace live musicians in a theatre. Neither Hope-Jones or anyone else ever suggested that the theatre organ, with its orchestra bells, xylophones, piano, drums, tibia pipes with heavy tremolo, English horn, and other effects, should be used in churches, although Hope-Jones pointed out that some of these devices, such as drums, had been used in certain churches in the past. The romantic attraction of the theatre pipe organ has not faded, and many makers of modern electronic organs have called them "theatre organs" and have adopted such Hope-Jones innovations as the horseshoe console, colored stop tabs, and the like.

While the theatre organ saw its finest hour after the nickelodeon era had ended, it was the nickel theatre, such as the Paris Theatre in Denver, which helped launch it. No one at the Paris Theatre in 1913, or at the nearby Isis Theatre two years later in 1915, could have envisioned that half a century hence, when the Paris and Isis had crumbled to dust and had been forgotten, the glory of Robert Hope-Jones and the thousands of organs which were to bear his name would be regarded with awe and admiration, or that a prominent historian, Ben M. Hall, in the midst of an age of computers and space exploration, would refer to the Wurlitzer organ as "one of the most versatile instruments ever devised by man."

CARYATIDES AND HEADS

APPENDICES

- Recent Developments of Organ Building
- Wurlitzer Theatre Instruments
- Farny Wurlitzer Reminisces

Recent Developments of Organ Building

By Robert Hope-Jones
of North Tonawanda, N.Y.

Being a lecture delivered before the National Association of Organists at the Auditorium, Ocean Grove, N.J., U.S.A. August 6th, 1910 (abbreviated)

Mr. President, Ladies and Gentlemen:

I deem it a privilege to be allowed to address this, the largest association of organists in the world. Some of you have traveled over 3,000 miles to attend these meetings, some have come from countries flying another flag, and it is with diffidence that I presume to occupy your time. Should I speak too much of my own work, pray forgive me. It is difficult to avoid what lies so near to my heart.

Experienced organists are usually conservative. For this there is a reason. Twenty or 30 years ago they approached the comparatively crude instruments of that day and by patient study and incessant practice mastered their manifold difficulties, achieving success and perhaps fame. These gentlemen are not likely now to approve some modification in the organ that will necessitate their unlearning their life-acquired methods and beginning the study of the instrument afresh. How, for instance, could such an artist as Edwin H. Lemare ever advocate the double touch?—a device that your Secretary (Mr. Beebe), a man trained in technique by modern scientific methods, declares presents no difficulty whatever—a device that you younger organ students know will be adopted universally. Mr. Lemare is perhaps the greatest living performer on the old fashioned organ. In his student days almost all organs had very heavy touch and as he was preparing to play these in all parts of the world, he cultivated a touch calculated to break down the resistance of the most stubborn tracker action he might ever meet with in his travel. When one sees him in attempting to play a modern instrument unconsciously hammering the keys to their lowest possible limit—double touch and all!—one can well understand his dictum that double touch is impracticable.

Similar reasons tend to set the experienced organist against well nigh every change introduced—make him in fact ultra-conservative.

Has it ever struck you how almost every improvement has met with determined opposition at the hands of organists?

Within the lifetime of some of us, organs were so tuned that music could be rendered in only a few of the keys. These keys were more perfectly in tune than anything we are now accustomed to but woe betide the musician who by straying into any of the forbidden keys encountered the "wolf."

Who opposed the beneficent change to equal temperament? Some of the leading experienced organists of the day. The great S.S. Wesley insisted on the fine new Willis organ in St. George's Hall, Liverpool (Engl.) being tuned to the old (unequal) temperament.

Willis did succeed in winning over that great musician to his radiating and concave pedal board—but the majority of the leading organists strenuously, and for many years successfully, opposed its introduction. The Royal College of Organists met in solemn conclave and the votes of the "experienced organists" led them to condemn the Willis board. Fortunately Willis had the courage to defy. The younger men—the ris-

ing generation—supported him, and today his pedal board is accepted as the standard in England and America and will be throughout the world.

Sir Walter Parat of St. George's Chapel, Windsor, the Royal Academy of Music, etc., was but one of the majority of the accepted authorities who strenuously opposed the introduction of higher wind pressure. Fortunately some of us were daring enough to ignore the conservatism, with the result that almost all builders are now adopting this great improvement.

The abolition of the absurd "mixture work" so vigorously defended by the older school forms another illustration of the opposition to reform often offered by those who acquired their skill on the old style of organ—whose ears had become vitiated—. Speaking broadly, it was the young men who held up our hands and enabled us to show the world the absurdity of the cherished idea that excessive mixtures were a necessity and a help to musical and effective organ tone.

Twenty odd years ago, when I took up the study of the organ, one frequently found a great organ provided with one double, one 8 foot open diapason, one 8 foot stopped diapason, one 8 foot trumpet, then principal, 12th, 15th, fouriture sesquialtera, cornet and perhaps cymbal, four foundation stops and near twenty ranks of mixture!

In introducing the first really small scale keen string tone in my organ in Worcester Cathedral, England, some 15 years ago, I encountered strenuous opposition. The Precentor of the Cathedral, that gifted musician, the late Canon Woodward, required me to disconnect these stops from the combination pistons so as to remove any temptation to use them when accompanying the choir! The majority of older organists protested against the introduction of such tones as "unchurchly," "foreign to the spirit of the organ," etc. Even today a few have hardly given up the erroneous assertion that these keen and strongly marked tone colors "do not blend." This organ (the Hope-Jones "unit organ" in the Auditorium, Ocean Grove, N.J.) contains the thinnest and most pungent orchestral oboe ever made and perhaps the keenest strings, and you have all heard how perfectly its various tone colors unite (applause)—I recall with a smile how one listener to the keen strings in my organ at St. Lukes, Montclair, (which is played by your gifted President, Mr. Mark Andrews) first condemned the strings as utterly unmusical and impossible of blend—some months later spoke of them as agreeable when the swell box was closed but unpleasant when open—and some months later still had the nearest imitation procurable inserted in an organ in which he was interested.

It is fortunate indeed for the art that some of us have been bold enough to brave the opposition of the great ones and insist upon introducing these new tone colors, till at last conservative prejudice is disappearing in their favor and the organ is becoming a more interesting and musical instrument.

Similar remarks apply to the new keen orchestral reeds and other extreme tone colors.

We have just read in The New Music Review from an authority of the older school, (Mr. E.H. Lemare) that the arrangement you see here of

inclining the various keyboards so that they meet the fingers naturally, is wrong.

An hour ago Mr. McClellan, the gifted concert organist, (who has traveled from the Mormon Tabernacle at Salt Lake City on purpose to attend this convention) declared it to be right; and as I notice you younger organists are unanimous in its favor I predict it will be universally adopted before long. Already that progressive firm the Austin Organ Company, supplies inclined keyboards—so does Willis of England.

Another reform spoken against by the older and more conservative organists is the enclosure of all the pipes of every organ in swell boxes.

Another is the introduction of a percussion department into the organ.

The "suitable bass," "pizzicato touch," "unit organ," each meet vigorous opposition from many members of the older school.

The introduction of the balanced swell pedal was so strenuously fought by many of those whose practice was done on instruments having the old self-closing pump handle device, that (despite Lemare's efforts to the contrary) it is but little used in England to this day.

I beg you gentlemen to bear these matters in mind and beware of the danger that besets us all of becoming fossilized—ultra conservative—much power lies in your hands. I plead with you to condemn nothing in ignorance. Test long, deliberately and thoroughly. Take the opinions of the younger men into consideration—then, decide and your opinion will not be likely to prove a hindrance to advancement of the art of organ building.

I do not forget that there is danger in departing too freely from accepted traditions and to this I especially should pay heed, for I have been publicly accused of being the author of nine-tenths of the innovations introduced during the last twenty years. The accusation is, I fear, true—but do not let us be alarmed. Of all the new things we various organ builders bring out, only the fittest will survive.

You, gentlemen, will be the judges. All we ask is that you will make allowance for your natural tendency to condemn that which is different from that you have so laboriously learned to use.

Some there are who cry out for standardization. "It matters little what pattern is selected, provided all consoles are similar." "All pianos are alike, why not all organs."

Before it was standardized, the piano went through a long period of evolution. It was of varied compass—had sometimes one, sometimes two or even three keyboards. The keys were of various lengths, of various widths and compass. Sometimes the naturals were black and the sharps white; sometimes mother of pearl was used and they were neither one nor the other. When evolution had run its course the piano standardized itself; the same will certainly happen in the case of the organ. The evolution is still in progress and must not be frustrated or cramped by premature efforts at standardization. Already, many points are settled and accepted by all. C.C. and 61 note compass for the manuals; radiating and concave pedal board; balanced swell pedals, etc., etc.

We poor organists must put up with the terrible handicap of want of uniformity for some time longer—for the sake of posterity. One thing we

193

may, however, reasonably ask for at once, and that is that all consoles be made adjustable, as this one is. You see that by a pull or push I can instantly move the keys to any relative positions; also that I can raise or lower the seat. Organists are of different size and build, and there is no reason why consoles cannot be made adjustable so as to suit all. The cost is trivial. (Applause.)

Let us now consider a few of the "recent developments of organ building."

Expression: Until the year 1731, when Jordan invented the swell box, every organ stop was entirely devoid of expressive power. Since then it has become the practice to enclose the pipes of the swell and of the choir organ in wood boxes which modify the power of tone to a small extent.

It is not obvious that every stop and every pipe of every organ should, as a matter of course, be enclosed? For some years now I have never built an organ on any other plan, and I opine that the plan must eventually be universally adopted.

What would we think of the orchestral conductor who said, "You double basses, trombones, bass tubas, etc., represent the pedal organ. You must never play with expression. Always either play at full power or stop playing altogether. You strings represent the diapason tone of the great organ. You also must either play full power or stop altogether. The flutes, clarinets and oboes will put in the expression."

Could you tolerate an orchestra played in this manner? No—Yet you not only tolerate it in the organ, but many of you strongly oppose the introduction to this reform.

Gentlemen, your ears are vitiated. You can not bear to hear the power of the pedal tone rise and fall in sympathy with that of the manuals. Simply because for a score or two score years you have always heard pedal tone, expressionless. When a man who has long played on a concave pedal board chances to use a flat one he feels that it is not merely flat but actually convex. So you gentlemen when for the first time you hear the pedals expressive think that such expression is exaggerated.

In this organ that we are examining, all stops are enclosed but one—the diaphone—that stop was not included in the original contract but was ordered at a later date, after the swell boxes had been made. The stop would be ten times as useful as it is, were it but enclosed and rendered expressive.

In these organs I build, the swell shutters are located immediately over the open ends of the pipes so that when they are opened the tone passes straight upward into the building without any impediment.

Swell boxes should not be made of wood. Though this be the cheapest material, it is about the worst that could be selected. It is light and is a most excellent conductor of sound. By using a cement construction I am able to obtain vastly superior results. A cement box when closed with my patent aluminum vacuum shutters, with sound trap joint, will reduce the power of any stop many thousand percent.

Listen to this smooth 16 foot tuba voiced on 50 inches of wind. With the box open it gives more tone than the whole of any 60 stop organ you can name—yet with the box closed it is soft enough to form agreeable accompaniment to a child's voice in solo. This was made two and a half years ago. Those made today are far more efficient.

With sound trap boxes of this kind the costly

necessity for putting soft stops in an organ disappears. Every stop may be powerful when its box is open; for we know that closing its shutters reduces the power of the largest open diapason below that of the softest dulciana or aeoline. What a saving in space and cost this effects.

Listen to the tremendous crescendo obtainable from these three stops—32 foot diaphone, 16 foot tuba, 16 foot tromba, with octave couplers. (Applause.) Is it exaggerating to say that no organ of 60 stops produces such a majestic, brilliant and well balanced effect? (Applause.)

Now having secured such wonderful results from our swell boxes, it is essential the organist shall always know and be able instantly to control the positions of the various sets of swell shutters. For this purpose you will see each pedal has connected with it, an indicator key, fixed on the lower edge of the music deck. As the shutters are opened this indicator key descends. Observe closely and you will see that this key is electrically sensitive so that the slightest touch on its upper or lower surface results in its being moved and carrying with it the swell pedal and the shutters connected therewith. The organist has therefore the power of moving his shutters into any position, either by foot or finger, and he is always aware of the position in which he has left them.

At the extreme right you see an extra swell pedal with its indicator and controlling key. This is termed the "general" pedal—normally this "general" pedal does nothing, but by means of these couplers we can cause it to operate any one, any selection or all of the swell pedals.

High Pressures: In spite of continued opposition in certain quarters, it must be growing clear to all of you that the old order of things has passed and that the organ of the future will be a high pressure instrument. When taking up organ building some twenty years ago, I found high pressures practically unknown save for the "tuba" stop in some very large instruments. Now most of the organists have relinquished opposition and all progressive builders are adopting the new practice. Twenty years ago a pressure sufficient to lift a column of water three or three and a half inches was practically universal. In this organ before you the pressures employed are ten inches, twenty-five inches and fifty inches. You deem this reed voiced on twenty-five inches one of unusual refinement and grandeur (applause)—but listen to the superior tone quality of this one voiced on fifty (applause). Listen again to this soft and smooth "oboe horn." It is voiced on twenty-five inches (applause.) If you will be very still you will hear that I am, and have for sometime been, playing on a "vox humana" of unusual delicacy. It is voiced on ten inches. A good vocalist employs a pressure of fifty inches and over, why then should we be afraid of it in the organ—only let us beware that like the good vocalist we use this increased pressure to obtain greater refinement not increased power of tone. Power will take care of itself.

The leathered lip for flue pipes and the "pneumatic blow" to strike reed tongues that would otherwise prove too thick to start promptly enable us to secure increased refinement from increased pressure.

It takes (approximately) no more power to deliver 500 cubic feet of wind at ten inch pressure than 1,000 at five, so that suggestion of increased cost is erroneous.

Let me beg you to assist us who are at the head of this reform in organ building by your artistic

self restraint. Some few of the performances given here have been ludicrous and damaging to the cause. Having multiplied the powers and range of expression twenty-fold you must use them with care and discretion.

Action (Patent)

Not in one organ in a thousand is the action free from fault. In none of the cheap forms of windchests having round pallets, is it possible to produce absolutely sympathetic response and connection between the finger of the player and the pipes. Your secretary—Mr. Chester H. Beebe and some others who have studied this subject are alive to the tremendous musical revolution that is starting from the admission of the organ into the class of instruments that are sensitive to the finest touch of the finger. Nine-tenths of you do not know what I mean. You are blinded by long use and cannot realize that the action of the organ you play is defective. But ladies and gentlemen, I assure you a great awakening is beginning and it is raising the organ to the rank of a "truly musical instrument." A few years ago hardly an organist could be found to share this faith—now hundreds have been converted and each month sees the number increase.

Diaphone (Patent)

The basis of this organ we have been examining is the diaphone. It is the most powerful foundation stop in the instrument. This particular diaphone resembles a diapason in tone quality, but many distinct colors of tone can be produced from a diaphone. This one that I hold in my hand is a diaphonic flute. It consists, as you see, of a small aluminum piston which rapidly and freely vibrates in an enclosing cylinder. Though the whole thing is scarcely larger than my two fists it would (if supplied with air of sufficient pressure) produce a sweet musical note that could be heard twenty miles away. You three gentlemen who have come to this meeting from Toronto, where one is used by the Canadian government on the harbor, know that I should not exaggerate if I said thirty miles. The diaphone will play an important part in the organ of the future. Its possibilities have not as yet been fully explored. Sectional drawings of the instrument are given in some of the more recent text books on the organ, such as Miller's *Recent Revolution in Organ Building,* Chas. Francis Press, New York; *Wedgwood's Dictionary of Organ Stops,* Vincent Music Co., London, England, etc.

Unit Organ (Patent)

This Ocean Grove instrument is a 'Unit Organ,' though from the limitation in funds, necessarily a skeleton one. Months before its completion the "Unit Organ" had developed on the following published lines.

The old departments of Pedal, Great, Swell, Choir and Solo are abandoned in favor of Foundation, String, Woodwind, Brass, and Percussion departments. Each of these latter is enclosed in its own independent cement swell box. The whole organ is treated as a unit. Practically any of the stops may be drawn upon any of the manuals (or on the pedal) at any pitch.

The Foundation department contains the diaphone; the tibias, and two or three diapasons, The String department contains a couple of mild and robust gambas, two or three very keen viol d'orchestres, a quintaton flute for furnishing the deep body tone often heard in strings, a vox humana celeste, and perhaps my new vox Viola—in fact any stops that go to make up a thrilling mass of "live" string tone.

The Woodwind department contains the oboe, orchestral oboe, clarinet, cor anglais, kinura, concert flutes, etc.

The Brass department contains the trombones, trumpets and tubas.

The Percussion department embraces the tympani, drums, triangle, glockenspiel, chimes, etc.

A set of stop keys representing all or most of these stops, at various pitches, is provided in connection with the great manual. Another set is provided in connection with the swell; another in connection with the choir, another with the solo, and another with the pedal. By their means any selection of the stops from the various departments may be freely drawn and mixed on any keyboard quite independently of what may at the same time be in use on the other keyboards.

By means of this radical departure from the old and accepted style of organ building we gain immensely in flexibility and in tonal resources, and we save much money.

Because of limited funds this organ has but 14 stops. It is easily the most powerful instrument in the world, and I fancy it would be difficult to find any fifty stop organ giving equal variety of effect (applause). Far otherwise would it have been had those 14 stops been distributed in the usual way, say 3 on the great, 3 on swell, 3 on choir, 3 on solo, and 2 on the pedal. How could recitals have been given on such an instrument as this?

This auditorium seats ten thousand people and is a mere shell made of thin matchboarding. The greater part of the organ tone immediately passes through and is lost. Had the few thousand dollars available been expended upon obtaining say thirty stops of the type used in ordinary organs of larger dimensions, a complete failure would have resulted. It was felt that very large scales, great weight, and heavy wind were essential. Such stops are of course expensive. The small funds provided furnished only fourteen of them. Electric switches for transferring stops from one manual to another do not cost five dollars apiece, so at the cost of less that $500 we were able to adopt the "Unit Organ" principle. As a result we have from these fourteen stops a four manual organ upon which several of the greatest organists have given most enjoyable recitals (applause). The "Unit Organ" is the simplest possible form of instrument and the least costly when judged by results.

It may not be foolproof but in the hands of an organist of any musical feeling, its tones will always be well balanced. For instance, if the large 8 foot diapason be drawn on the great, and a 16 foot or 4 foot diapason is to be added, one will naturally select one or both of the smaller diapasons for the purpose. The relative strength of 16, 8, 4 and 2 foot tone can be graded to suit the particular effect it is desired to produce etc., etc.

I have been asked to reply to criticism of the "Unit Organ" published in the present issue of the New Music Review, but will not take up your time. In the first place the writer shows fundamental misconceptions of the instrument and in the second he is so entirely and utterly impregnated with the style of instrument he has struggled with from his youth as to be incapable of shifting his point of view.

Of ten organs that I build scarcely one is a Unit Organ. I consider it the organ of the future, rather than that of the present—An instrument for progressive organists rather than for those who have become wedded to the old order. I see

that, unknown to me, your president, Mr. Mark Andrews, has just publicly stated:

"I consider the Ocean Grove organ to be the most remarkable instrument I have played. The possibilities of variety and flexibility of tone are well nigh endless, and I have been more and more interested in it every day. The instrument is particularly effective in the performance of orchestral transcription."

Mr. Ferdinand Dunkley, the well known concert organist and composer, writes of a Unit Organ:

"Though containing only ten extended stops, it has more variety of tone, sweet, delicate and beautiful or thundering and majestic, as you may wish, than an organ of sixty built on the old fashioned lines—but no organ however large of the old style could ever compare with it in powers of expression.

"With your 'unit' system and four cement swell boxes, you have given me a more beautiful organ that could have been obtained from any other builder for three times as much money."

Mr. Tali Esen Morgan, concert master and conductor, of New York, writes:

"The great Unit Organ in the Ocean Grove Auditorium, built by Mr. Hope-Jones, is an unqualified success and has been pronounced by hundreds of organists from all parts of the world to be one of the greatest organs ever built."

Mr. A.T. Webster, conductor of the Buffalo Music Festivals, writes:

"I am convinced that the Unit system in large organs is a very great advantage. Few pipes, built on large scales, heavily winded and enclosed in practically sound-proof boxes, according to their families—foundation, string, woodwind or brass—this brings into the range of possibilities, effects hitherto unknown in organ playing. Furthermore it should be greatly easier to keep such an organ in tune."

We see therefore that the "Unit Organ" principle will receive consideration at the hands of the rising generation of organists.

Suitable Bass (Patent)

A performer on the organ has so much more to think of and do than he can accomplish without distracting his attention from the music he is rendering, that no chance of helping him should be ignored. He should always have pistons or pedals giving him independent control of the pedal organ stops and couplers, but the automatic "Suitable Bass" attachment in addition to these will save him an immense amount of thought and unnecessary work. On each keyboard there is provided a double touch tablet or piston labeled "Suitable bass." Upon touching this tablet the pedal stops and couplers instantly group themselves as to provide a bass that is suitable to the stops at the moment in use upon that particular manual. If the tablet be pressed much more firmly it will become locked down and then the pedal stops and couplers will continue to move automatically so as to keep the bass suited to that particular manual, whatever changes may be made in registration. This locked suitable bass tablet will release itself the moment the performer touches any of the pedals, stops or couplers by hand or touches the suitable bass tablet belonging to any other manual.

All the combination pistons in the Unit Organ are provided with double touch. The first touch moves the manual stops only, but a much firmer touch will provide the suitable bass for the particular combination in use. (Patent) This

Suitable Bass device is condemned by the writer in New Music Review, but is described by your president, who has used it for years, as "The greatest help given to the organist since the introduction of combination pedals." (Applause.)

Double Touch

In the Unit Organ all keys and pedals are provided with double touch. The first touch is an ordinary or normal one and the key is brought to rest against an apparently solid bottom in the usual way. When, however, great extra pressure is used the key will suddenly give way again about a sixteenth of an inch and a strengthening of tone, either of the same or of another quality, will be brought into play. The second touch on the pedal organ is used to control the tympani, drums, triangle, etc. Second touch can be shut off from both manuals and pedals when not required.

Combination Control

Whether the stops of an organ should be under the control of combination pistons placed below the manual they affect, or of combination keys placed just above the manual, is much debated. The thumb has a longer range than the fingers and can readily reach pistons placed underneath; but it has to grope in the dark, as it were, for these pistons are not so easily seen as are the combination keys. An expression of opinion from you, ladies and gentlemen, upon this point will be appreciated.

It is my practice to fit ten combination keys or pistons to each manual, whether the organ be large or small. Seven of these are arranged to be "graded" from p.p. to f.f.f., and three of them are "free" for special combinations. All these combination keys or pistons are adjustable from the keyboards so that the organist can alter his combinations at a moment's notice—even whilst playing. All the combination keys or pistons have double touch, so that a suitable bass can be obtained when desired, simply by pressing the movement much more firmly. Five toe pistons are provided for giving independent control of the pedal organ and five for governing the entire organ, including couplers and tremulants.

All these contrivances of course visibly move the stop keys and stop knobs. It is hoped that the absurd plan of altering the tone without moving the stop knobs is at death's door. The Canadian builder, Casavant, has often been advance of his confreres in this matter.

Reed Tuning Devices (Patent)

The old idea that reeds are unreliable and need frequent tuning must be abandoned. You see here thick reed tongues that are once and for all screwed into place and tune—no tuning wires are provided. The reeds stand in tune as well as the flue pipes.

Temperature Troubles

In the organs I build all pipes are enclosed in cement boxes and thermostats and tiny electric radiators insure temperatures always being equal. The organs are in tune at all times, whether the church be warm or cold.

Slanting Keyboards

You will notice that the great organ keys are level, because in playing upon them the forearm is level. But when playing on the swell the forearm inclines upward, therefore the swell keys are made to slope upward at the same angle. For a similar reason the solo keys slope at a greater angle, and the stop keys at a greater angle still. On the other hand, the choir keys incline slightly in the other direction. This is without question the natural arrangement and in the opinion of the great majority of you, will become universally adopted—despite the opposition to be expected from those who cannot shake off old methods. (Applause.) The idea that the fingers may be cramped is founded upon a misconception.

Pizzicato Touch (Patent)

The Pizzicato Touch was first used in the organ I rebuilt about the year 1895 for Mr. J. Martin White, Balruddery, Dundee, Scotland. I have put up several examples in this country; and am now incorporating it into all organs I build—though, unfortunately, funds did not permit of its being introduced into this Ocean Grove organ. It yields many effects that are truly beautiful and musical—and others that may best be described as curious.

It is generally applied to the couplers. Let us draw the swell to great coupler at Pizzicato Touch and have a diapason speaking on the great and an eight foot flute on the swell. If now we strike a chord on the great keys the swell also will speak at the moment of striking, but will instantly become silent again, leaving the great diapason alone to sustain the chord. The percussion effect thus produced is at times valuable. By the employment of contrasts in tone and pitch between great and swell more marked effects are furnished.

Percussion Department

In the organ I constructed in St. John's Church, Birkenhead, England, in 1888, I introduced a bass drum and used it frequently in accompanying the church services. I escaped ostracism at the hands of my English friends only because I made the drum so soft and refined that few of them knew it was there, though they felt the charm of its rhythm and attack. I soon grew bolder and introduced chimes, etc. I am now courageous enough to say that every concert organ should have a percussion department of equal importance to any of the other departments. The continuous manual tones that can be produced by percussion are of great beauty, and are of as much use in what has been spoken of as "legitimate organ music" as in orchestral transcriptions. A complete octave of "tympani" is a valuable addition to any organ and is not costly.

Vowel Cavities

These, used in connection with reed stops, are of great value in securing new tone colors. Here is a kinura pipe that gives a small plaintive, wailing tone. By placing one or other of these vowel cavities above it I can entirely alter its tone and make it sing ah, eh, e, i, o, or u. You hear this altogether unusual orchestral oboe in this organ. Its effect is due to a vowel cavity on each pipe, governed by a sliding stopper. I commend this subject to my brother organ builders as a fruitful field for investigation.

Reflectors

Will play an important part in the organ of the future—not only do they solve many architectural problems, but when rightly used they lend poetry to the music. This organ, as you know, is located 20 or 30 feet below where you sit, and its tone is directed into the auditorium by reflec-

tors made of cement. If placed in the hall it would have left no room for the chorus.

Robust Reliability

None need fear for an organ of this simple type, enclosed in cement chambers—such instruments can be set out of doors in public parks or private gardens and may be relied upon summer or winter. This great auditorium is a mere shell constructed of thin boards. It is located on the shore of the Atlantic and is devoid of heating plant.

Next month a tarpaulin will be thrown over the console and the place will be abandoned to the mists, storms and fogs till next summer. The organ has already stood two winters and the iron screws used in its construction are still bright.

The Sphere of the Organ

No one who has heard the organs I built for the great English churches and cathedrals will accuse me of detracting from the dignity of the church organ, or deny that my influence has been entirely in the other direction—the suppression of excessive mixtures and other trivial stops, the provision of fuller diapasons, smoother reeds and more dignified pedal tone. I, however, frankly declare myself in favor of the bold introduction of the organ into the secular field as well.

With the advantage of these great powers of flexibility and expression that I have described and with the new range of tone colors now available, there is no reason why the instrument shall not be modified and introduced freely into public halls, theatres, hotels, restaurants, parks and other pleasure resorts—in fact, I am at the moment building several such instruments.

But, gentlemen, if we are going to do this we must frankly set on one side all our conservatism—all our traditions born of church use and we must approach the modified organ as a new instrument. We have heard much said against "degrading the organ" and "prostituting our art"—I cannot see the matter in this light. Such remarks are indeed forceful when applied to the church organ; but I fail to see their applicability to a new instrument avowedly designed for amusing a large section of the public. This public will have light and popular music, and if any of you organists are minded to meet the demand and have an instrument to enable you to do so, I fail to see that you thereby hinder yourselves from performing the highest classical compositions on the church organ when the proper times and seasons arrive.

Our president, Mr. Mark Andrews, has thrown us into fits of laughter by the funny "stunts" he performs on the piano. After turning to this lighter music for a few moments, is he less able to thrill us with the dignity of a Bach fugue or Rheinberger sonata played on the organ?

"Degrading our art" indeed! Let me tell you that there is scope for the exercise of the highest art any of you can bring to bear, in rendering effectively good popular compositions on the new orchestral organ or "Unit Orchestra" as I prefer to call it. If any of you will successfully study this new art I can promise you will not lack remunerative employment. I am asked to provide a performer for the instrument that will be completed this winter at the Statler Hotel, Buffa-

lo, and I cannot find a man with sufficient flexibility to allow to his throwing to the winds all church organ traditions—with sufficient knowledge of orchestration—with sufficient musical feeling and with high enough technique. I have other posts of the kind to fill at salaries ranging from $2500 to over $5000 per year, but where are the men to fill them? Are the members of this Association going to ignore this new field and enjoy smug satisfaction in having resisted the temptation to degrade their art? Or are some of them going to make a serious study and endeavor to fit themselves for such service?

I have heard the overture to William Tell played by excellent orchestras; but neither I nor the friends who were present will ever forget the pleasure, the thrill, the enthusiasm aroused here last fall, when that overture was played to us on this organ by S. Archer Gibson.

Many have found fault with Ocean Grove's musical director, Mr. Tali Esen Morgan, for "debasing the organ" and allowing Mr. Clarence Reynolds to compose and render daily his Storm Fantasia. They say that it is the mission of the organist to "elevate the people." I ask how the people are to be elevated by the performance of a faultless classical program when they remain on the boardwalk and leave the auditorium empty, save for a handful of people whose tastes are already elevated. No! Morgan is right—he first draws thousands of people into the auditorium by giving "The Storm" fantasia (which, by the way, contains much that is elevating) and then awakens such a love of music and of the organ that many of them are seen next day paying their 25 cents to hear the regular recital which precedes the Storm. If you are going to raise the people, you must first get your arms around and underneath them.

I doubt if there is anyone here present who enjoys the work of Bach, when played with grand unemotional dignity, more than I do. Yet I think that Mr. Morgan and Mr. Reynolds have rendered a great service by awakening in the hearts of thousands and thousands of people a renewed and increased love of music through the medium of their joint composition "The Storm." It is perhaps forgotten that such composers as Beethoven, Mendelssohn, Rossini, Lemmens, Neukomn and others have done their best to depict a storm through the agency of music. Judged from the result of efficiency I doubt whether any of these compositions will compare with the storms played on this organ last year by Mr. Will C. MacFarlane and this year by Mr. Clarence Reynolds.

Each city of 30,000 inhabitants or more will shortly have its great organ in a public hall and will provide, for five or ten cents, daily feasts of popular and good music to gratify, amuse and uplift its citizens. Mr. Morgan has proved in this very auditorium during two summer seasons that brilliant financial success attends such an effort if rightly directed.

Not many decades hence there will be more organs in hotels, theatres, restaurants, parks and seashore resorts than are today to be found in churches and the chief instrument in every orchestra will be the orchestral Unit Organ.

I thank you, Mr. President, Ladies and Gentlemen for your patience and your courtesy. (Applause.)

Wurlitzer Theatre Instruments

The following is a listing of Wurlitzer photoplayers and theatre (mainly) pipe organs shipped from 1911 through 1915 inclusive, as taken from Wurlitzer factory records, supplemented by information provided by David L. Junchen. The dates, when shown, are shipping dates. This list, which includes only the nickelodeon era, is part of a much longer list comprising over 2,000 organs made through the late 1930s.

Photoplayers

Style F photoplayer. Piano with side cabinet containing percussion and novelty effects. Uses Wurlitzer 65-Note Automatic Player Piano rolls. Sold for $950 in 1915. 1913 54 shipped; 1914 30; 1915 26; 156 total sold through 1921.

Style G photoplayer. Piano with single side cabinet containing violin and flute pipes, percussion and novelty effects. Uses Wurlitzer 65-Note Automatic Player Piano rolls. Introduced by 1912, during which year many were sold; however, 1912 production records have not been seen by the author. In 1912, these units were referred to as Piano Orchestras. Later, the One Man Orchestra name was employed for this and other models. 1913 176 shipped; 1914 222; 1915 119; total 708 shipped from 1913 to 1926.

Style O photoplayer. Piano with two side chests containing violin and flute pipes (including bass pipes), drums and novelty effects. Uses Wurlitzer 65-Note Automatic Player Piano rolls. 82 sold in 1915 (474 eventually made through 1927). Style YO, using 88-note home player piano rolls, was made to the extent of 5 units in 1915 (100 eventually made through 1924).

Style R photoplayer. Piano with single very large side chest containing several ranks of pipes, percussion and novelty effects. Uses Concert PianOrchestra rolls. 1913 2 shipped; 1914 54; 1915 8; apparently made only from 1913 through 1915, during which period 64 were produced.

Style U photoplayer. Piano with two large side chests containing extended ranks of bass and flute pipes, orchestra bells, percussion and novelty effects. Uses Wurlitzer Concert PianOrchestra rolls. In 1915 64 were shipped (from 1915 through 1927 a total of 171 were made).

Style H photoplayer. Piano with two large side chests containing three ranks of pipes, including bass pipes, orchestra bells, percussion and novelty effects. Uses Wurlitzer Concert PianOrchestra rolls. In 1915 the Style H sold for $3500. 1913 35 shipped; 1914 16; 1915 5; total of 63 made through 1919. Style YH, using 88-note home player piano rolls, was made to the extent of 3 examples, 1 in 1912 and 2 in 1919.

Style K photoplayer. Similar to the Style H, but with vox humana pipes and xylophone. The largest of the regular pit instruments. Sold for $4500 in 1915. 1913 42 shipped; 1914 67; 1915 43; total of 293 made through 1927. One example of the Style YK, using 88-note home player piano rolls, was made in 1915, and 30 totally were made through 1924.

Theatre Organs

Style L theatre organ. Two manuals, 6 ranks. Piano console with Wurlitzer Concert PianOrchestra roll mechanism, attached by an electric cable to a large chest fronted with display pipes and containing pipes, xylophone, bells, percussion, and various novelty effects. In 1915 these units listed for $7,500. 1913 7 shipped; 1914 3; 1915 3; 14 units totally made through 1916. The Style L was listed among photoplayers in several Wurlitzer catalogues.

Style J theatre organ. Two manuals, 7 ranks. Somewhat similar to the Style L as preceding, but some models used Wurlitzer Concert Organ rolls. The Style J was listed among photoplayers in several Wurlitzer catalogues.

Styles L and J were roll operated and used Concert PianOrchestra or Wurlitzer Concert Organ rolls. It is believed that many if not most of examples of styles M (2 manuals, 4 ranks), N (2 manuals, 7 ranks), and V (2 manuals, 8 ranks) were roll operated. The listing of the Style L units in the following enumeration duplicates that given in the earlier paragraph describing this style.

Styles 1 through 6 are early models of the Wurlitzer Hope-Jones Unit Orchestra, with Style 3 being one of the most widely advertised. Style 1 was a 2 manual, 4 rank instrument; Style 3 was a 2 manual, 7 rank instrument; Style 4 was a 2 manual, 8 rank instrument; and Style 6 was a 3 manual, 13 rank instrument. Style 35, the largest of the regular models shown in the following listing, was a 3 manual, 15 rank instrument. "Special" styles differed from the regular specifications, sometimes only slightly. Rebuilt units represent earlier instruments brought back to the North Tonawanda factory, rebuilt, and shipped to new locations. In numerous instances, organs were repossessed and sold to new owners. Listed here are early models. In later years, Wurlitzer produced many other styles as well.

Wurlitzer theatre organ shipping list. The following opus numbers are from the Wurlitzer factory shipping list. Each listing includes the opus number, the style, the name of the theatre or buyer (when known), the destination, and the shipping date.

Opus No. 1. Special house organ of 2 manuals, 5 ranks. Dr. Woodward residence. Philadelphia, Pennsylvania. 1911. Cost $6,662.

Opus No. 2. Style 6. Cort Theatre. Chicago, Illinois. 1911.

Opus No. 3. Special model. Hotel Martinique. New York, New York. The pipes and percussion effects were housed in a large freestanding wooden cabinet. Wurlitzer issued a special brochure featuring this installation. Moved in 1919 to the Burland Theatre, New York, New York.

Opus No. 4. Style 6. Century Theatre. New York, New York. 1912. Later repossessed. See Opus 33.

Opus No. 5. "Style A Woodwind Orchestra." 1912.

Opus No. 6. Style J. Philadelphia, Pennsylvania. 1912. Equipped with tubular pneumatic action. Cost $4,000. Later electrified and shipped to Cincinnati. Installed in the Franklin Theatre, Philadelphia, this "Style J" consisted of a central piano unit flanked by two wooden cabinets, each faced with dummy pipes—similar to one version of the later styles H and K.

Opus No. 7. Style J. Kansas City, Missouri. 1912. Equipped with 75-note player mechanism. Exhibited at the Chicago Moving Picture Convention, then sent to Kansas City, where it was installed in the Maze Theatre.

Opus No. 8. Style M. Ideal Theatre, Louisville, Kentucky. 1912. Equipped with 88-note player. Exhibited at the Chicago Moving Picture Convention, then sent to Louisville. Later moved to New York.

Opus No. 9. Style 3. Tremont Theatre. Bronx, New York. 1912. Cost $10,000. On August 24, 1915, Samuel H. Trigger, proprietor of the Tremont, wrote to Wurlitzer: "After using the Wurlitzer Hope-Jones Unit Orchestra for a period of over three years every day with our pictures, we wish to say that we have found this instrument to be a wonderful help to the pictures and to our business. It has practically paid for itself many times over, and we feel certain that the manager or owners of a theatre would never make a mistake by purchasing one of these instruments. The music which it furnishes is quite superior to that of a 15 or 20 piece orchestra, and in addition to that there is a large pipe organ of ample volume, and as it can be used for all purposes, including accompanying vaudeville acts, we do not hesitate for one moment to recommend it highly to all people who are considering it for their theatre. It has given us very little trouble and from a mechanical standpoint is satisfactory. We are very much pleased with our purchase and certainly assure you of any other business when we are considering instruments for other theatres." Located on Webster Avenue between 177th and 178th streets, the theatre seated 1,100 people and was said to be the second theatre in New York to install a Hope-Jones Unit Orchestra. This "immediately built up its formerly lagging attendance and kept the theatre alive in the face of strenuous competition," a Wurlitzer catalogue noted. "With the assistance of the Wurlitzer Hope-Jones Unit Orchestra, the management was enabled to change the theatre from a stock and vaudeville house to pictures exclusively." The console was located in the orchestra pit under the screen, while the pipes and other effects were in a large furniture-style cabinet fronted with display pipes, mounted on a balcony on the side of the theatre to the right of the screen.

Opus No. 10. Style 3. New York Children's Theatre. New York, New York. 1912. Cost $10,000. Repossessed. Sold in 1913, also for $10,000, to the Montclair Theatre, Montclair, New Jersey.

Opus No. 11. Style 3. Wurlitzer store. Chicago, Illinois. Later moved to Cincinnati, Ohio.

Opus No. 12. Style 3. Shipped to Philadelphia in 1912. Sold to the Germantown Theatre, Philadelphia, Pennsylvania, 1913, for $10,000. The organ in the Germantown Theatre played for years and attracted wide admiration. According to a Wurlitzer catalogue, "Mr. Stuempfig, the proprietor, has a large collection of letters from people, commenting upon the Unit Orchestra and requesting special selections. The instrument is featured at every performance by an announcement that a certain selection will be played, and the spotlight thrown on the player."

Opus No. 13. Style J. Chicago, Illinois. 1912. Cost $4,900. Repossessed.

Opus No. 14. Style J. Used in a skating rink in Syracuse, New York. 1912. Cost $6,000, less $1,000 trade-in allowance.

Opus No. 15. Style 6. Cort Theatre. New York, New York. 1912. Cost $15,000.

Opus No. 16. Style J. Chicago, Illinois. December 14, 1912. Cost $5,000. Repossessed.

Opus No. 17. Style J. Tremont Theatre. New York, New York. December 30, 1912.

Opus No. 18. Style J. Family Theatre. Cincinnati, Ohio. March 7, 1913. Cost $7,500, less $1,750 trade-in allowance.

Opus No. 19. Style 6. Shipped to the Imperial Theatre, Montreal, Canada, March 11, 1913. The Imperial Theatre was part of Keith's Circuit. A catalogue noted: "Seats, 2300. Cost half a million dollars. Wonderful building devoted entirely to pictures. Theatre opened with Wurlitzer Hope-Jones Unit Orchestra. Most modern architectural features, including special cooling and ventilating plant. One of the best paying houses in the Keith Circuit. Wurlitzer music has proven so successful that another Wurlitzer Hope-Jones Unit Orchestra has been ordered for the new Keith St. Denis Theatre, now under construction. It is the best patronized theatre in Canada. The big diaphone, orchestra chimes, and other traps of the instrument are located above the boxes, and on Friday afternoon it is the custom to discontinue the pictures entirely and give the Unit Orchestra recital for two hours, the Unit in itself being a sufficient attraction to draw crowds.."

Opus No. 20. Style 6. Paris Theatre. Denver, Colorado. March 22, 1913. Located at 1751 Curtis Street, the Paris was billed as: "Unquestionably the largest theatre in the United States giving a high-grade program for 5c. Seats 2,200. Represents a capitalization of $250,000 paid up." The first Wurlitzer Hope-Jones Unit Orchestra installed in Denver, the instrument attracted wide admiration. Cost $20,000. Additions were made to the organ in September 1913.

Opus No. 21. Special model. Elks Lodge No.1. New York, New York. 1913. Additions to existing organ performed at a cost of $5,450. On December 24, 1915, Clayton J. Hermance, a prominent New York attorney who served as organist at the Lodge, described the recent rebuilding of an earlier installation: "In conversation with your representative a few days ago I was asked to express an opinion as to your Wurlitzer Organ or Unit Orchestra, as it is sometimes called. As you know, I have used one of these instruments at the Elks Home in this city for a period of about four years. As originally installed the organ was somewhat limited in size, but as I wrote you with respect to that particular instrument, I have never in all my experience seen so much organ in so small a space. As remodeled by you, we now have an instrument which we challenge anyone to reproduce in quality of tone and character of workmanship and in the number of effects that can be produced. I have played the instrument for hundreds of thousands of people and have yet to hear any but the highest praise for its beauty."

Opus No. 22. Style J. Philadelphia, Pennsylvania. April 12, 1913.

Opus No. 23. Style 3. Fitzhugh & Hall Amusement Company. Rochester, New York. May 14, 1913. Cost $10,000. Repossessed. Shipped on December 16, 1916 to the Rialto Theatre, Fort Wayne, Indiana. Chimes added March 6, 1917. Later repossessed and sold as Opus 174.

Opus No. 24. Style J. Nordland Plaza Theatre. Cincinnati, Ohio. June 8, 1913. Cost $8,000, less $1,000 trade-in allowance. New console in 1927.

Opus No. 25. Style L. Sold for $9,000 to the Quincy Amusement Co., New York, New York.

Opus No. 26. Style L. Western Automatic Music Co. Dallas, Texas. September 6, 1913. Cost $7,500, less $2,250 trade-in allowance. Sold to the Crystal Theatre, Dallas. A Wurlitzer catalogue noted: "Cost $60,000. Seats 600. The first theatre in the Southwest to install a Wurlitzer Hope-Jones Unit Orchestra. In ten months this theatre drew a patronage of over one million." On February 14, 1914, G.K. Jorgensen, owner of the theatre, wrote: "The Style L Motion Picture Orchestra, which has been in my theatre for about six months, has certainly fulfilled its promises. In making a special feature of the music that is permissible with this instrument, I feel that my theatre is the most refined and attractive motion picture theatre in the state of Texas. The manner in which this instrument makes it possible to follow the rapidly changing pictures with the right effects, lending itself readily to any phase, comedy or tragedy, has won the plaudits and admiration of all my customers. I firmly believe that my theatre is the showplace of the town."

Opus No. 27. Style 6 Special. Pitt Theatre. Pittsburgh, Pennsylvania, August 10, 1913. Wurlitzer was very proud of this installation and issued at least two brochures featuring it. The proprietor of the theatre often featured concerts, advertising them in local papers and on posters. At the dedication, *Thais* was performed. Soon after its installation, the organ suffered extensive damage during a flood which inundated much of the city.

Opus No. 28. Church organ. New York, New York. September 8, 1913.

Opus No. 29. Style 3. Joy's Theatre (Strand). Toronto, Canada. August 29, 1913. Cost $10,000. Later moved to the Beaver Theatre, then to the Rex Theatre, both in Toronto.

Opus No. 30. Style L. Grand Opera House. Wilmington, Delaware. December 4, 1913. Cost $7,500.

Opus No. 31. Style L. Shipped to San Francisco California. December 31, 1913. Later sold as Opus 71.

Opus No. 32. Style L. Orpheum Theatre. Cincinnati, Ohio. January 10, 1914.

Opus No. 33. Style 6 Special. Formerly Opus No. 4, with 32-foot diaphone and 16-foot tuba added. Installed in the Vitagraph (formerly the Criterion) Theatre, New York, New York, February 2, 1914. A letter from J. Stuart Blackton, a principal of The Vitagraph Company, was reproduced in many Wurlitzer advertisements. An early account relates that a $35,000 Unit Orchestra had been ordered but was not ready in time for the inauguration of the theatre on February 7, 1914, so a smaller model—"one of the cheapest the company makes"—(a Style J)—was successfully used as a stand-in. The formal dedication of the finished organ took place on March 9, at which time Robert Hope-Jones gave a recital on the instrument.

Opus No. 34. Style 1. Cincinnati, Ohio. March 18, 1914.

Opus No. 35. Style J. March 14, 1914. Rebuilt instrument.

Opus No. 36. Style L. New York, New York. February 28, 1914.

Opus No. 37. Style 3. New York, New York. April 9, 1914.

Opus No. 38. Style L. Lafayette Theatre. Philadelphia, Pennsylvania. May 2, 1914.

Opus No. 39. Style L. Lexington Theatre. Cleveland, Ohio. May 18, 1914.

Opus No. 40. Style L. Set up at the Convention of Motion Picture Exhibitors, Dayton, Ohio. June 26, 1914. Subsequently sold to the Pageant Theatre, St. Louis, Missouri.

Opus No. 41. Style 3. Regent Theatre. Paterson, New Jersey. July 10, 1914. The organ was installed in two wooden cabinets fronted by display pipes, each mounted on a balcony to the side of the theatre, 8 feet from the floor, 70 feet distant from the console. Jacob Fabian, proprietor of the theatre, stated: "I feel certain that more than 50% of my patrons come especially to hear the good music."

Opus No. 42. Special 3 manual model with 4 rank echo organ. Liberty Theatre. Seattle, Washington. July 29, 1914. Played by Henry Murtagh, this organ created a sensation when the theatre was opened and was responsible more than any other installation for the popularization of the theatre organ in America. From this point onward, Wurlitzer's star rose rapidly. Additions costing $1,137.50 were made October 14, 1915, bringing the organ to 20 ranks.

Opus No. 43. Style 3. Crescent Theatre. Brooklyn, New York. August 8, 1914.

Opus No. 44. Style L Special (with 16-foot diaphone). Claremont Theatre. New York, New York. September 17, 1914. A Wurlitzer catalogue had this to say about the Claremont Theatre: "Located in one of New York's most fashionable residential districts. Seats 1,200, cost $150,000. Land occupied worth half a million dollars. House opened with Wurlitzer Hope-Jones Unit Orchestra, and no other kind of music has been used since. Unique feature of the equipment is the weekly 'Photoplayers' Night,' upon which occasion various photoplay celebrities appear in person and talk to the audience. The instrument is placed upon both sides of the platform, and the console in the center, about 20 feet away from the screen, so that the performer may get a good view of the picture and make quick changes appropriate to the action.".

Opus No. 45. Special 3-manual model. Regent Theatre. Rochester, New York. September 21, 1914. "It may interest you to know that we use the organ with and without our regular orchestra," the owner of the theatre informed the Wurlitzer Company. "The results are wonderful; the organ backs up the orchestra and seems to give it that sort of backbone. It is very pleasing to be in any part of the theatre and hear the soft, rich and mellow tones of the organ that seem to come from nowhere, but appear to be in the atmosphere as a spirit." The cost of the theatre was stated to be $125,000, with a seating capacity of 1,800, increased from a former seating of 1,600. "Increased patronage made it necessary to add the 200 additional seats," it was stated. Additions were made to the organ on September 27, 1916, bringing it to 11 ranks.

Opus No. 46. Style L. New Ulm, Minnesota. October 6, 1914.

Opus No. 47. Style 3. Wurlitzer store. New York, New York. October 8, 1914. At one time, Clara Kimball Young, a well-known movie actress, played a concert on this organ, much to the delight of several onlookers, including a reporter from *Moving Picture World*. Later installed in the National Theatre, Jersey City, New Jersey, 1916.

Opus No. 48. Style 3. Grand Theatre. Columbus, Ohio. October 29, 1914. "Recitals upon the Wurlitzer Hope-Jones Unit Orchestra are given regularly with great success, the music being highly praised by the patrons," a Wurlitzer catalogue noted. The theatre cost $50,000 and seated 1,500 people.

Opus No. 49. Style L. Strand Theatre. Cincinnati, Ohio. November 17, 1914. The house had a seating capacity of 1,500 and operated continuously from 9:00 in the morning until 11:30 in the evening. It was reported that Mr. I. Libson, manager, controlled three other Cincinnati theatres and used Wurlitzer music in all, "representing an investment in the four Wurlitzer instruments of $30,000. These theatres are also affiliated with the Harris Syndicate of Pittsburgh, which uses 11 Wurlitzer instruments," according to a catalogue. Undoubtedly, the Pittsburgh instruments referred to were primarily photoplayers.

Opus No. 50. Style 3. Empire Theatre, San Antonio, Texas. November 18, 1914. Seating 2,000 people, the Empire Theatre cost $100,000. A Wurlitzer catalogue noted that the theatre was "one of the most magnificent houses in Texas, and was opened with the Wurlitzer Hope-Jones Unit Orchestra. Mr. Clarence Eddy, world's greatest organist, played Handel's *Messiah* upon the Wurlitzer Orchestra installed in this theatre, accompanying 250 voices in a brilliant music festival. Mr. Eddy says that the Wurlitzer Orchestra has more volume than six ordinary orchestras, and the director of the festival changed all his plans and went to extra expense to hold the festival in the Empire Theatre, because of the Wurlitzer Hope-Jones Unit Orchestra. Many stars of grand opera took part. Musical critics, writing in the newspapers, spoke of the Wurlitzer Unit Orchestra as being the most wonderful instrument they had ever heard."

Opus No. 51. Special model. Liberty Theatre. Spokane, Washington. November 28, 1914. "The Unit Orchestra is giving entire satisfaction here," the manager of the theatre wrote to Wurlitzer on August 19, 1915. "We cannot recommend it too highly for photoplay purposes. Its orchestral quality is particularly adapted to theatrical work, while at the same time the ordinary pipe organ effects may be easily obtained and without sacrificing entire performances to the straight pipe organ music that to many is not what is desired in a varied photoplay organ. Our next theatre will be equipped with a Wurlitzer Unit Orchestra." Additions costing $1,735 were made on October 14, 1915.

Opus No. 52. Style 3. Shipped on January 16, 1915, to the Panama-Pacific International Exposition, San Francisco, California, where it was set up at the United States Steel Company exhibit. After the fair it was sold to the Strand Theatre, Reno, Nevada. Additions to the organ were made on June 30, 1919.

Opus No. 53. Style L. Harris Theatre. Detroit, Michigan. January 26, 1915.

Opus No. 54. Style 3. Broadway Theatre. Louisville, Kentucky. January 29, 1915. This theatre seated 1,400 people and was built at a cost of $100,000. According to a Wurlitzer catalogue, "The proprietor, Mr. Louis Steuerle, is interested also in six other theatres, and in each he has installed a Wurlitzer instrument. Mr. Steuerle frankly states that much of his success has been due to the high quality of music produced by the Wurlitzer Hope-Jones Unit Orchestra."

Opus No. 55. Style 3. Victoria Theatre. Harrisburg, Pennsylvania. February 1, 1915.

Opus No. 56. Style 3. Opera House, Lowell, Massachusetts. March 4, 1915. Later moved to Passaic, New Jersey (April 28, 1916); later moved to Jamestown, New York.

Opus No. 57. Style L. Knickerbocker Theatre (Whittier). Detroit, Michigan. March 17, 1915.

Opus No. 58. Style J. Cincinnati, Ohio. March 20, 1915.

Opus No. 59. Style V. Flatbush Theatre. Brooklyn, New York. April 8, 1915. This instrument was described as having a 2-manual console, with 8 ranks divided in two chambers.

Opus No. 60. Style 3. Old Mill Theatre. Dallas, Texas. May 1, 1915. This theatre cost $250,000 and seated 1,924 people who paid from 10c to 20c admission. An early Wurlitzer catalogue noted the economy effected by the installation of the organ: "Formerly employed an orchestra at a cost of $1,180 per month. Since the installation of the Wurlitzer Hope-Jones Unit Orchestra, the total cost, including paying for the Unit Orchestra, is $590 per month."

Opus No. 61. Chicago, Illinois. May 29, 1915. Subsequently installed in the Delthe Theatre, Detroit, Michigan.

Opus No. 62. Style L. Orpheum Theatre. Cincinnati, Ohio. June 4, 1915. A catalogue noted concerning the Orpheum: "Seats 2,500. A wonderful building six stories high, cost $300,000. The Orpheum Theatre has purchased two Wurlitzer Orchestras, both of which are played simultaneously in the theatre and on the roof." Opus 62 was the roof garden instrument.

Opus No. 63. Style J. Cincinnati, Ohio. June 11, 1915. Repaired earlier instrument from Buffalo, New York.

Opus No. 64. Special 4-manual, 28-rank model. Isis Theatre. Denver, Colorado. June 12, 1915. Cost $40,000.

Opus No. 65. Style 35. Broadway-Strand Theatre. Detroit, Michigan. June 26, 1915. Costing $400,000, the Broadway-Strand Theatre seated 1,600 patrons. "It is indeed with great pleasure that we can write and say that the Wurlitzer Hope-Jones Unit Orchestra installed in the Broadway-Strand Theatre has been unanimously voted a success," the manager wrote on August 3, 1915. "It was the one thing needed to make our house the success that it now is, judging from the crowds that we have been handling since the opening of the instrument by Detroit's foremost music lovers, and commercially we consider it to be one of our best investments. We now know that no motion picture can give a scientific show without one of your instruments."

Opus No. 66. Style 3. Alamo Theatre. Louisville, Kentucky. July 18, 1915. Theatre name later changed to Ohio, then back to Alamo.

Opus No. 67. Style V. Opera House. Bayonne, New Jersey. August 23, 1915.

Opus No. 68. Style 3. Standard Theatre. Cleveland, Ohio. August 29, 1915. Earlier, this theatre used a Style K photoplayer, as evidenced by a letter from the manager to the Wurlitzer Company, September 19, 1915: "We want to thank you for the prompt manner in which you have installed the Wurlitzer Hope-Jones Unit Orchestra at the Standard Theatre in place of the Style K Orchestra formerly used and which has given such eminent satisfaction to our patrons during the past year. Our decision to supersede the Style K with the Hope-Jones Unit Orchestra was based entirely on the demand of the hour by photoplay patrons for the largest musical attraction in the world, something out of the ordinary, along with the greatest pictures ever produced."

Opus No. 69. Style V. Philadelphia, Pennsylvania. August 30, 1915.

Opus No. 70. Style 3. American Theatre. Bellingham, Washington. September 17, 1915. The owner subsequently informed the Wurlitzer company: "We opened our new 1,800 capacity house, The American, on October 16th with the Wurlitzer Unit Orchestra, and at the first performance, which was at 2 o'clock, we filled the house, and at the evening performance Saturday people were standing from 7 to 10 o'clock, and on Sunday we were unable to handle the crowds at all. The Unit Orchestra is certainly wonderful. People applaud the concert as if to tear the house down. Every musician in the city says that the instrument is the most wonderful organ ever heard. In phoning the theatre, our people never ask what time the picture starts but what time the concert starts."

Opus No. 71. Style L. Ringling Theatre. Baraboo, Wisconsin. September 29, 1915. Originally Opus 31. Rebuilt and then shipped to Wisconsin.

Opus No. 72. Style 3. Avon Theatre. Utica, New York. October 8, 1915. The Avon seated 1,800 and was elaborately decorated in white and gold. The house opened each day at 1:00 and ran continuously until 11:00 in the evening. Later sold to H. C. Colberg and moved to Buffalo, New York.

Opus No. 73. Special model. Elks Lodge. Columbus, Ohio. October 9, 1915. This installation was widely advertised by Wurlitzer and was a showcase instrument. This organ may have been a rebuild of an earlier instrument of unknown manufacture.

Opus No. 74. Style 3. Philadelphia, Pennsylvania. October 26, 1915.

Opus No. 75. Style N. Chicago, Illinois. October 30, 1915.

Opus No. 76. Style V. Chicago, Illinois. November 6, 1915. Later installed in Racine, Wisconsin.

Opus No. 77. Style J. Detroit, Michigan. November 26, 1915. Earlier instrument rebuilt.

Opus No. 78. Style 3. Colorado Springs, Colorado. November 29, 1915.

Opus No. 79. Style N. Crawford Theatre. El Paso, Texas. December 14, 1915. Equipped with a duplex roll playing unit.

Farny Wurlitzer Reminisces

Address by Farny R. Wurlitzer, chairman of the board of The Wurlitzer Company, before members of the American Association of Theatre Organ Enthusiasts, at Melody Fair, Wurlitzer Park, North Tonawanda, New York, Monday, July 6, 1964. From Mr. Wurlitzer's personal transcript of the talk.

Mr. Norvel, members of the ATOE and their wives, who have done so much to help their husbands, guests and friends. This is really a red letter day for me because it brings back many happy memories of the past.

I go back to January 1909, when we purchased the business from the DeKleist Musical Instrument Manufacturing Company, and I was chosen to come up here and take charge of the business. I was 26 at the time. I feel, however, that you will be interested in having a brief history of the events that brought us into the theatre organ business.

The family traces its history back to the first Wurlitzer that we have a record of, in 1596, Heinrich Wurlitzer, and in 1659, Nicolaus Wurlitzer, the first Wurlitzer was born who made a musical instrument. It is unusual perhaps that in every generation that succeeded him, there was either a maker or dealer in musical instruments. My grandfather, Christian Gottfried Wurlitzer, dealt in musical instruments in the small village of Schoeneck, in Saxony where my father was born in 1831. The musical instrument business at that time was a home industry to a large extent. Grandfather bought the musical instruments from the peasants, who made them largely in the winter season when they weren't busy in their fields, and then he resold them to jobbers and to exporters.

My father, of course, had experience in this business and he hoped to become a partner in his father's business, he was the eldest son. But his father decided that was not the arrangement he had in mind. He wanted to keep the business for the youngest son, who was a child at the time. So my father decided to come to America. I'm making this very brief, although there are many details of this history that I know you would be interested in if I had the time to tell them all.

He came to the United States in 1853. It is a coincidence that in the same year, my mother crossed the ocean; she was French and my father German. My father imported the first musical instruments from his father in 1856, and it is from that date on that our business started. I will skip to the time when we were musical instrument dealers in Cincinnati, Ohio, and Mr. DeKleist, who had been brought over here by the merry-go-round manufacturers—there were three of them in North Tonawanda at that time—from England to build merry-go-round organs for them because the duty had been increased and they decided it was necessary to manufacture the instruments here.

Mr. DeKleist, with one or two helpers, came over from England. His name really was Eugene vonKleist, and he belonged to a famous German family, but having been in England, changed it to DeKleist. He made merry-go-round organs for the manufacturers, but the business got a little slack and he decided to see whether he couldn't get some additional business by making trumpets for the U.S. Army. He called on Lyon and Healy, one of the largest dealers in musical instruments in Chicago, and spoke to them. They said, "Oh, if you want to sell trumpets to the U.S. Army you'd better see Wurlitzer in Cincinnati because they have that business. So he came down to see my older brother, who was 12 years older than I, and we did buy trumpets from DeKleist. You see, merry-go-round organs had brass trumpets so this was just a short step to making the instruments such as used in the army. DeKleist said, "Couldn't you sell some merry-go-round organs?" My brother said, "Well we might sell one or two a year, but there's very little demand for them. If you would make a coin-operated piano for us we could sell a lot of them."

At that time the merry-go-round organs that DeKleist made had a wooden cylinder that varied according to the size of the organ. It usually had ten tunes on it and by turning a lever on the side you could choose any one of the ten. He made the piano the same way, a long wooden cylinder with ten tunes on it. When the model was finished, my brother came up to look at it, and after a number of changes decided it was satisfactory, and ordered 200. Mr. DeKleist did not have the funds at that time and so he went to the bank and borrowed money on the strength of the order. Well, that business developed and Mr. DeKleist became prosperous. We had sole selling rights to all of the instruments. Paper music rolls followed very shortly after that and wooden cylinders were discontinued. There were many types of coin-operated musical instruments and there was an era there when skating rinks were very popular, and the band organs, as we called them, also were useful and many of them were sold.

There were nickelodeons, and for those we had developed an instrument, various models of them with piano, and the small ones with one cabinet on the side, the larger with two, and they had two music rolls. One would be rewinding while the other was playing, and in that way the music could accompany the picture. Motion pictures were very short—they were short reels—and you paid a nickel or a dime to go in and see the show, that is how they became known as nickelodeons.

That business was growing and we felt there was an opportunity to build instruments for theatres. We weren't thinking of the motion picture theatre because the real motion picture theatre did not exist. We thought of replacing orchestras and heard of Robert Hope-Jones. He had some financial difficulty, and his company failed in Elmira, with a distinguished lot of stockholders in it—Mark Twain, Mr. Vail, president of the American Telephone Association, and quite a few others, but Robert Hope-Jones, whom we investigated quite thoroughly before we entered into business relations with him, had been a continuous failure with everyone he had associated with. He first began remodeling an organ in his own church at Birkenhead, England. He electrified it and that was something new. He brought the console out of the church and put it outside and then played the organ on the inside of the church, which created quite an impression on the church world of England.

He lost his own money in building organs. He lost that of his wife, who was a very fine woman, and then he was backed by various people, one to the extent of $250,000, but Hope-Jones was an inventor. He had a very brilliant mind and was very persuasive. He was an unusual looking man. But every time he finished an organ it wasn't good enough, he always had in mind building a better one the next time. And that was why he lost money because every time he built an organ it was different; he didn't duplicate anything. He was with two large firms in this country, Skinner, Austin—and then he formed his own company in Elmira, which was a failure.

While at Elmira he built the Ocean Grove organ which really was an outstanding instrument and is still in use today at the Ocean Grove camp meeting place in their auditorium there.

Hope-Jones came up to see us and gave us a demonstration on the organ in St. Paul's Episcopal Cathedral in Buffalo which he built, and he tried to interest us in taking over his company which was then in receivership. My two brothers and I were there. We were very impressed. I'd never heard an organ sound like that before, it was beautiful. We then went down to Ocean Grove and heard the organ, which was marvelous. We heard Clarence Reynolds play *The Storm*, a thing that he did during the summer months. Church organs were slow in response while Hope-Jones had instantaneous response, which made it possible to play all types of music.

We knew of all these failures of Hope-Jones, and knew that it had been continuous. Perhaps we were conceited enough to think that we knew how to make money with Hope-Jones and be a success. We entered into a contract with him in April 1910 and closed the deal with the receiver in May 1910.

I am glad to say that one of the two first men to come up here from Elmira is with us today, Earle Beach. There are others here who were with us in those days.

Our thinking in the early days when we took the business over was in the church field, and hotels and theatres which Hope-Jones had been working with. We didn't realize that the large movie theatres were coming.

Hope-Jones had a contract with the Hotel Statler, which is now the Hotel Buffalo. Of course the company having gone into receivership it was necessary to renew that contract. I went down to see Mr. Statler with Hope-Jones and we did renew the contract. It was a most peculiar installation. Mr. Statler had just built an addition to his hotel and had a large banquet room in this addition on the second floor. His grille room, really the dining room, was used most by him, and the problem was that he wanted the music to be heard in the second floor banquet room and the ground floor dining room, which had a glass dome over it. We installed the organ in these two bedrooms, putting the chambers for the pipes on two sides of a hall that we built between them so that the tone could go both to the banquet hall and to the grille room dining hall on the ground floor. When we installed the organ we had a most peculiar result. When the full organ was played it was softer than when only the pipes on one side of the hall were played. This was due to the tone waves melding together, a thing that is well-known in physics but it was a demonstration in this instance. We cured it by putting up a narrow wall about two inches thick the length of the corridor and that solved the trouble.

That installation was quite interesting to me, and later on when Mr. Statler built his new hotel that is still there in Buffalo, we sold him two organs, one for the main dining room and one for the ballroom.

But to go back a little bit, Hope-Jones obtained some contracts for churches and he'd come to me and say, "You know, this is really an important installation, and if we could just add this stop and that stop to it, it would make it perfect and would mean so much to us in getting other contracts." Well, we were willing to go along with things like that, and we did, but at the end of two years we had lost two hundred thousand dollars in the Hope-Jones organ department.

We tried many things to develop the business. We were new at it and it was a new field. No one had built organs for theatres before and we got an order from the Cort Theatre in New York and also from the Cort Theatre in Chicago. We installed those and replaced the orchestras. I didn't learn until yesterday that just at that particular time there had been a year's strike of the musicians in New York and that made it much easier for us to enter the theatre field. They made it possible. They have been unreasonable once in a while since then.

One of our earliest installations was in the theatre that most of you have never heard of— The Century Theatre on Central Park West. It was built by a group of very wealthy men because they wanted to do something outstanding for the theatre world. They had only spectacular shows.

The one I remember quite distinctly, when we installed our organ without expense to the theatre, was called *The Daughter of the Gods*. Oscar Hammerstein, I think, had written the music for it, and he was there. We put in this fairly large instrument and it was demonstrated. Not long after this the Criterion Theatre, the name of which was changed to the Vitagraph, put on the first long film show in the history of moving pictures. It lasted an hour. Our organ was the only music that was used, and that was really an historical event in motion picture history.

I recall that when we used the diaphone pipes which most of you know were used to imitate thunder, the city authorities of New York forbade the use of them because they were afraid the plaster ceiling would come down, which it might have. This, of course, was not a movie house built for the purpose; it was an old theatre changed over for the purpose on 43rd and Broadway. This was the first and earliest installation of an organ where a long film was used.

To continue with Robert Hope-Jones—he had a most unusual crop of hair. It was pure white and I've never seen one like it before nor since. His hair stood up straight and he really enjoyed walking down Fifth Avenue or Broadway holding his hat in his hand and everyone turned to look at him because he was so unusual. He was a very fine man in many respects, a real inventor and a gifted man.

He was very persuasive. He could talk you into believing black was white, and I think he succeeded sometimes. Well, at the end of this period of time we decided that the only way we could make a success of the business was to have Hope-Jones stay out of the factory and have nothing to do with the actual manufacturing operations of the business. We talked to him and wrote him a letter and told him he no longer had permission to come into the plant, that we would continue to pay him just as the contract provided for. He had a percentage of the sales price on all the organs that we sold, and we told him that as soon as the business was profitable we would then establish an experimental shop for

him where he could do the experimental work, but would not interfere with the current work that was going through. This was necessary because you just cannot manufacture and make every instrument different from the last one you built. And that, unfortunately, with his inventive mind was the only way he could manage it. It discouraged Hope-Jones that he could no longer come into the plant. It discouraged him that he was no longer in the public eye as much as he had been before, and as many of you know, he committed suicide on September 13, 1914. It was a great pity. Had he believed in us he would have been well compensated because the business did a little later on grow prosperous.

His wife, in my opinion, was a very wonderful woman, very kind. She did so much for all the employees whom she had known for years. Most of these people had come over from England with Hope-Jones.

We had many, many problems, many serious problems in those early days because the loss we had was a big one for us. But throughout it all we never lost faith in what the Hope-Jones organ was and what he had done. We believed in his work, and we believed that we could be a success—and we were!

The first outstanding organ, it isn't by any means the first organ we built in a theatre, was the one that we sold to the Liberty Theatre in Seattle. We shipped that in late 1914. That was a tremendous success!

The theatre was built especially as a motion picture theatre. They had no provision for an orchestra, they depended entirely on our organ for music, and the theater was quite original. Up to that time, nearly all theatres were remodeled theatres, and it had one feature that at that time was unusual—a ramp to go up to the balcony instead of stairs. The theatre was such a tremendous success from the start—I'm not exaggerating in telling you this—that for three weeks the Seattle police had to take care of the crowds that stood for three blocks waiting for their turn to get into the Liberty Theatre!

Well, that, of course, was a great help to us and the business grew, especially on the Pacific Coast. I recall that there was a theatre, so I was told, in San Francisco way out on Market Street that had closed 23 times. Maybe they exaggerated when they told me. We put an organ in there and then it was a success. it wasn't a large model, and at that time Sid Grauman, who had a theatre in San Francisco on Market Street, became interested in our organ and he installed one in his Market Street theatre. A little later he arranged to install an organ in his new theatre in Los Angeles called the Million Dollar Theatre on Broadway. That was a very successful installation.

To my mind, Sid Grauman was perhaps the greatest moving picture showman that we have ever had. He was a most unusual character. I could tell you stories by the hour of many things he did that were very unusual. He was very absent-minded but he was very gifted. When he put on a show at the Million Dollar Theatre he had usherettes, not men ushers, in the costume that suited the picture. If it was an Oriental film they had Oriental costumes. If it was something else, they wore that type of costume. His shows were usually on for more than a week, more like six weeks or so. He was enthusiastic about our organ and he did so much to sell the idea of our organ to other moving picture people.

For instance, to Balaban and Katz. Sam Katz came out to Los Angeles, and Sid Grauman

made it a special chore for him to sell Sam Katz. The same thing with Mr. Zukor, who was the father of the Paramount organization. When Mr. Zukor came out he gave him a special demonstration after the show was over, and our representative, who was also a director of our company, Buzz Lyons, met Mr. Zukor and started to talk to him about organs for all their theatres because they had many throughout the United States. Mr. Zukor said, "I'm too busy to talk to you now, but I'm leaving tomorrow evening on the train for San Francisco. I have a drawing room and if you will be on that train, we'll talk about it." So it was arranged that the Board of Directors of the Wurlitzer Company and the Board of Directors of the Paramount organization were to meet and discuss the buying of Wurlitzer organs for all their theatres. Well, three of us went down, I went down, Mr. Lyons was there from the Coast, Mr. Ryan, who was also a member of the Board was present.

But we didn't meet with their Board—we met with Mr. Connick, who was running the Paramount organization for the banks because the chain had gotten involved financially. Mr. Connick knew a good deal about church organs and his thought was that how many stops did we have in this model and how many in that, and we changed the subject always because that was the one thing we didn't want to discuss because with the Hope-Jones system, the unit system, we didn't use as many stops as the church organs did, but we got the results. To make the story short, Mr. Connick said, "It appears as if none of us knows much about organs."

But we did get the orders and we did install Wurlitzer organs in all the Paramount theatres, and the same way with Balaban and Katz in Chicago. As you know, Mr. Balaban is today president of the Paramount organization.

We had the business of practically all the chains—Keith Circuit, Loew's and really all of them. Our organs cost more than those of any other makes and there was a reason for it; the materials and the design were expensive, and the workmanship that went into them. We used only the very finest grade of sugar pine, first and second, and solid mahogany or solid cherry because they didn't chip when you bored into them, and of course, Hope-Jones had laid the foundation for this quality which we believed in and followed.

In 1918 we installed the organ in the Denver City Auditorium. That was the largest organ that we eve built. I remember being out there when we were trying to get the contract. Madam Schumann-Heink sang in the Auditorium. She was very much loved in Denver and a very good friend of the mayor—and the mayor was the one who would decide the question of the organ. Well, she was returning to Chicago. The next day at noon there was a meeting of the Rotary Club and I met Schumann-Heink. She had a big sign across her chest saying "Baby Ernestine." So when I met her in the sleeping car that night— it took much longer to go to Chicago in those days than it does now, the trains are faster now—why I said, "Good evening, Ernestine." She just stepped back quite shocked and said falteringly, "I don't remember your name." I told her who I was, and she knew our family in Cincinnati. She had sung there many times.

She had a drawing room and her accompanist with her, a woman, was in another compartment. The next morning I got up earlier than she did. When her drawing room was being made up, I said, "Don't you want to sit in my seat?" I only had a berth, so she joined me and spent the whole morning telling me the history of her life. It was most interesting. She was a wonderful woman. She told me about each of her husbands, there were four of them, what their characteristics were and about her present husband, and that she had a large number of children. This was in February 1917. It was just at the time when vonBernsdorf, German ambassador, had been given his walking papers by Washington because I think the *Lusitania* had been torpedoed and we were about to break off relations with Germany.

She said to me, "You know, my heart bleeds because I have sons in the German army and I have sons that are in the American army. They'll be fighting each other." She, at that time, had a home in San Diego, California. I met one of her sons who was with her in Denver. She was a very warm-hearted individual. When she got on the stage, why the audience was just with her—they knew they were a part of her; she had that ability. She was idolized in Denver.

We got the order for the organ. We had a lot problems. The organ had 50 inch wind pressure, and to get 50 inches of wind pressure the wind is heated an awful lot in the blower from the friction. We could not keep the organ in tune. Temperature up in the organ chambers was 120 degrees, and Louis Lockwood, who was superintendent of the plant, spent almost a year out there. We had blower companies come out and help us, but they couldn't do anything. He finally solved the problem in a very simple way—there was an immense volume of air blown through these blowers. He took a garden hose, turned the water on and put it in the blower. It cooled the air immediately. The evaporation of the water brought the temperature down and we had no trouble after that. There were many things like that we would run into.

We had many problems with architects. They didn't realize the necessity of giving us the right location for our organs so that the tone could come out. All they thought of was the design of the theatre and the beauty of it. We'd have to put up quite a fight, and we would appeal to the buyer and say, "Now do you want to buy an organ from us and pay that much money and get only 25 or 50 percent results? That is what is going to happen if you don't let us have proper openings for the tone that comes out of the chambers." Well, we won out in I think almost all of the cases.

One of our early problems was finding men to play our organs. You see, church organists didn't know how to play a theatre organ and follow the film. In the early days films were silent and they had to depend on music to interpret the picture. So we tried to train people to play our organs, and gradually, of course, the famous names developed that really did interpret what could be done with the Wurlitzer organ, as well as the other makes of organs. I don't wish to slight the competition. Names that I knew most of you know—Jesse Crawford is the best known of all, I think. He played here in Buffalo for Mike Shea at the Shea's Buffalo. Albert Hay Malotte had played for Mike Shea at the Hippodrome; he is the composer of *The Lord's Prayer*, and there were many others. Henry Murtagh was the man who opened the Liberty Theatre in Seattle. He was followed by a very brilliant man, Oliver G. Wallace, whom I just learned passed away about a year ago. He was a brilliant musician.

I might tell you a little more about failures. We put an organ in the new Pitt Theatre in Pittsburgh in August 1913. Unfortunately, the Ohio River got higher than it should and entered the theatre and the organ was drowned. That ended rather unfortunately, but that was one of the many experiences we had in disappointments.

Perhaps the most powerful organ we ever built was for the Roosevelt Memorial Park Cemetery. They wanted the organ powerful enough so that it could be heard for a mile or two as a funeral procession approached the park. That was built on 50 inches of wind pressure on several of the stops. That organ was played by rolls as well as having a console so that it could be played by hand. It is still in use.

I do want to mention something about the roll attachment. We made two different rolls. One had 165 holes in the tracker bar, and the other had 105. We were building organs for homes, most of them with the smaller rolls. The large one has never been duplicated; with 165 holes crosswise, we operated 340 different things, either keys or stops. Now the way we did that was—there were ten holes vertical as well as those crosswise. One was a firing hole, and, depending on which one of these holes was passing over the bar of the 100, you see, there were ten times ten, why that would fire that or any number of them and in a way we were able to play this organ as a two manual or a three manual organ at times. We had an organ in the studio and a perforating machine, and when the organists recorded for us—Jesse Crawford recorded for us—one minute after they were finished playing we could play the roll back and let them hear what they had done. In those days there wasn't the tape or the arrangements we have today for the organist to hear himself play.

I think nearly every one of them who came here to record for us, and we had many prominent organists come, they were all quite astonished to hear themselves play because an organist doesn't hear himself when he's at the console. He's busy, you know, playing. I know one of them, perhaps more than one did it, said, "Give me that roll." He just tore it up and said, "I want to do it again." He wasn't happy with what he had done.

One of my great regrets is that we didn't keep all this here, but the Depression came along and we sold the recording organs and all the equipment that we had and didn't keep it. I wish that I had it today. It was a question of our survival during the Depression.

As many of you know, we installed an organ in Radio City Music Hall, and that is the largest theatre organ that we built, and it is used today in all their shows. Radio City, they purchased that organ from us, not only purchased one, but four organs from us—the one for the Music Hall, the large three manual organ upstairs above the theatre for the organists to practice on so that they could practice what they were gong to play in the show; and then they had an organ in the Rainbow Room, which is the restaurant on the top floor of Radio City, and they built a theatre just across the street from the Music Hall on 50th Street in New York and they installed an organ in there. That one, however, has been discontinued, so it is no longer there. I am happy that Radio City continues to use the organ.

When talking pictures came along we realized that the days of the theatre organ were approaching an end. Our business continued in other parts of the world. We did quite a business in England, in Australia, in fact most of the countries of the world—some in Germany, a few in France, and one in Spain, one in India, in Japan—I believe that is still in use today—it is in one of the large department stores there. The business, however, dwindled. Radio City Music Hall was one of the last organs that we built in this country for a theatre, but we kept on shipping abroad.

Then the war started in '39 and that was the end of the export business. Even though there were talking pictures, they continued to use the organs in England. In this country they didn't to any great extent.

I imagine many of you wonder why we didn't continue in the pipe organ business. The main reason is that our costs were so much higher than those of church organ builders that we felt we had no chance of selling to churches. They couldn't afford to pay the price we had to charge. Furthermore, we had the antagonism of 99 percent of the church organists of the United States. They didn't like the unit system. They did not like the theatre organ. Many of them, I think, have been converted since then, but I'm sure there are still a lot of them that feel the same way. Those were the reasons we didn't carry on with the business. To my mind it was a wonderful business, I mean it was fascinating. We had a marvelous crew of men. They were devoted artisans, and they put their hearts and souls into the work.

In building organs for theatres, it was always a problem to have that organ there for the day of the opening, and that was sometimes difficult. I recall one instance where our men worked for 35 hours without sleep in order to get that organ finished and packed and expressed. We had to send it by express to the theatre so it would be there on time for opening day.

And those openings were always a trying time because we installed the organ when they were still doing plastering work and all kinds of other work, and dust and dirt, and you know that's one thing that doesn't agree with an organ is dirt. It causes ciphers, and a cipher of course is terrible, when the audience is there to hear that pipe squeal that shouldn't squeal. And so I have always avoided openings, I didn't go.

I feel that it may be of interest to you to have me read a list of the people that came from Elmira in May 1910. There was Fred Smith, Dave Marr, James Nuttall, Joe Carruthers, John Colton, Earle Beach (and he is here today), Gus Erickson, Jack Hurst, who was in charge of the metal pipe department. James Nuttall, I forgot to say, was the head voicer. There was John Badger, Charles Russell, Carl Johnson, Gus Notterman and his son, Gus, Jr., and then Mrs. Linhairs, who came up from Elmira to teach our girls and women to do this intricate work on the Hope-Jones organ, because we ran all our own cables and for every organ that was built the cables were different. We had long tables that we'd run these cables on and form them out in advance. Of course, our drawing office had to lay everything out on paper before it was built, and that was an intricate part of the work, and very important.

Then there were many men who came a little later on who weren't here originally, and I do want to mention the names of some of them. There was W. Meakin Jones, no relative of Robert Hope-Jones, but he had been associated with Hope-Jones in England. He came over in 1912. Louis S. Lockwood took over as superintendent when some of the other men left, because a number of them melted away from us between the time that we moved them up here and the time when Hope-Jones died. So Lockwood was responsible for a great deal of the success of our later work, our important work. He was responsible along with Howard Maurer (who is here today) for developing the roll system and this marvelous tracker bar. I forgot to mention this tracker bar—you see, with paper you have the problem that it shrinks and expands with the humidity—this tracker bar had two cuts in it. There were two small leaves outside the tracker bar. If the paper expanded, those leaves were pushed out and the tracker bar would open up electrically. It couldn't open very much, of course, otherwise the music wouldn't track. It opened up just enough so that it would not cause any trouble, and then, if the paper shrank again, why the bar would come back to the correct size. It was just a tiny fraction of an inch that opened up each one of these slots. Howard Maurer helped to develop that and I regard his work very highly.

There is Manly Cockcroft, Fred Wood, Walter Berry, David Arthur, who was one of our voicers. Tom Ruggles succeeded to be chief voicer and I always felt very indebted to him for what he did for us because he carried on the Hope-Jones type of voicing. The most important factor was that he trained young men to follow, something that the original voicers didn't want to do. They didn't want to teach anybody, they wanted to keep it a secret. The business was expanding so much and we had to have more voicers.

There's Bob Shreeve (who is here today). He succeeded to the management of the Metal Pipe Department after Jack Hurst left us. Louis Markovitz is here today. Elmer Brodfuehrer for many years was in charge of our Drawing Office, and he is here today, although retired from the business. Some of our old other members are here and I'm very grateful to all of those people who helped us and who did such a marvelous job in building the Wurlitzer organ.

I am also very grateful to all the many organists who made it possible for the Wurlitzer organ to achieve fame. They did a wonderful job. You know Jesse Crawford, his wife Helen; there was Eddie Dunstedter; one of the early ones was Henry Murtagh. I didn't consider him as great a musician as many of the others. There was Dick Leibert, who is head organist at Radio City Music Hall, Milton Charles and Clarence Reynolds. I must mention again he was organist at Denver and had been the organist at Ocean Grove. Then there was C. Sharpe Minor, who was a great showman but a poor musician. He really did show off the organ and people liked him. Carl Coleman here in Buffalo and Tom Grierson from Rochester played here in Buffalo and is one of our very good friends.

I'm grateful to all of them, and please don't be offended if I didn't mention the names of all of them who helped us so much.

I want to thank especially the "Wurlitzer Widows" because I know it took a lot of patience and help from the wives of American Theatre Organ Enthusiasts members when they purchased an organ and installed it. Without the support of their wives, it couldn't have been accomplished. Many of them helped with the actual work, and all of them showed patience. This not only applies to Wurlitzer Widows but to the wives of all ATOE members whatever make of organ they have. And my appreciation to all of you for your patience and loyalty. And, of course, my very great appreciation goes to all of you who have purchased theatre organs—naturally, I appreciate most of all the purchase of the Wurlitzer organs from theatres so that these are preserved, because otherwise their lives would have been very short and the present generation would have forgotten them.

I can't close without thanking Ben Hall for the marvelous book that he wrote, *The Best Remaining Seats*, and the study that he made of the early history of the motion picture industry. I think that was very important to preserve for future generations.

I thank all of you for having been so patient to listen to me and I hope it hasn't been too boring for many of you. I've tried to tell you of some of the early periods, and the problems we had. Let me tell you that I appreciate your being here, and thank you very much.

Bibliography

Audsley, George Ashdown. *The Art of Organ Building.* New York: Dover Publications, Inc., 1965. Reprint of original 1905 edition. A comprehensive treatise on organ building with notations concerning several Hope-Jones devices.

Balshofer, Fred J. and Arthur C. Miller. *One Reel a Week.* Berkeley and Los Angeles, California: University of California Press, 1967. A thoroughly readable and very enjoyable account of the early years of motion picture production, especially 1905-1915, written by two pioneers.

Barnes, William Harrison and Edward B. Gammons. *Two Centuries of American Organ Building.* Glen Rock, New Jersey: J. Fischer & Bro., 1970. Discussion of organ building in America, with a chapter on theatre organs.

Bergsten, Bebe (Editor). *Biograph Bulletins, 1896-1908.* Los Angeles, California: Locare Research Group, 1971. Compilation, introduction and notes by Kemp R. Niver. A reproduction of film notices and plot synopses of one of the pioneer American firms.

B'hend, Tom. *The Console.* Pasadena, California, published by the editor. Various issues from the 1960s through 1984 were studied. A journal of the theatre organ hobby and also a forum for the reprinting of early information.

Billboard, The. Cincinnati, Ohio: Billboard Publishing Company. Various issues 1903 to 1916. *The Billboard,* published weekly, is one of the most important periodical sources for information relating to the very early days of film making.

Blum, Daniel. *A Pictorial History of the Silent Screen.* New York: Grosset & Dunlap, 1953.

Bowers, Q. David. *The Encyclopedia of Automatic Musical Instruments.* Vestal, New York: The Vestal Press, Ltd., 1972. Contains histories and model information concerning theatre photoplayers and their builders.

— *Put Another Nickel In.* Vestal, New York: The Vestal Press, Ltd., 1966. History of The Rudolph Wurlitzer Company, with much information on theatre instruments.

— "Theatre Photoplayers," article in the Musical Box Society International *Bulletin,* reprinted in the Silver Anniversary Collection, Musical Box Society International, 1974.

Bramlet, Roland. "Robert Hope-Jones' Shadow in the Organ Loft," chapter in *Reaching for the Infinite.* Rochester, New York: The First Universalist Society, 1983.

Brownlow, Kevin, *Hollywood - The Pioneers.* New York: Alfred A. Knopf, 1979.

Conot, Robert. *A Streak of Luck.* New York: Seaview Books, 1979. A biogrpahy of Thomas A. Edison. Contains information concerning the development of the Kinetoscope.

Csida, Joseph and June Bundy Csida. *American Entertainment.* New York: Watson-Guptill Publications, 1978.

Fell, John L. (editor). *Film Before Griffith.* Berkeley, California: University of California Press, 1983.

Foort, Reginald. *The Cinema Organ,* second edition. Vestal, New York: The Vestal Press, Ltd., 1970. A first-hand account of playing the theatre organ by one of the best known old-time organists.

Gorish, Roy. "The Wurlitzer Hope-Jones Unit Orchestra in the Isis Theatre, Denver, Colorado," article in *The Tibia,* journal of the American Theatre Organ Enthusiasts, Fall 1955 issue.

Grau, Robert. *The Theatre of Science.* New York: Broadway Publishing Co., 1914.

Griffith, Richard and Arthur Mayer. *The Movies.* New York: Bonanza Books, 1957. A widely-circulated volume on the history of the movies from the early days forward, a book which has inspired much interest on the part of collectors and historians since its publication.

Hall, Ben. *The Best Remaining Seats.* New York: Bramhall House, 1961. A fascinating account of theatres of the "palace" era and theatre organs, written by one of the foremost historians in the field.

Herzog, Charlotte. "The Nickelodeon Phase (1903-1917)." Article in *Marquee,* journal of the Theatre Historical Society, First Quarter 1981. An excellent overview of the nickelodeon.

Hinton, J. W. *Story of the Electric Organ.* London: Simpkin, Marshall, Hamilton, Kent & Coe, Ltd., 1909.

Hope-Jones, Robert. *Recent Developments of Organ Building.* North Tonawanda, New York: The Rudolph Wurlitzer Company, 1910. Reprint of a lecture delivered before the National Association of Organists, Ocean Grove, New Jersey, August 6, 1910, which outlines many of Hope-Jones' ideas and philosophies.

Hulfish, David S. *Cyclopedia of Motion Picture Work,* Volumes I and II. Chicago: American Technical Society, 1911. An excellent study of the field of motion pictures of the time, with chapters devoted to operating theatres, projecting film, taking motion pictures, and other aspects of the business.

Johnson, Osa. *I Married Adventure.* Philadelphia: J.B. Lippincott Company, 1940. An account of early film making, 1907 onward, by the wife and traveling companion of a photographer who visited many distant areas to film travelogues and adventures.

Junchen, David L. *Encyclopedia of the American Theatre Organ,* Volume I. Pasadena, California: Showcase Publications, 1985. The introductory volume of a planned three-volume set produced by one of the world's foremost authorities in the field of theatre pipe organs. Contains shipping lists and detailed information on a company-by-company basis, plus excellent accompanying text.

Landon, John W. *Behold The Mighty Wurlitzer.* Westport, Connecticut: Greenwood Press, 1983.

— *Jesse Crawford, Poet of the Organ, Wizard of the Mighty Wurlitzer.* Vestal, New York: The Vestal Press, Ltd., 1974. A biography of one of America's best-known theatre organists.

Lauritzen, Einar and Gunnar Lundquist. *American Film-Index 1908-1915.* Stockholm: Film-Index, 1976.

Lindsay, Vachel. *The Art of the Moving Picture.* New York: The MacMillan Company, 1915. Lindsay discusses social and artistic aspects of films and comments on the behavior of theatre audiences.

Macgowan, Kenneth. *Behind the Screen.* New York: Delacorte Press, 1965.

Mast, Jerald. *A Short History of the Movies.* Indianapolis: The Bobbs-Merrill Company, Inc., 1976.

Meloy, Arthur S. *Theatres and Motion Picture Houses.* New York City: Architects' Supply and Publishing Comany, 1916. A discussion of theatre construction and recommended practices, especially with regard to large houses.

Miller, George Laing. *The Recent Revolution in Organ Building.* New York: The Charles Francis Press, 1913. A very readable book on the development of organs with electric actions, particularly with regard to the innovations of Robert Hope-Jones. Contains biographies of important organ builders of the era. Reprinted by The Vestal Press, Ltd.

Motion Picture Magazine. Brooklyn, New York, various issues 1913 to 1916. Each issue contains stories and plots of current films, interviews with actors and actresses, and other news, particularly from the viewpoint of things interesting to the theatregoer.

Moving Picture World. New York. Various issues, 1912-1916, particularly the "Convention Number," July 15, 1916, with various articles concerning the evolution of motion picture exhibition.

New York Clipper, The. Various issues 1895 to 1916.

Patterson, Joseph Medill. "The Nickelodeons: The Poor Man's Elementary Course in Drama," article in *The Saturday Evening Post.* Philadelphia: The Curtis Publishing Company, November 23, 1907.

Ramsaye, Terry. *A Million and One Nights.* New York: Simon and Schuster, 1926.

Rhode, Eric. *A History of the Cinema From Its Origins to 1970.* New York: Hill and Wang, 1976.

Richardson, F. H. *Motion Picture Handbook,* third edition. Published by *Moving Picture World,* New York City, 1916, earlier editions in 1910 and 1912.

Reblitz, Arthur A. and Q. David Bowers. *Treasures of Mechanical Music.* Vestal, New York: The Vestal Press, Ltd., 1981.

Roehl, Harvey N. *Player Piano Treasury.* Vestal, New York: The Vestal Press, Ltd., 1961 and subsequent editions.

Schoenstein, Louis, J. *Memoirs of a San Francisco Organ Builder.* San Francisco: Cue Publications, 1977.

Savage, Henry W. "The Dilemma of the Theatre," article in *The Saturday Evening Post.* Philadelphia: The Curtis Publishing Company, May 11, 1912.

Sinclair, Upton. *Upton Sinclair Presents William Fox.* Los Angeles: Published by the author, 1933.

Smith, Albert E. *Two Reels and a Crank.* Garden City, N.Y.: Doubleday & Co., Inc., 1952.

Sumner, William Leslie. *The Organ.* New York: Philosophical Library, 1953.

Theatre Organ. Journal of the American Theatre Organ Enthusiasts (name later changed to the American Theatre Organ Society), various issues 1955 to 1985, including early issues published under the names of *The Tibia* and *The Bombarde.*

Whitworth, Reginald. *The Electric Organ.* London: Musical Opinion, 1940.

Wurlitzer Company, The. *The World's Greatest Achievement in Music for Theatres.* Cincinnati, Ohio, 1916. Sales catalogue picturing various theatres and organ installations mainly circa 1912-1915.

Wurlitzer Unit Organs, sales brochure issued by the Rudolph Wurlitzer Company, Cincinnati, Ohio, mid-1920s.

Index

ENTRANCE TO STAR THEATRE, HUDSON, N. Y.

Scene on Pine St. Showing Grand Theatre,
Orlando, Fla.

ABOUT THE AUTHOR

Q. David Bowers has been interested in the history of theatres and their music, and the history of the silent era of motion pictures, for many years. He is the author or co-author of over two dozen books on various subjects, including the following titles published by The Vestal Press: *Put Another Nickel In* (1966), *Guidebook of Automatic Musical Instruments,* Vols. I and II (1969), *The Encyclopedia of Automatic Musical Instruments* (1972), *Treasures of Mechanical Music* (with Arthur A. Reblitz, 1981), and *The Moxie Encyclopedia* (1985).

A 1960 graduate of the Pennsylvania State University, the author received in 1976 the Alumni Achievement Award from that institution's College of Business Administration. He has contributed to the *Encyclopedia Americana,* articles by him have appeared in such diverse publications as *American Heritage, Reader's Digest,* and *Barron's,* and he has appeared on ABC, CBS, NBC, Metromedia and other television networks.

His reference collection of theatre memorabilia includes such items as early postcards, posters, trade publications, pictures, and printed material relating to early films and movie houses; a Wurlitzer Style K Pipe Organ Orchestra photoplayer (originally installed in the Pastime Theatre, Coshocton, Ohio in 1915); and a four-manual, 20-rank Wurlitzer theatre pipe organ (first installed in the Minnesota Theatre, Minneapolis, in 1928). His interest in the subject continues, and readers with information are invited to contact him at the following address: Q. David Bowers, Box 1224, Wolfeboro, NH 03894.

☞ NICKELODEON THEATRE MUSIC
on cassette

You've enjoyed seeing and reading all about the fascinating nickelodeon theatre era from 1905 to 1915. Now you can hear the music!

The Vestal Press offers two top-quality cassette tapes for your listening pleasure.

[1] NICKELODEON THEATRE MUSIC

. . . with the famed theatre organist Dennis James playing the Fotoplayer. His live performance includes accompaniment music for the Edison film "The Great Train Robbery" with a full repertoire of sound effects, two great Joe Lamb rags—*Ragtime Nightingale* and *Ragtime Bobolink*, plus *Struggle Music*, *A Mysterioso*, and *a Furioso*.

Filmusic player piano mood music rolls especially manufactured for silent movies are on side 2, as embellished with sound effects by Mr. James: *Serenade Grotesque, Sorrow Theme, Implorations, Treachery and Vengeance,* and *The Gawky Rube.*

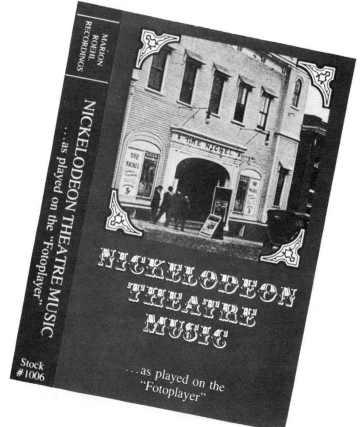

This tape and the one on the other side of this sheet feature three instruments.

The Style 25 Fotoplayer was used in the Strand Theatre in Ephrata, Pennsylvania.

The Seeburg coin-operated speakeasy piano was used in a tavern in upstate New York, near the Canadian border.

The Reproduco portable piano-pipe-organ was used in the Gem Theatre in Derry, Pennsylvania.

☞ all three are from the private collection of Harvey and Marion Roehl of Vestal, New York

THE VESTAL PRESS Ltd
P.O. Box 97 · 320 N. Jensen Road
Vestal 10, New York 13850

THE VESTAL PRESS publishes a complete line of books on Player Pianos, Carousel Organs, Antique Radio, Carousels, Antique Phonographs, Reed Organs, Piano Servicing, and related subjects. It also produces and sells a wide variety of recordings of antique music machines and theatre pipe organs. Send $2 (refundable) to the address above for a complete catalog.

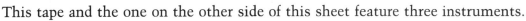